WOMEN IN WHITE COATS

WOMEN
IN WHITE
COATS

HOW THE FIRST
WOMEN DOCTORS CHANGED
THE WORLD OF MEDICINE

OLIVIA CAMPBELL

PARK
ROW
BOOKS

PARK
ROW
BOOKS™

Recycling programs
for this product may
not exist in your area.

ISBN-13: 978-0-7783-8939-2

Women in White Coats: How the First Women Doctors Changed the World of Medicine

Park Row Books
22 Adelaide St. West, 40th Floor
Toronto, Ontario M5H 4E3, Canada
ParkRowBooks.com
BookClubbish.com

Printed in U.S.A.

To Mom, Grandma, Laura, Ellen, Louisa, MaryAnn, Lara, Sarah and all of the other ladies in my life who showed me that there's nothing tenacious, independent women can't do.

TABLE OF CONTENTS

WOMEN IN WHITE COATS

PROLOGUE

The Forgotten History of Healing

When Elizabeth Blackwell decided to become the first woman doctor, in many ways she wasn't actually the first. Women have delivered healthcare across the globe for centuries as herbalists, healer-priestesses, shamans, apothecaries, healers, wise women, witch doctors, diviners, surgeons, nurses, and midwives.[1] But this rich history is largely overlooked, and very few names have weathered the passing of time.

Agnodice is one of the earliest named female physicians in the historical record. The story goes that she became a doctor in the fourth century BCE to save the women of Athens from dying of treatable illnesses because they didn't want to see male physicians. It was illegal for women to be doctors, so Agnodice set up practice disguised as a man. To show her patients who she really was, she flashed her genitalia. Soon, jealous male doctors found out and convicted Agnodice of illegally practicing med-

---

1   Midwifery wasn't typically considered medicine, per se.

icine. In the final dramatic showdown, the women of Athens rushed into the courtroom to defend her and the ban against women physicians was overturned.

There's only one problem with this tale: there was no law against women practicing medicine in ancient Greece. This inconsistency, paired with the fantastical elements of the story, is enough to convince some scholars that Agnodice didn't exist. Other scholars believe she was a real person, who surely encountered persecution even if she wasn't breaking any official law.

This is how we are introduced to historical medical women: biographies sprinkled with doubts, caveats, clauses; lives methodically dissected under a microscope by scholar after scholar looking for any hint of error, any crumb of fabrication to wave around gleefully as proof that this woman wasn't what we thought. We don't often hear about the historical contributions of women's medical brilliance, but when we do, we are taught to question the very core of such claims. Men rarely enjoy such scrutiny.

A relative scarcity of women officially labeled as professional medical practitioners in historical texts is not because they didn't exist, but rather because their occupations were not labeled as frequently as men's. As "wise women" healers or midwives, their activities may not have been believed to warrant recording. Throughout much of history, a man's entire household would have been involved in his occupational activities. Spouses and children of physicians or apothecaries would have helped mix medicines, visit the sick, and administer treatments; the family of a barber surgeon helped him pull teeth and set broken bones. And widowed wives took over those family businesses.

Most areas in Europe would have had a wise woman or man who inherited the role of village healer, and women were largely the ones called upon to tend sick or dying family members; the ones sent to care for sick or dying neighbors who had no other family to care for them. As late as the 1500s, King Henry VIII was still granting the occasional medical license "to certain women to attend the sick poor who could not afford to pay the fees of regular practitioners." In medieval France, about one hundred women have been identified as medical practitioners (alongside seven thousand men). Nuns soon became the main practitioners of the healing arts; convents could be considered proto-hospitals. Nuns would tend medicinal herb gardens, dress soldiers' battle wounds, and nurse ill villagers back to health.

When medicine began to be solidified as a profession during the thirteenth century—its practice now requiring university training and licensure—patriarchal control swept in. Women could not become "official" doctors since most universities wouldn't admit them. Outside of England and France, some institutions were more amenable. In 1390, Italian physician Dorotea Bucca took over for her father as chair of medicine at the University of Bologna, a post she held for more than forty years. Still, such women were the exceptions, not the rule.

Professionalization further sidelined women because book learning was now viewed as superior to any wisdom passed down orally, like most of women's folk medicine was.

Women's claims of medical prowess began to be questioned in real time, not by history scholars, but by the women's newly professionalized male contemporaries. Lay women healers were vilified as dangerously incompetent because they lacked a classical education (which they couldn't obtain even if they wanted to). In 1421, English physicians petitioned parliament and King Henry V to request that no women practice medicine "under payne of long imprisonment" and steep fines, declaring those who tried "worthless and presumptuous women who usurped the profession." Women who were found guilty of practicing medicine illegally were excommunicated and fined. Things took a deadly turn when the Church stepped in.

The Church controlled most university medical schools and wanted to ensure they also monopolized its practice. Between 1400 and 1700, the Catholic and Lutheran churches executed a massive campaign to rid Europe of wise women, branding them witches or sorceresses—even the nuns! They reasoned that only through God could a person be healed, and since women weren't ordained by Him to wield such powers, their ability to make sick people well must originate from the devil. While the Church claimed it was fighting dark magic—not medicine or women—their campaign saw more than a hundred thousand women healers burned at the stake.

This legacy of discrimination against women healers cast a wide shadow over the medical profession. Even if women did somehow manage to achieve professional qualifications, they were relegated to specialties deemed feminine: they could deliver healthcare, but only as nurses or midwives.

For Victorian women like Elizabeth Blackwell, Lizzie Garrett, and Sophia Jex-Blake to seek entrance into the male realm of medicine was a radical request to be seen as equals. It meant these women couldn't just be students, they also had to be women's rights activists. If they wished to fully reenter the realm of medicine as doctors, they'd have to put up a hell of a fight.

Each woman's journey to a medical degree would vary; each was driven by vastly different motivations. One sought a degree in Scotland with disastrous results. One was forced to travel to France for her degree. One's college application was considered a practical joke. Each would grapple with defining women's work and purpose—as sister, wife, mother, daughter, adoptive mother, single parent, lesbian partner.

But even in the early days of their studies, each one recognized their role as trailblazers paving the way for others. They knew their actions would allow future generations of women to forge their own paths, craft their own definitions of what women's work could be. They would never stop fighting, because they saw how women physicians could revolutionize medicine, not just for the benefit of female patients, but for everyone. History would be made by these medical women.

ONE

A Lady Doctor

Mary Donaldson was dying. One day in early 1845, Mary's neighbor Elizabeth Blackwell stopped by to offer the ailing woman some solace and comfort. This casual chat over a cup of tea in suburban Cincinnati would turn out to change the course of medical history. Elizabeth was a frightfully small woman with a thin nose, a sweet voice, and remarkably soft, fine hands. Everything about her seemed petite, except for her mind.

The third child of the family, it was no secret that Elizabeth was her father's favorite. He lovingly referred to her as "Little Shy." While she may have been socially awkward, she could also be quite stubborn, happy to put all of her energies into a cause to prove a point. At a time when most women were raised to be subservient to men, Elizabeth's parents encouraged all of their children to be knowledge-seeking independent thinkers unafraid to speak their minds.

Elizabeth's family was somewhat new to Cincinnati, having

moved frequently when Elizabeth was growing up. First, when she was eleven, her father uprooted their entire household—his eight children, pregnant wife, their governess, two servants, and two aunts—to move from Bristol, England, to New York, New York. It was a seven-week voyage on the merchant ship *Cosmo*, during which Elizabeth suffered terrible seasickness. Next, they moved to Jersey City, then Cincinnati where her father spent his final days.

Now, twenty-four-year-old Elizabeth sat perched by Mary Donaldson's bed, listening to her catalog the agonizing months she'd spent in increasingly worsening abdominal pain. Mary was more than likely suffering from advanced uterine cancer. She hadn't sought medical treatment for her symptoms at first, and when she had, her doctor only seemed to make her more uncomfortable.

"The worst part of my illness is that I am being treated by a rough unfeeling man," Mary confided in Elizabeth, complaining that her checkups and treatment were nearly as excruciating as the illness itself. "If I could have been treated by a lady doctor, my worst sufferings would have been spared me."

Elizabeth agreed that this was an unfortunate state of affairs and offered sympathy and comfort as best she could. Short wisps of Elizabeth's wavy, reddish-blond hair escaped from its pulled-back confines and spilled across her forehead.

"You are fond of study, have health and leisure," Mary nudged Elizabeth. "Why not study medicine?"

The question hung in the air. This time, Elizabeth disagreed, finding it difficult to hide her shock behind her wide-set blue-gray eyes. "I hate everything connected with the body and could not bear the sight of a medical book," she protested. "The very thought of dwelling on the physical structure of the body and its various ailments fills me with disgust."

Elizabeth's exposure to the medical field would have been limited at the time. Most women healers in history had a family member in the trade who sparked their interest, but this was not the case with Elizabeth. Her father had been a sugar refiner, her mother a devout Christian kept busy with raising their nine children. Her uncle and grandfather were both jewelers. Elizabeth's maternal grandmother ran a successful millinery shop to support her family after her husband was convicted of forging £5 notes and banished to Australia.

Elizabeth's most recent experience with medicine was seven years prior, when her father had become gravely ill. She watched as his doctors dosed him with brandy and arrowroot laudanum and rubbed his joints with mercurial ointment. When they left, she and her sisters took over: giving him sponge baths of muriatic acid solution, feeding him broth and brandy, and administering his medicines. He died shortly after falling sick. This firsthand exposure to medical care did nothing to pique then-seventeen-year-old Elizabeth's interest in medicine.

It's no wonder Elizabeth was initially repulsed by the prospect of becoming a doctor. The practice of medicine in the first half of the 1800s was a gruesome business. "Heroic" measures were the go-to treatments, such as bloodletting, blistering, and purging. Hippocrates's theory of humors still reigned supreme. It asserted that illness was the result of an imbalance of the four humors: melancholic (cold and dry), choleric (warm and dry), sanguine (warm and wet), and phlegmatic (cold and wet). Different foods or treatments could return balance and therefore restore health. Infections were thought to be caused by an excess of blood, so bloodletting should fix a fever.

Toxic metals made up some of the early Victorians' favorite medicines. Calomel, or mercury chloride, was believed to cure anything from cancer, tuberculosis, and cholera to syphilis, ingrown toenails, and influenza. Babies were given the white, odorless powder to soothe teething pain. Around the 1840s, megadoses were the fashion: twenty grains four times a day. Treatment was working when violent, dark diarrhea was achieved (the body trying to rid itself of the poison) and three pints of saliva was produced via excessive drooling, which we now know is actually a sign of mercury poisoning.

Arsenic, though an infamous poisoning agent, was considered to be therapeutic in small doses. Arsenic tinctures were used to treat maladies ranging from fevers and emotional disturbance to loss of libido and asthma. It was listed in the British Pharmaceutical Codex until 1907 and in the US pharmacopoeia until 1950. Another popular remedy was the *everlasting pill*. Made of the toxic metal antimony, ingesting it would induce a "cleansing" bout of vomiting and diarrhea. The pill was then retrieved from the patient's excrement, washed, and tucked away to be used again by the next person in the family who took ill.

Diseases of the reproductive organs were considered a woman's burden to bear, cancer believed to be a feminine malady. "There is no fact in the history of cancer more absolutely demonstrated than the influence exercised by sex on its development," pioneering oncology researcher Dr. Walter Walshe proclaimed in 1846. "The female population of this country is destroyed to about two and three quarters times as great an extent by cancer as the male."

For instance, of the 9,118 cancer-related deaths in Paris between 1830 and 1840, nearly three thousand were the result of uterine cancer. There were several reasons for this grim statistic, among them that symptoms of reproductive cancers in women often don't show up until later and tend to mask themselves as more benign ailments. Another issue was that women often put off, or couldn't bring themselves to consult their male physicians, and cancer is much easier to treat successfully in its earliest stages. Since cancer was known to be hereditary, seeking treatment might also reveal you to society as tainted. Even if she survived, such a diagnosis could ruin a woman's romantic, social, and professional prospects.

In the end, doctors had little to offer a patient like Eliza-

beth's friend Mary. The best they could do was ease suffering
with morphine or opium and suggest some lifestyle changes
they hoped would promote a healthier constitution: reduce their
food intake, maintain open bowels, avoid exertion, and refrain
from sex. Among the many cancer cures touted at the time were
yellow dock root, Turkish figs boiled in milk, zapping tumors
with electricity or injecting them with lead and sulfur, applying
a poultice of dough and lard, or mesmerism, which purported
to harness the healing power of the invisible natural forces of
all living creatures.

"My friend died of a painful disease, the delicate nature of
which made the methods of treatment a constant suffering to
her," Elizabeth wrote about Mary. "I resolutely tried for weeks
to put the idea suggested by my friend away; but it constantly
recurred to me." The more she thought about it, the more plau-
sible the idea became.

Elizabeth had just returned from a disappointing stint teaching at a girls' school in Kentucky after working many years as a
governess and teacher to help her family make ends meet after
her father died. These jobs didn't particularly interest her, but
because they were practically the only non-working-class professions available to reasonably educated women, she did them.
Her older sister Anna was off teaching in New York accompanied by their younger sister Emily, who was still in school. The
family's new home in the Cincinnati suburbs seemed unusually
quiet, giving her plenty of time to think.

Elizabeth dreamed of discovering a "more engrossing pursuit" and felt like a spark without fuel. It was more than for-
tuitous, then, that Mary implored her to consider a career in
medicine at this exact moment. Witnessing her friend dying a
needlessly uncomfortable death—exactly because there were no
women doctors—proved the jolt Elizabeth needed. She would
become a doctor.

In addition to healing sick women like Mary, practicing medicine was attractive to Elizabeth because she believed it would be the perfect field in which to begin to push the boundaries of women's reach. If other women would join her in becoming a physician, then no woman patient would have to suffer like Mary.

From an early age, Elizabeth believed her intelligence and strength as equal to a man's. Despite her slight, diminutive frame, she was surprisingly strong. Once, as a young girl in their Bristol home, a gentleman houseguest was regaling Elizabeth and her family with his views on women's physical inferiority: how even the weakest man could best the strongest woman.

"That is certainly a mistake," Elizabeth's brothers protested. "For Elizabeth, when she chooses to give herself the trouble of measuring strength with us, is more than a match for either of us at wrestling or at lifting, and can carry us about with perfect ease."

"She could not lift *me!*" the man protested with contemptuous incredulity. "No woman living could lift me against my will. Try it, Elizabeth," he goaded, sizing up his pint-size competition. "Do your utmost; I defy you to move me out of this chair." Young Elizabeth slowly crossed the room, then easily hoisted the man up and settled him into her left arm. As he squirmed to free himself, she paraded him around the parlor three times.

"You see," Elizabeth quipped as she returned him to his chair. "Some women are as strong as some men." The room erupted in laughter. Elizabeth continued to enjoy wrestling as a diverting hobby into adulthood, often physically tussling with landlords in her spare time.

Her goal with medicine was social change: a place to stick a wedge in and begin the expansion of women's educational and career opportunities. Elizabeth's desire to widen women's sphere and her ideas about how best to accomplish such a goal were heavily influenced by the writings of feminist Margaret Fuller, whose book *Woman in the Nineteenth Century* was published around the same time as Elizabeth was consoling her ill neighbor.

Fuller served as editor of the transcendentalist magazine *The Dial* along with Ralph Waldo Emerson. Elizabeth was an avid subscriber. Fuller's feminism favored a gentler brand of gender equality, one achieved via persuasion and persistence rather than aggression and antagonism. Both Fuller and Blackwell wanted to see women gain more opportunities and influence without taking any away from men. Alienating men, they decided, would do nothing to further their cause.

In fact, Elizabeth didn't blame men for women's subordinate social position. She felt women could stand to express a deeper desire to broaden their own horizons and often found her female companions frustratingly interested only in idle gossip. Women were narrow-minded and frivolous, Elizabeth believed, "ignorant of their own capacities." She thought she could help them realize their full potential.

Her other neighbor, Harriet Beecher Stowe, discouraged Elizabeth's newfound career plans. Stowe, who would go on to author the novel *Uncle Tom's Cabin*, called the idea of a woman becoming a doctor "impracticable." Elizabeth said Harriet warned her of "the strong prejudice which would exist, which I must either crush or be crushed by."

Elizabeth was practically giddy at the thought of such universal opposition. She relished the idea that the path she was about to embark upon would be filled with resistance. Such paths were surely noble. "I was severing the usual ties of life and preparing to act against my strongest inclinations," Elizabeth opined. "But a force stronger than myself then and afterward seemed to lead me on; a purpose was before me which I must inevitably seek to accomplish. Winning a doctor's degree gradually assumed the aspect of a great moral struggle, and the moral fight possessed immense attraction for me."

An absorbing profession would also help Elizabeth get her

mind off of men. Her religious upbringing made her ill at ease about her strong libido. "I had always been extremely susceptible to this influence," Elizabeth wrote. "From my first adoration, at 7-years-old, of a little boy with rosy cheeks and flaxen curls, I never remember a time when I had not suffered more or less from the common malady—falling in love."

Becoming a physician, she reasoned, would act as a barrier between her and the expectation of marriage. She was attracted to men, but often found them intellectually disappointing or else found the prospect of sexual contact shameful. Having something to engross her mind, distract her thoughts from wandering to romance, "some object in life which will fill this vacuum" would "prevent this sad wearing away of the heart." She'd already resigned herself to the possibility that she might never find a worthy partner, and therefore would need to be able to support herself financially.

With her mind made up, Elizabeth began her inquiry into medical schools. Obtaining a degree would be no easy feat. People would diminish her, laugh at her, taunt her, try to stop her. The road ahead would be filled with obstacles of every kind. Her resolve would be tested in ways she never could have imagined.

TWO

Surely, She Is a Joke

No road map existed for what Elizabeth hoped to achieve. At the time, only two or three established American colleges were open to women applicants, and none had a medical school. Many higher education institutions just for women existed, but nearly all held the sole goal of preparing women to be teachers: one of the only acceptable professions for their gender. A few lucky women were also able to support their families with a career in writing, though many used male-sounding pen names. The idea of coeducation of the sexes at universities was starting to take shape in the US, but it was far from the norm. Elizabeth would have to carve out her own lonely path.

Her first obstacle would be a personal one—overcoming her revulsion at the sight of bodily fluids and functions. One of the stereotypes of the time was that women were ill-suited to medicine because they could not handle all of the grotesqueness involved. There must be something wrong with women who wanted to become doctors, so the common wisdom went. Medical education involved dissection and other unpleasant sights, which should surely make any real lady scream or faint. Practicing medicine was decidedly unladylike. To even be interested in medicine was to forsake your femininity.

The *Australian Medical Journal* supported this belief in 1865. "A woman who dissects, who makes post mortem examinations, who tests urine, who perhaps carries diseased specimens in her dress pocket, who can pass the male catheter, who punctures buboes, probes sinuses, examines purulent discharges, applies ligatures to haemorrhoids, and may have just come from operating for anal fistula, is not a person in whom you would look for the tenderer domestic qualities."

Elizabeth's squeamishness may have been a female stereotype, but nevertheless, it was a hurdle that would take a lot of nerve-steeling to overcome. "The struggle with natural repugnance to the medical line of life was so strong that I hesitated to pass the Rubicon and fought many a severe battle with myself on the subject," Elizabeth said.

But her mind was made up. She wrote to all of the doctors she knew through her family to gather their opinions on her becoming a lady doctor. Elizabeth describes their responses as curiously unanimous. They thought it was a great idea but would be impossible to accomplish.

Before she could even think about applying to medical college, Elizabeth would need money to pay for it. She calculated she would need $3,000[2] to cover her living expenses and tuition. Her dream would have to wait a few years while she earned the money.

She took a post teaching music at a school in Asheville, North Carolina. Here, Elizabeth's medical self-education would begin. A job was a job, but the fact that the school's principal, Reverend John Dickson, had previously worked as a doctor, likely

---

2 About $95,000 in today's money.

piqued Elizabeth's interest in accepting the post. Dickson's strict religious beliefs meant he didn't approve of board games, novels, or other frivolous amusements, but what he did approve of was Elizabeth's medical aspirations. He was more than happy to allow her access to his medical library. So, in her downtime, she studied his volumes on physiology, nutrition, and theories of popular medicine.

When that school shut down for good at the end of the year, Elizabeth went to stay with Reverend Dickson's younger brother Samuel in Charleston, South Carolina, and took a new post teaching music at the local girls' boarding school. Samuel was a prominent doctor and professor of medicine with an even bigger library. When she wasn't teaching, Elizabeth was knee-deep in medical books in Samuel's library, which included more than one thousand texts. Within a year, she exclaimed, "I really now feel like a *medical student*."

Elizabeth insisted nothing could sway her now: "My mind is fully made up. I have not the slightest hesitation on the subject; the thorough study of medicine I am quite resolved to go through with. The horrors and disgusts I have no doubt of vanquishing. I have overcome stronger distastes than any that now remain. As to the opinion of people, I don't care one straw."

Now that she'd finally saved up enough money, Elizabeth was ready to begin her studies at a bona fide medical school. Admission to American medical schools didn't require anything much in the way of advanced educational credentials, and applying was essentially a formality for most men. The subject was basically just another undergraduate career track. Medical schools had only recently begun replacing the system of apprenticeship for learning the practice of medicine, but they caught on quickly. Between 1830 and 1845, the number of medical schools in America more than doubled. Elizabeth could've easily found someone to apprentice under, but she wanted to adhere to the educational status quo as tightly as possible. She wanted to earn a legitimate MD and be as highly educated as her modern medical peers.

Elizabeth turned her sights to Philadelphia, the birthplace of medical education in America and currently home to four medical schools. In 1765, the first medical school in North America was established at the College of Philadelphia, later renamed the University of Pennsylvania. Founded by two American men who studied at the University of Edinburgh, the school followed the Scottish system: to graduate required two years of lecture-based courses and one year of clinical instruction in a large hospital setting.

By the start of the 1800s, medical schools had been around for centuries in Europe, but many still taught only theory, while others taught only practice. It was Scotland's medical schools at the universities of Edinburgh and Glasgow, founded in 1726 and 1751, respectively, that realized the importance of doctors learning both. In addition to accompanying doctors on wards, clinical lectures emerged as an exceptional method of clinical training. Doctors and surgeons would trot sick or injured patients out onto the stage to teach the student audience how to identify symptoms and administer treatments.

Around midcentury, it only took two years to complete a degree at most American medical schools, and your training may or may not have included any practical or clinical experience, depending on the school. In Europe, by contrast, a medical degree took about four years to achieve.

Elizabeth wrote to Philadelphia physician Dr. Joseph Warrington, a devout Quaker, to ask for his advice on medical schools. Warrington was dedicated to providing the city's poor women the quality maternity care they deserved. In 1828, he founded the Philadelphia Lying-in Charity for Attending Indigent Women in Their Own Home. (Lying-in was a period of extended bed rest after childbirth.) In 1839, he created the Philadelphia Nurse Society which, among other things, provided training in obstetric nursing. Such a champion of women's health and medical train-ing would surely be supportive of Elizabeth's plan.

"I confess, my dear lady, that I see many difficulties in the way of attainment," Warrington replied. He told Elizabeth he had given the matter much reflection—even "personally ap-pealed to some of the most intelligent and liberal-minded la-dies of my acquaintance how far the services of a well-educated female physician would be appreciated by them."

Their response, uniformly, was that no woman would be ac-ceptable to them as a practitioner of medicine. Perhaps these liberal ladies feared the erosion of the status quo, or perhaps they worried no woman could achieve enough education to provide quality medical services. After listening to society con-stantly trumpet the inferiority of the fairer sex, some women couldn't help but believe it true. It's also likely these ladies were wealthy enough to be quite discerning in their choice of physi-cians. Had Warrington polled the working-class women of the city, he may have gotten a more favorable response to the idea of a lady doctor.

Despite these warnings, Warrington invited Elizabeth to come to Philadelphia. He hoped to convince her that "woman was designed to be the helpmeet for man" and that it was more ap-propriate for a woman to be the nurse and not the physician; hoping that it would then possibly occur to Elizabeth that her real mission was to fulfill the holy duties of nursing.

While she had nothing against nurses, Elizabeth simply saw no reason why she shouldn't be allowed to become a doctor. "So revolutionary seemed the attempt of a woman to leave a subordi-nate position and seek to obtain a complete medical education," Elizabeth declared.

With what she described as her carefully hoarded earnings, Elizabeth headed to Philadelphia. Here again, she stayed with a former doctor, William Elder, who offered her support and advice. She needed all the encouragement she could get. When she began requesting entrance into Philadelphia's medical schools in 1847, the reactions were grim.

The first school Elizabeth attempted to gain admittance to was Jefferson College. She called upon Dr. Samuel Jackson, one of the oldest professors in Philadelphia, in person. As she entered his office, a short, gray-haired man glanced up from his newspaper. He was clearly annoyed.

"Well, what is it? What do you want?" he demanded.

"I want to study medicine," Elizabeth announced.

Jackson began to laugh. "Why?" he asked.

After she detailed her plans, slowly and methodically, his demeanor changed. He began to take her seriously. "There are great difficulties, but I do not know that they are insurmountable," Jackson admitted. He told her that he would consult with the other medical professors at the college and see what the consensus was as to admitting a female student. "I will let you know on Monday."

When she returned to his office, Jackson told her he had done his best, but all of the professors were opposed to her entrance. It was a devastating first blow, but Elizabeth did her best to remain optimistic. There were still three more schools to apply to in the city. Next on her list was the Pennsylvania Medical College. That June she visited Professor William Darrach who she would later describe as "the most non-committal man I ever saw. I harangued him, and he sat a full five minutes without a word."

"Can you give me any encouragement?" she finally demanded of Darrach, tired of waiting in silence.

"The subject is a novel one, madam," Darrach sputtered at last. "I have nothing to say either for or against it… I cannot express my opinion to you either one way or another."

"Your opinion, I fear, is unfavorable," Elizabeth replied dejectedly.

"I did not say so…the way in which my mind acts in this matter I do not feel at liberty to unfold," William answered.

"Shall I call on the other professors of your college?" countered Elizabeth.

"I cannot take the responsibility of advising you to pursue such a course," Darrach conceded.

"Can you not grant me admittance to your lectures, as you do not feel unfavorable to my scheme?" she prodded.

"I have said no such thing; whether favorable or unfavorable, I have not expressed any opinion," Darrach insisted. The professor may have been wholly against her scheme, but too timid to reject such a determined woman in person. He also may have been so taken aback by the proposition of a woman becoming a doctor that he simply needed more time to truly fathom the idea.

Agitated by Darrach's waffling, Elizabeth got up and left.

Frustrated, but undeterred, Elizabeth went to visit Warrington. In his letters, he may have stressed the difficulty of her chosen path, but he was more encouraging than most of the other medical men she'd encountered in the city. Even someone who was vaguely open to her plans might prove a good ally, or at the very least a sounding board.

Despite his preference that she pursue the less contentious path of nursing, Warrington became a sort of confidant from whom she frequently sought advice. And the more time he spent with her, the less objectionable her idea became. He invited her to use his medical library, visit his patients, and attend his medical lectures.

Elizabeth enjoyed her self-guided study of medical textbooks, but understood its limitations without a teacher to guide her. Not one to sit idly by, she also began studying anatomy at a private school. Upon encountering the inner workings of an actual human body for the first time, it was not revulsion or disgust she felt, but quite the opposite—awe.

"The beauty of the tendons and exquisite arrangement of this part of the body struck my artistic sense," she beamed after dissecting a human wrist with a calm and curiosity that surprised even her. "I begin to think there is more love of science in me than I have hitherto suspected." Once given the opportunity to study every subject in school that men did, many women discovered they could in fact be fascinated by and even excel in fields they were told would offend their sensibilities or overwhelm their mental capacities.

Elizabeth continued applying to medical schools, now widening her search beyond Philadelphia. Her private lessons were a stepping-stone to college classes, not a stand-in. Elizabeth was always keenly aware of her trailblazer status, always thinking of what kind of example she would be setting. She feared that taking the private study or apprenticeship route might inspire a fleet of ignorant women into haphazard medical practice after enduring low-quality training. Catastrophizing, perhaps, but Elizabeth was determined to attend a traditional medical college and acquire an MD, both as a sanction for her own course and as a precedent for other women. She wanted nothing to do with the many so-called irregular medical schools that had been popping up nearly as rapidly as traditional ones.

Society's interest in alternative medicine and untested, trendy wellness cures is far from new. Not everyone agreed in the curative abilities of the harsh treatments favored by regular physicians of the time. Indeed, bloodletting and blistering could easily induce a secondary infection in already-weakened patients. Thanks to ignorance of antiseptics and disease transmission, you might come out of the hospital with more illnesses than you went in with—if you came out at all.

As Western medicine transformed into an educated profession, myriad forms of untested therapies promising the sick more "natural" solutions became fashionable. Such sects included homeopathy, botanical medicine, hydrotherapy, mesmerism, eclecticism, faith healing, and Thomsonianism. The Thomsonian System, developed by self-taught botanist Samuel Thomson, championed herbal purgatives and the warming of the body with steam baths and cayenne peppers. Hydrotherapy "water cures" flushed out toxins with baths, sweating, and wet bandages.

Even if these practitioners offered the same old blue calomel pills, patients often preferred their services. The newly professionalized physicians, also called allopathic physicians, were too self-important, and with little-to-no bedside manner to boot, some patients felt. They allocated less and less time to listen to their patients at appointments. It's the same grievance that drives many people into the arms of alternative medicine today.

Since medically inclined women were unable to gain entry into traditional medical schools, many chose instead to train and practice in these alternative sects. Harriot Hunt was one such well-known practitioner. At her Boston practice, she treated patients with a healthy mix of herbs, rest, hydrotherapy, and psychotherapy.

Elizabeth refused to be relegated to the medical sidelines, lumped in with the "irregulars." To create the kind of social change she envisioned and demand the same respect given to male physicians, she needed to be educated as officially and as fully as a traditional male physician.

The possibility of studying in Paris was always in the back of Elizabeth's mind. It was an idea that many of the doctors and professors she visited brought up because its universities were more welcoming to female students. But one well-known Cincinnati doctor was positively horrified when she suggested she might stay in Paris as a single woman. Warrington echoed this viewpoint.

"You, a young unmarried lady!" Warrington protested. "Go to Paris, that city of fearful immorality, where every feeling will be outraged and insult attend you at every step; where vice is the natural atmosphere and no young man can breathe it without being contaminated! Impossible, you are lost if you go."

"If the path of duty led me to hell, I would go there," Elizabeth snapped. "I do not think that by being with devils I should become a devil myself."

Warrington was so taken aback by this sentiment, all he could do was sit and stare at her in amazement.

In truth, while she knew there was a better chance of achieving her goal in Paris, she didn't want to take her fight for education to Europe. She thought America was ripe for her social revolution and refused to be forced into traveling to a different continent to earn a medical degree.

Perhaps America wasn't as ripe as she hoped. Over the months, the disappointments mounted. Rejection after rejection hit, each one stinging a bit more than the last. Her applications to twenty-nine different American medical schools, both large universities and smaller "country" schools, had all been turned down. Soon, every option would be exhausted.

A flat, heavy sadness began to descend upon her. Yet her determination never wavered. "I have tried to look every difficulty steadily in the face," Elizabeth explained. "I find none which seem to me unconquerable."

One difficulty Elizabeth experienced was that medical men were scared of the competition female practitioners might present. In a surprisingly frank response to her admission application, the dean of one smaller college wrote back, "You cannot expect us to furnish you with a stick to break our heads with." All this led Elizabeth to the sad conclusion that medical schools were strongly opposed to a woman entering the profession in any official capacity.

"Elizabeth, it is of no use trying. Thee cannot gain admission to these schools," Warrington sighed in exasperation. He had a new idea about how to make Paris feasible. "Thee must go to Paris and don masculine attire to gain the necessary knowledge." He was not the first doctor to suggest Elizabeth disguise herself as a man to earn her degree, but this strategy didn't fit in with her grand plans, either. She wanted to make a point of being a *woman* achieving a medical degree, to make a statement about the capabilities of women.

Finally, in late October 1847, she received a letter from Geneva Medical College in western New York state. Upon reading it, she jumped for joy—she was invited to begin her studies there straightaway! The school boasted seven professors and a new building that housed state-of-the-art laboratories, spacious lecture theaters, and a robust specimen collection. It was much better appointed than similar small medical colleges around the country. School terms ran from October to January, so she had only missed the first few weeks of classes.

Unbeknownst to Elizabeth at the time, her admission was unintentional. Warrington had taken it upon himself to write to the school's professors to entreat them to admit her. His being a prominent Philadelphia physician, the professors didn't want to offend him, so they opted to let the students decide whether to allow a female student into their ranks. That way when she was surely rejected, it would be the students' fault, not theirs.

But when it was put to a vote, the students assumed it was a practical joke—the doings of students at a nearby rival school—and they voted unanimously to allow her entry. That a woman would seriously be desiring entry into medical school was surely a joke.

The students would very quickly learn that Elizabeth Blackwell was far from a joke.

Elizabeth left for Geneva on November 4, only a couple of weeks after receiving her acceptance letter. A few days later, she trudged through the cold, drizzly weather to meet with the college dean and be inscribed on the role as student 130. At age twenty-six, she was a first-time college student; the first woman medical student in the nation.

After being turned away from several boardinghouses because the other boarders threatened to leave if she was allowed to stay, she had begun to worry she might never find a room. At last, Elizabeth found a comfortable room to stay in on the top floor of a large boardinghouse a mere three minutes down the road from her college. The brief walk took her along the high bank of the town's scenic Seneca Lake. The room cost $2.50[3] a week including fuel and lights, but she felt a bit lonesome on the top floor all by herself.

To graduate from Geneva, students were required to attend two sixteen-week terms, submit a thesis, then take an oral exam. Between 1790 and 1820, most states created medical licensure requirements, but essentially, there was nothing in place to prevent anyone from advertising themselves as a healer. To differentiate themselves from all the irregular practitioners and assure their particular allopathic—or science-based—branch of medicine was ensconced in the culture as mainstream, physicians decided they needed national standards.

In 1847—the same year Elizabeth began college—the American Medical Association was born: more than 250 delegates representing forty medical societies and twenty-eight colleges gathered in Philadelphia to define national policies on education and licensing. They decided medical school should be at least six months instead of only four and the curriculum must include anatomy, physiology, pathology, chemistry, therapeutics, surgery, pharmacy, midwifery, diseases of women and children, medical jurisprudence (forensic medicine), materia medica (pharmacology), and theory and practice of medicine.

On Elizabeth's first day of school, Dean Charles Lee instructed her to wait outside until he introduced her to the class. It was an exciting moment—she was about to attend her first official medical school lecture! Lee stepped into the lecture hall in an unusual state of agitation. The students, alarmed by his mood, worried that he might be about to announce the school's closure or proclaim some other dreadful news.

"The female student…has arrived," he said gravely, his voice trembling. The door creaked open and in she walked. "This is Miss Elizabeth Blackwell," he announced.

---

3   About $80 in today's money.

A hush fell over the room as all of the students sat and stared in shock. These 129 medical students were typically boisterous—some days you couldn't even hear the professor's lecture over their din—but today, their unusual stillness continued throughout the lecture. Elizabeth was the only one who took notes that morning.

The rest of her day was gloomy and busy. The rain poured as she scrambled around the building looking for the right rooms for her four subsequent lectures. She had no textbooks and hadn't been told where to get them. The anatomy professor was absent that day and the demonstrator, a kind of assistant to the professor, hesitated to allow her to perform a dissection.

After her first day of attending live lectures, Elizabeth exclaimed, "How superior to books! Oh this is the way to learn!" The next day, the anatomy professor, Dr. James Webster, was back. Elizabeth didn't know what to expect when Dean Lee introduced her to him before class.

"Your plan is a capital one," Webster declared as he shook Elizabeth's hand warmly. Webster was a big man with an even bigger personality; a quick wit who didn't mince his words. After poking fun at the novelty of teaching a female student, he asked, "What branches of medicine have you studied?"

"All but surgery," Elizabeth replied confidently.

"Well, do you mean to practice surgery?" Dean Lee chimed in.

"Why, of course she does!" Webster interjected on her behalf. "Think of the cases of femoral hernia; only think what a well-educated woman would do in a city like New York! Why, my dear sir, she'd have her hands full in no time, her success would be immense. Yes, yes, you'll go through the course and get your diploma with great éclat, too. We'll give you the opportunities. You'll make a stir, I can tell you."

Elizabeth beamed. She handed Webster her letter of introduction from Dr. Warrington.

"Stay here in the anteroom while I read it to the students," he instructed her. She hoped he would remind them of the promise they made when they voted to admit her, that they would be on their best behavior. Webster walked into the amphitheater, and Elizabeth listened at the door as he read aloud the letter. At the end, they erupted in applause.

Such a spirited welcome surprised and pleased Elizabeth. A smile radiated across her face as she entered the lecture hall and sat down quietly. As the delicate surgery demonstration proceeded, she again took studious notes. The only peculiarity Elizabeth noticed that day was that the amphitheater was unusually full, and many of those present were eyeing her with seemingly benign curiosity.

After the lecture, Webster and Dean Lee approached Elizabeth again.

"You attract too much attention, Ms. Blackwell," Webster laughed. "There was a very large number of strangers present this afternoon. I shall guard against this in the future."

"Yes," Dean Lee agreed. "We were saying today that this step might prove quite a good advertisement for the college. If there were no other advantage to be gained, it will attract so much notice. I shall bring the matter into the medical journals. Why, I'll venture to say in ten years' time one-third the classes in our colleges will consist of women. After the precedent you will have established, people's eyes will be opened."

Reporters' eyes were definitely popping. Men had come to gawk at the nation's first woman medical student because news of her admission had already spread to medical journals and newspapers across the country. The Massachusetts *Republican* provided a concise assessment of Geneva's newest resident and the wide-reaching press she'd already garnered. Perhaps the reporter was one of the uninvited guests at that very lecture.

"A very notable event was the appearance at the medical lectures of a young woman student named Blackwell. She is a pretty little specimen of the feminine gender. She comes into the class with great composure, takes off her bonnet and puts it under the seat, exposing a fine phrenology. The effect on the class has been good, and great decorum is observed while she is present. The sprightly Baltimore *Sun* remarked that she should confine her practice, when admitted, to diseases of the heart."

In a letter to her sister, Elizabeth claimed to be perfectly indifferent to the notice she attracted. "I sit quietly in this large assemblage of young men, and they might be women or mummies for aught I care. I believe the professors don't exactly know in what species of the human family to place me, and the students are a little bewildered. The other people at first regarded me with suspicion, but I am so quiet and gentle that all suspicion turns to astonishment."

The small town of Geneva didn't know what to make of her. As she walked back and forth to college each day, little boys, gentlemen, and ladies alike all stopped to gawk at her. A curious animal indeed.

"Here she comes! Come on; let's have a good look at the lady doctor!" she heard well-dressed ladies cry as they darted into her path. Elizabeth refused to take any notice of them. Eventually, the novelty of her being an oddity wore off.

While the surprise of the townspeople was hard to miss, Elizabeth remained initially unaware of the more malicious gossip. "I had not the slightest idea of the commotion created by my appearance as a medical student in the little town. Very slowly I perceived that a doctor's wife at the table avoided any communication with me," she later admitted. "I afterward found that I had so shocked Geneva propriety that the theory was fully established either that I was a *bad woman*, whose designs would gradually become evident, or that, being insane, an outbreak of insanity would soon be apparent."

Elizabeth decided it would be safest if she kept to the school grounds and her boardinghouse. The college became her refuge.

"I knew when I shut the great doors behind me that I shut out all unkindly criticism, and I soon felt perfectly at home amongst my fellow students."

Yet it was only a matter of days before a few of her classmates began pestering her during lectures: a pesky tap on her head from behind, a nasty hiss from across the amphitheater. She shook them off, not giving anyone the satisfaction of her perturbation. During a particularly trying lesson, a folded paper note flew down from the upper seats and landed on her arm as she was taking notes; a conspicuous white flake contrasted against her jet-black sleeve.

"She felt, instinctively, that this note contained some gross impertinence, that every eye in the building was upon her, and if she meant to remain in the College, she must repel the insult, then and there, in such a way as to preclude the occurrence of any similar act," her sister Anna claimed.

Without so much as raising an eyebrow, Elizabeth continued taking notes, pretending she hadn't seen the paper. When she finished, she lifted her arm up to ensure everyone in the room could see it, then, keeping her eyes fixed on her notebook, with the slightest flick of the wrist, she dropped the unread missive flat onto the floor. Loud cheers exploded around the hall, with some students hissing their distaste at the perpetrator.

"Her action, at once a protest and an appeal, was perfectly understood by the students," Anna asserted. She had banked on her quiet manner and utter nonengagement to quickly quell any nonsense. And it worked. Elizabeth had passed the test; the students never bothered her again. Indeed, the students easily acclimated to her presence. Because she was much older than most of them, her classmates began treating her like an older sister.

But her troubles weren't entirely over. Soon, she was being asked to abstain from attending certain classes when the more delicate subject matter would be covered. When Webster, who was one of her earliest supporters at the school, requested she

not come to an anatomy demonstration involving the reproductive system, she decided it was time to put a stop to these
requests once and for all. Elizabeth wrote to him requesting he
reconsider.

"The study of anatomy is a most serious one, exciting profound reverence," her note explained. She demanded that she was
there as an earnest student, and should be regarded in the same
manner as any other student. She conceded, however, that if her
classmates desired her to remove herself, she would yield to their
wishes. Webster read the note aloud to the class while Elizabeth
again waited in the anteroom. She listened as the students responded with hearty approval, then quietly entered and took her
seat. Elizabeth would not be asked to sit out any classes again.

Her determination was put to the test during one particular
dissection early in the term. While she never alludes to what was
being dissected, Elizabeth thoroughly depicts the reactions of
the students. Around the room, some blushed, some were hysterical, while others put their heads down and began shaking.

"My delicacy was certainly shocked," she wrote in her diary.
"I had to pinch my hand till the blood nearly came, and call on
Christ to help me from smiling, for that would have ruined ev-
erything; but I sat in grave indifference."

The more Elizabeth learned about it, the more beautiful she
found human biology. "The wonderful arrangements of the
human body excited an interest and admiration which simply
obliterated the more superficial feelings of repugnance," Elizabeth proclaimed as her studies continued. "I passed hour after
hour at night alone in the college, tracing out the ramification
of parts, until, suddenly struck by the intense stillness around,
I found that it was nearly midnight, and the rest of the little
town asleep."

In January, after the end of her first term, Elizabeth headed
back to Philadelphia. Sadly, she went empty-handed as none of
her professors had provided her with their promised letters of

introduction needed for her to secure an apprenticeship in between terms. Perhaps they felt being associated with a woman
medical student might be professionally disastrous. She lodged
with the Elders again and earned some income by selling a few
short stories and teaching private music lessons and set about
securing an apprenticeship on her own.

The director of Blockley Almshouse received her most kindly.
Blockley was a four-story, two-thousand-patient charitable hospital that cared for Philadelphia's poorest physically and mentally
ill residents. Almshouses were an English tradition carried to
America by Pennsylvania's founder William Penn. As the need
for such institutions grew with America's population, most cit-
ies had a poorhouse by the early nineteenth century.

To get her apprenticeship approved, Elizabeth had to convince
each of the three political parties on the board of the almshouse
to support her. After much lobbying, her petition was put forth
at the next board meeting, the vote to admit her was unanimously in favor.

A large room on the third floor in the middle of the women's
syphilitic ward had been prepared for her to stay in while interning. After hearing several curious patients scurrying up and
peeking in her door, she arranged her stacks of books and papers
on her table so they would line up with the keyhole, obstructing
her from view.

The head doctor allowed her entry onto every women's ward.
She was quite taken with his tender bedside manner, describing
him as "truthful, energetic, and spirited as he is kind." In time,
the nurses warmed to her. But as for the young resident physicians, when Elizabeth walked onto the wards, they walked out.

To these newly graduated men, a woman who dared to muscle onto their hard-earned turf was insulting, her motives suspect. What if she caught them making a mistake? They hindered
her study by ceasing to write the patient's diagnosis, treatment
plan, and case notes on the card at the head of the bed. To avoid

confrontation, she studied in her room until they finished their rounds, when she could wander the wards unimpeded. This lack of cooperation left Elizabeth frustrated. She could have learned so much more if only they hadn't avoided her.

The experience was a crash course in observing suffering, mental illness, and the human condition for Elizabeth. She learned more about treating patients than she could have in a decade of college classes. Her older sister Anna had explained to her that sex wasn't only confined to a marriage bed, but nothing could prepare her for what she witnessed at Blockley. For the first time, Elizabeth encountered the everyday ravages of poverty and male licentiousness: sex workers devastated by STDs, servants impregnated by their employers, and other victims of rape and incest, some pregnant and many still children themselves.

"I see frequently many painful sights. Within one week, a lunatic scalded himself to death, one woman cut her throat, another fell down a cellar opening and broke both legs, they died the following day, another jumped over the bannisters, breaking both ankles," she revealed.

"Last night, just as I had got to sleep, I was roused by running and screaming in the gallery. I jumped out of bed, ran to my window and looked out. There in the moat that surrounded the building, a depth that made me dizzy, lay a white heap covered in blood uttering a terrible sound half groan, half snort. It was a woman who had been confined in the room next to mine and had jumped out of the third story window," Elizabeth described. "There she lay in the moonlight in agony while lamps held out of the windows by pale, half-dressed forms threw a strange glare upon the terrible sight."

Overall, she declared her time at Blockley painful, both in body and mind. Once her eyes had been opened to the suffering and social inequity in the world, there was no closing them.

Elizabeth continued to maintain a surprisingly low opinion of women. Between men and women, there would always be an intellectual difference, she told her little sister Emily. Of the early feminists who gathered in Seneca Falls, New York, that summer—just ten miles east of Geneva—to rally support for women's education and suffrage, she was less than supportive.

In October, Elizabeth returned to Geneva. The townspeople seemed to take less and less notice of her. If she'd had more time for socializing, she might have even been able to make friends with them. As it was, classes and studying occupied most of Elizabeth's waking hours. She had to make do with her interactions with professors and fellow students. "The outside world made little impression on me."

She continued to be an attentive, dedicated student. Her notes from one of Dr. Lee's materia medica lectures show how studious she was and give us a glimpse into what medical students were learning at the time.

When it came to women, the teachings were that their sensitive nervous systems required "the same precaution necessary as in infancy. A delicate woman should not be dosed like an Irishman." Physicians should always inquire as to the presence of menstruation, Lee explained, during which time a woman's nervous system is continually excited. Powerful remedies should be avoided during menstruation, menopause, and pregnancy, otherwise hysteria or miscarriage could result. It was good to be cautious about medication use during pregnancy, but surely many women might have appreciated a healthy dose of pain relievers to combat cramps during menstruation.

Before long, Elizabeth found herself sitting for the arduous final exams. "My face burned, my whole being was excited," Elizabeth exclaimed after it was over. Moreover, "a great load was lifted from my mind." Soon she could reap the rewards of all of the time she'd dedicated to arduous study, revision, and classwork, of the sacrifice of eschewing any semblance of a social life.

The week before graduation, her little brother Henry came

up to be by her side. He had traveled through terrible blizzards to be there with her on her special day.

"I found E. in good spirits, as you may suppose," Henry wrote home. On Monday morning, Henry accompanied Elizabeth to the college, where she underwent a second examination along with the other members of the graduating class. The students welcomed him most warmly. Their intelligence and hospitality impressed him. During the exam, the other students sat by the stove chatting with Henry.

"Well, boys, our Elib feels first-rate this morning. Do you notice how pleased she looks?" one student commented.

"Yes, indeed," another agreed. "And I think she well may after the examination she passed yesterday."

"So Lizzie will get her diploma after all!" a third exclaimed. Then they all agreed that "our Elib" was "a great girl." Henry quickly realized his sister had become a universal favorite of professors and students alike.

"Our Sis came off with flying colours and the reputation of being altogether the leader of the class," Henry raved to his family.

In the afternoon, students were called upon to take turns reading from their theses. Henry got to watch this part, but Elizabeth wouldn't get her chance to read because her thesis was in Buffalo being printed.

Finally the big day arrived: graduation. On Tuesday, January 23, 1849, bright sunshine reflected off the snow and soaked through the windows of the Presbyterian House Church in Geneva. The seats were packed. This year, the room was abuzz with an unusual sound—the crinkling of crinolines. The church was a vast expanse of bonnets and curious female eyes. All the ladies of the town had filled the audience to witness this historic spectacle. As a hearty supporter of Elizabeth and a man who reveled in spectacle, Webster was ecstatic to find the church so full.

At around 10:30 a.m., the procession of graduates entered the building headed by the bishop of New York and the faculty, and accompanied by a rousing Native American band. Webster was anxious that Elizabeth should march in the procession, but she refused. Elizabeth wanted to enter the church with Henry. Her heart beat proudly in her chest as she gripped her brother's arm. The nerves of exams now dissipated, all that remained was excitement. As they ascended the church steps, Webster again urged her to join them.

"It wouldn't be ladylike," she insisted.

"Wouldn't it indeed? Why, no, I forgot—I suppose it wouldn't," he replied, evidently struck for the first time with the idea.

Going against her typical modest attire, Elizabeth had saved up enough money to have a sumptuous black brocaded silk gown and cape made especially for the occasion. It was trimmed with black silk fringe and delicately accented with a narrow lace collar and cuffs. It was an expense, she concluded, that she couldn't avoid. "I can neither disgrace womankind, the college, nor the Blackwells by presenting myself in a shabby gown." She paired the dress with green-black gloves and black silk stockings. Her hair was beautifully braided and unlike most ladies, she was without a shawl and hat.

Once everyone was seated, college president Benjamin Hale said a prayer, then the fiddlers began to play and the choir to sing. The one woman in the choir commanded the audience's attention with her alarmingly loud tones and peculiar emphasis on different words of the songs. Next, Hale called the graduates onstage four at a time to accept their diplomas, each scroll sealed and wrapped with a blue ribbon. Hale doffed his cap at each set of students, but remained seated as he said a few brief words in Latin confirming their degrees. The students replied with a short word of thanks and headed back to their seats.

After all of the calls for *dominus* had been made, finally, the call came for "*Domina* Blackwell." Hale touched his cap and then arose to his feet as she ascended the steps. A hush fell over the entire church. After handing over her diploma, Hale bowed. Elizabeth paused for a moment.

"Sir, I thank you," she proclaimed. "It shall be the effort of my life, by God's blessing, to shed honor on this diploma." The audience roared with applause. Elizabeth's face flushed deep scarlet. She bowed and hurried offstage to take her seat in the front pew with her fellow newly minted MDs. She had graduated at the top of her class.

For those who would follow in Elizabeth's footsteps, the doors would not open so easily. One woman might have been able to slip through the gates as a fluke, an oddity. But if they were to start making a habit of it, well, that was something the profession couldn't abide.

Blackwell's attendance was an experiment, not a precedent, a Geneva professor insisted when the next woman applicant presented herself soon after Elizabeth's graduation.

THREE

Another Elizabeth Blazes the Trail

Nine years later, across the Atlantic Ocean, twenty-one-year-old Elizabeth Garrett was reading the April 1858 issue of the *English Woman's Journal*, where she first encountered the idea of a lady doctor. Lizzie[4] lived in the mansion her father built his family in Aldeburgh, a coastal English town about one hundred miles northeast of London. Lizzie's long, reddish-brown hair was parted neatly down the center and pulled back, swooped up into a broad swirling bun at the nape of her neck.

That summer was one of the hottest on record in England. While Lizzie was enjoying the biting, salt-tinged sea breezes of the Suffolk County coastline, London's residents could scarcely breathe. Later dubbed the Great Stink, the heat caused the sewage-choked River Thames to produce an ungodly smell.

---

4   Elizabeth Garrett's family and friends called her Lizzie. For the sake of clarity, to distinguish her from Elizabeth Blackwell, she is referred to as Lizzie throughout the rest of the book.

In an effort to filter out the rank odor, lime-soaked rags were hung across the riverside windows of the Houses of Parliament; lawmakers covered their noses with perfumed hankies.

The *English Woman's Journal* was a new monthly periodical costing one shilling, the first magazine in England to be published by a feminist organization. At its height, it would be printing 1,250 copies a month. The publication outlined the deplorable conditions many working women suffered and advocated for women's professional sphere to expand. It made a point of highlighting notable professional accomplishments of modern women.

The first article in this particular issue was about the famous Crimean War nurse Florence Nightingale and her efforts to effect radical, immediate changes to the shockingly unsanitary conditions at military hospitals. These institutions had been entirely overwhelmed by the volume of sick and wounded soldiers during the war. When Florence and her team of thirty-eight nurses first arrived at the British encampment outside Constantinople, the doctors were decidedly inhospitable. But as patient numbers increased, they finally acquiesced and accepted the women's help.

The second article in the journal was "Elizabeth Blackwell, M.D.," written by Blackwell's older sister Anna. A lady doctor! What an extraordinary idea, Lizzie must've thought.

Lizzie relished these rare moments of quiet solace when she got a chance to read or write letters to her friends. With ten siblings and her father's busy shipping and malting business being run out of their vast property, silence was in short supply.

Her older sister, Louisa, affectionately called Louie, had recently gotten married, leaving Lizzie with a full docket of household duties to perform as the oldest daughter of the house. There were gardens, piggeries, stables, laundry, and granaries to manage, not to mention maintaining the Turkish bath her father had installed. But despite all of this work, she found her sheltered, comfortable existence increasingly dull. Her energetic body and bright mind longed to be engaged in work that did more to excite her intellect and curiosity. Surely there was more to life than tending her family's home, and then getting married off and tending her husband's home. Why should men be the only ones to pursue professions and politics?

Lizzie read the twenty-page biography of Elizabeth Blackwell with great interest. She learned about how this industrious woman, who lacked the wealth or connections she herself possessed, successfully navigated her way through every obstacle to obtain a medical degree and establish a practice, where she was helping New York's poorest women and children out of illness and destitution.

"Endowed by nature with an unusual energy and concentration of purpose, perfectly unselfish, and with a great amount of practical sagacity and latent enthusiasm combined with remarkable self-command and the utmost quietness of manner, she was perfectly fitted to be the pioneer in the difficult enterprise she had determined to undertake," Anna Blackwell wrote.

Anna also included an excerpt from a letter she received from Elizabeth, describing her reason for choosing to practice in the United States, instead of England, where she briefly studied after graduating: "I believe it is here that woman will be first recognised as the equal half of humanity. In England, where the idea can be intellectually comprehended, there is a deep-rooted antagonism to its practical admission which it may take generations to modify…the central reform has not yet found in England a single earnest advocate; and the time for woman to be acknowledged as the free fellow-worker and necessary complement of man is still in the invisible future."

Despite their fifteen-year age difference, Lizzie recognized the England Blackwell described—one where society limited women to a mind-numbing existence as baby factories and household managers. The "Cult of True Womanhood" that emerged in the early 1800s insisted women were biologically ill-suited to extensive education or work outside of the home. Nevermind the inconvenient fact that many women *had* to work to support themselves and their families, a lady should always know her place: the domestic sphere. Church was often women's only source of diversion outside the home since performing arts, cards, dancing, and reading novels were considered by most religious families to be useless, potentially morally degenerative frivolities.

Society preferred women to embody a sort of friendly ignorance. The 1829 publication *The young lady's book: a manual of elegant recreations, exercises, and pursuits* explained that "in whatever situation of life a woman is placed from her cradle to her grave, a spirit of obedience and submission, pliability of temper, and humility of mind are required of her." A few decades later, little had changed.

Women weren't just expected to be submissive, they were now being told there was only space in their dainty brains for morality *or* knowledge, not both. As women began to question their position in society and push for more education, society scrambled for reasons why that couldn't possibly happen.

While Elizabeth benefited from the slightly more open minds in America, Lizzie remained stuck in the Old World. Lizzie was born in June 1836, Louisa and Newson Garrett's second child. She inherited her father's determination and her mother's short stature and plain features: thin eyes, a long oval face, frizzy hair, and blunted nose. Whether it was a blessing or a curse, her youthful looks always had people assuming she was younger than she was. Her father was an entrepreneurial businessman. Recognizing a growing demand for malt in London breweries, within three years of establishing his grain-malting business, he was shipping seventeen thousand quarters of barley a year and providing a comfortable lifestyle for his family.

Lizzie's mother, Louisa, was a devout Anglican who took loving care of her many children, oversaw the home's cooking and cleaning, and managed the household finances and her husband's business accounts and correspondence. She was content in her life, busy and fulfilled in her domestic role. After marrying, Louisa found herself pregnant every two years or so. She lost one son in infancy, a loss she never truly recovered from.

The family believed in educating girls as well as boys, a growing but not wholly embraced idea at the time. In the mid-1800s, only 50 percent of girls were literate, compared with two-thirds of boys. While most of their peers sat confined in stuffy nurseries, the young Garrett children could be found outdoors, freely exploring the salt marshes, sailmaker's yard, and stony beaches of their neighborhood.

The boys enjoyed a tutor while the girls learned from their mother until the family eventually hired a governess. But this woman was not highly educated. A governess was expected to prepare girls for becoming ladies, and that future didn't involve much in the way of advanced scholarship. As a young girl, Lizzie was interminably bored with her governess's rudimentary lessons and would pester her with questions she knew she couldn't answer.

When she was thirteen and her sister Louie was fifteen, the pair were sent off to private boarding school in London for two years. Here, the teachers proved no more intellectually advanced. They were taught neither math nor science and the French they learned was heavily anglicized. In fact, recalling her teachers' ignorance as an adult made Lizzie shudder.

The sisters became known at school as "the bathing Garretts" because their father insisted they receive a hot bath once a week. Most Victorians settled for an occasional wipe-down with a wet cloth and liberal application of perfume. But for the Garrett girls, every Saturday, a wooden washtub was placed in front of the kitchen stove and, shielded by a towel horse, the girls took turns immersing themselves in warm, soapy water.

Being more familiar with the company of fisherfolk than gentlemen's daughters, Lizzie had trouble fitting in, though she did find a couple of friends. Her closest friend was Emily Davies, a small, plain woman six years older than Lizzie whom she'd met through mutual friends. Emily's mousy, prim appearance belied her caustic wit and progressive beliefs. Emily was an outlier in her conservative social circle, and her feminism had a profound impact on Lizzie. The pair maintained a close friendship throughout their lives, and she no doubt encouraged Lizzie to think of possibilities outside the domestic space.

When Lizzie read about Elizabeth Blackwell's exploits, she had already been out of school for six years, languishing at home as a housewife-in-training. Given the suitors available, the prospect of marriage seemed less than desirous. She felt agitated by a lack of purpose, just as Blackwell once did. A butterfly stuck as a caterpillar.

In January 1859, Lizzie read in the paper that Elizabeth Blackwell would be touring England giving the lecture, "Medicine as a Profession for Ladies." She would be making several stops in London and throughout the country. She had, in fact, already arrived.

Toying with the idea of opening a health sanatorium in the English countryside, Blackwell submitted her credentials to the General Medical Council to be considered for its List of Registered Medical Practitioners. Only those whose names appeared on the register were legally permitted to practice medicine in the country. Those who'd earned medical degrees outside of Great Britain were eligible for registry consideration so long as they had practiced medicine in the UK before October 1858, when the registry law was enacted. Elizabeth had treated a few patients in England when she interned at a London hospital after graduating from Geneva, so she was eligible. It was back then that she met Florence Nightingale, who now wrote her a letter of recommendation to include in her medical registry application. Having Florence vouch for her certainly went far in securing the

General Medical Council's favor. On January 1, 1859, Elizabeth Blackwell became the first woman on Britain's medical register.

Not everyone in England was excited about Blackwell's presence. Many regarded her with what one historian called "well-bred horror." Lizzie's father, Newson, repeated one such writer's assessment aloud to the family: "It is impossible that a woman whose hands reek with gore can be possessed of the same nature or feelings as the generality of women," he read.

"How can you judge a woman of whom you know nothing?" his daughter countered quickly. Lizzie was more and more finding her voice, finding the gumption to push back on the status quo. When pushing for social change, she felt it important to start in your own home. Newson may have been surprised by his daughter's strong defense of a woman she'd never met, but he was open to the possibility that he was wrong to make assumptions about the lady doctor.

Lizzie suggested her father ask his business partner, Valentine Smith, to tell him more about Elizabeth before he made up his mind about her. Valentine's cousin Barbara Bodichon was a close friend of Elizabeth's. Newson spoke to Valentine about Elizabeth, but there was a misunderstanding—Valentine thought Lizzie was looking for a private meeting with her, so furnished her with a letter of introduction. Without realizing it, Lizzie's father set in motion an introduction that would change his daughter's life.

Upon hearing about Lizzie's interest in Blackwell, Barbara invited her and their mutual friend Emily to tea. Barbara was a budding women's rights activist, having founded the *English Woman's Journal*. A tall, lively, well-traveled woman, the thirty-three-year-old Barbara warmly welcomed the younger women. She told Lizzie she'd love to arrange for her to meet Dr. Blackwell when she came to town. Barbara was actually helping arrange her lecture tour.

"For the purpose of opening the medical profession to women

before we are all dead," Barbara explained to her two guests, laughing. As they parted ways, Barbara invited Lizzie and Emily to stop by her magazine's offices in town.

At the office of the *English Woman's Journal*, they found the beating heart of the women's rights movement in England: a group of energetic, fashionable young women hoping to achieve more fulfilling and fair lives for women of all classes. Housed at 19 Langham Place, they were colloquially known as the Langham Place Group. They advocated for expanding the educational and professional opportunities available to women, and for women's right to vote.

In addition to a magazine, the group published pamphlets, crafted petitions, and ran initiatives such as women's arithmetic classes. They had established a social center, registry office, Ladies Institute, and the Society for the Promotion of Employment of Women (SPEW). The Society's goal: "It is work we ask, room to work, encouragement to work, an open field with a fair day's wages for a fair day's work." The long, grueling hours, dangerous environments, and insultingly low wages that awaited women in the working-class jobs open to them—domestic servant, sweatshop laborer, factory or mill worker—led many to turn to prostitution. Some reports say there were thousands of prostitutes in Victorian London.

Agreeing wholeheartedly with the need to broaden the stiflingly limited roles available to women, Lizzie readily joined the Society.

On the day of Elizabeth Blackwell's first London lecture, the sweet, sharp smell of primroses and evergreens filled the hall. Barbara had decorated her reading desk with flowers and wreaths of fresh greenery. Lizzie was among the "intelligent and appreciative" audience that Elizabeth said greeted her. In fact, Elizabeth later called Lizzie her "most important listener."

On stage, Elizabeth—who was thirty-eight by this time— exuded simplicity and quiet authority. Her sisters had been an invaluable resource in preparing her for this moment: Emily helped her draft her speeches, while Anna helped her pick out some elegant new dresses in Paris, which Elizabeth grudgingly purchased so as to appear presentable and professional in front of an audience.

In her speech, Elizabeth described the unique, far-reaching impact women physicians could have on the health of women patients and that of their families by teaching them about sanitation, nutrition, and hygiene. She argued that women being doctors was simply a natural extension of the healing and caretaking responsibilities they already undertook within their homes. By teaching mothers how to keep healthier homes, women physicians could impact the health of entire families. She assured the audience her declarations were not mere speculation, but borne of eight years spent practicing as a physician in New York. She also outlined the obstacles facing women interested in pursuing medicine.

"The chief difficulty in the way of women students at present is, as it always has been, the impossibility of obtaining practical instruction. There is not in America a single hospital or dispensary to which women can gain admittance," Elizabeth lamented. She was speaking from experience, when after graduating, the only place she could find practical training and hospital experience was France. Traveling all the way to mainland Europe was a troublesome and expensive solution—beyond the means of most women—but it was the only way a woman could obtain anything that deserved to be called a medical education, Elizabeth declared.

Elizabeth presented a call to arms to upper-class women to contribute to improving the social welfare of their country. Instead of being listless ladies, she proposed they should give back to their communities by working in hospitals, schools, and prisons. She meant them to engage in active work of good social standing and authority, working alongside intelligent coworkers. She wanted them to have purpose: "the feeling of belonging to the world instead of [leading] a crippled and isolated life."

Lizzie's heart must've skipped a beat. She was hearing her own feelings voiced onstage, and what's more, she was being offered a road map to a solution in the form of professional fulfillment.

After the lecture, Barbara whisked Elizabeth to her house to celebrate. Lizzie was invited to join. Here, she presented Elizabeth with the letter of introduction, but there was another misunderstanding. Recognizing her from the audience, Blackwell was sure Lizzie was interested in pursuing medical study. She spoke with her at length about how she might accomplish this.

"She assumed that I had made up my mind to follow her," Lizzie explained. "I remember feeling very much confounded and as if I had been suddenly thrust into work that was too big for me." In fact, Lizzie didn't have a specific occupation in mind at the time, with "no particular genius for medicine or anything else." While Lizzie may not have liked to admit it, Elizabeth clearly made an impression.

Fate had brought Elizabeth Blackwell into her life at just the right moment. Here was Elizabeth, suggesting medicine as a viable, enriching profession, claiming that while such a path was difficult, it certainly wasn't impossible. *Why* not *medicine?* Lizzie must have thought.

Lizzie went on to attend two more of Elizabeth's London lectures, given at the Portman Rooms on Baker Street a few blocks east of Barbara's house. While the tour made its merry way on to Manchester, Birmingham, and Liverpool, Lizzie and Emily were off to be bridesmaids in a friend's wedding. There, Lizzie continued entertaining the idea of studying medicine, encouraged by Emily.

"It seemed to us that the duty of ministering as a physician does to the care of women and children would be work not unsuitable to a woman, and also that it was work they ought to be free to take up if they chose," Lizzie later recalled of their talk.

"Naturally neither of us knew much of the details of medical education, nor did we realize how long and sustained an effort would be needed before our end could be reached."

As a clergyman's daughter, what Emily did know was that women doctors could make an immense difference in the lives of poor women and children. She had seen the way they suffered when accompanying her father on visits to his parishioners in the tenements of their industrial town of Gateshead in northern England. By the end of the wedding festivities, Lizzie's mind was made up.

Upon her return to Aldeburgh, Lizzie's younger sister Alice was waiting for her at the train station. As she climbed into the small pony-drawn carriage, Lizzie whispered exuberantly to her: "I'm going to be a doctor."

Emily came to stay with Lizzie a few months later. One evening, the girls were sitting in Lizzie's room brushing each other's hair by the fireplace. Lizzie's younger sister Millicent sat on a stool nearby, watching and listening. Emily was twenty-nine, Lizzie twenty-three, and Milly thirteen. Most of the younger Garrett children found Emily insufferably dry, a killjoy who never stopped harping on about education. They didn't know what Lizzie saw in her. But Milly's interest was piqued. As the young women brushed, they made plans that would transform society as they knew it: three witches conjuring changed fates.

"Women can get nowhere unless they are as well educated as men," Emily declared.

"Yes," Lizzie agreed. "We need education but we need an income too and we can't earn that without training and a profession. I shall start women in medicine. But what shall we do with Milly?"

Emily turned to the girl. "You are younger than we are, Milly, so you must attend to getting the vote for women."

When young women get together to imagine a better world, and inspire each other to start a revolution and not stop until it's over, incredible things can happen. Seven years later, Milly was asked to join the executive committee of the London National Society for Women's Suffrage. She then served as president of the National Union of Women's Suffrage Societies for many years. Little Milly indeed dedicated her life to tirelessly campaigning for women's suffrage. Her dream of voting rights was finally realized in 1918, and she retired the following year. For her work, she was awarded a damehood.

Lizzie wasn't the only one stirred by Elizabeth Blackwell's example. The London lectures led to the formation of a committee hoping to create a hospital for women, run by women. A circular was drafted seeking funding, which was signed by sixty-six well-known ladies. For a time, the efforts came to nothing, but eventually, their wish would come true.

In February 1860, Lizzie again found herself sitting down to read about Dr. Blackwell in the *English Woman's Journal*, this time with renewed attentiveness. This piece had been penned by the doctor herself. In reading Blackwell's "Letter to Young Ladies Desirous of Studying Medicine," Lizzie began to fill the gaps in her knowledge of how to begin her medical training and what would be required.

Students should be between the ages of twenty and thirty, in good health, and possess a liberal English education in addition to having a familiarity with French, Latin, and Greek, Blackwell explained. She outlined a four-year education plan: the first year should be spent living at home studying medical texts under the direction of a physician. She recommended a healthy stack: Carpenter's *Physiology*, Wilson's *Anatomy*, Pereira's *Materia Medica*, Watson's *Practice of Medicine*, Druitt's *Surgery*, Churchill's *Midwifery* and *Diseases of Women*, Alison's *Pathology*, Fownes's *Chemistry*, and Bell's *Legal Medicine*.

Assuming you finished all of those books, you should spend the first half of the second year working as a nurse in a hospital, and the latter half training in a laboratory and receiving private instruction. Next, students must travel to America, one of the few countries where they could earn a medical degree. Two women's medical schools had been opened in the years since Elizabeth graduated, but more importantly, more established American colleges were becoming coed. Finally, six months should be spent training at La Maternité midwifery training hospital in Paris, just as Elizabeth had done. Elizabeth firmly believed that the measly two years Americans spent earning a medical degree didn't provide nearly enough preparation or real-world training.

From the outset, Elizabeth didn't sugarcoat the hurdles that awaited these women. Speaking from her own experience, she warned, "The task is a very arduous one, and should not be lightly undertaken. Independently of the difficulties involved in the study itself, there are social difficulties which are far greater. Society has not yet recognised this study as fit woman's work. Gossip and slander may annoy the student, and want of confidence on the part of women, with the absence of social and professional support and sympathy, will inevitably make the entrance of the young physician into medicine a long and difficult struggle."

Lizzie understood her first difficulty would be gaining the approval and support of her family. Conventional wisdom held that a career of any kind would ruin any chance she had for attracting a worthy suitor. It was a point of pride for middle-class families that their daughters didn't need to work. And to be interested in the grotesque realm of medicine as a woman would convince friends and relations that she was surely unrefined, if not completely deranged.

Lizzie decided she would wait to tell her family about her newfound career plans until after she completed some of the educational prerequisites Blackwell mentioned. To do this, she convinced the schoolmaster who came to their house to tutor her brothers to give her Greek and Latin lessons in secret. Emily helped by correcting Lizzie's English compositions by mail. Her newfound goal and sense of direction had greatly improved her mood. But she knew that sooner or later she would have to tell her family what she was up to.

So on June 15, 1860, Lizzie approached her father. She'd had plenty of time to consider what she would say, many months to practice a speech or to prepare responses for the questions or concerns she imagined he might hurl at her. Still, trepidation must've bubbled inside her as she approached her father's study.

"I wish to study medicine," she declared matter-of-factly.

"The whole idea is disgusting!" Newson roared, cutting her off. "I could not entertain it for a moment."

"What is there to make doctoring more disgusting than nursing, which women are always doing and which ladies have done publicly in the Crimea?" she persisted. Newson could come up with nothing. "I must have this or something else; I cannot live without some real work."

"It would take seven years before you could practice," Newson pointed out, now trying to appeal to her practical side.

"Six, not seven," Lizzie corrected. "And if it were seven years, I should be little more than 31-years-old and able to work for 20 years probably."

"At least I cannot agree to it without more thought," Newson finally conceded. He had recognized his own stubbornness in his daughter. She was not about to give up.

"I think he will probably come round in time," she wrote to Emily. "I mean to renew the subject pretty often. He does not like it, I think…but he will soon be reconciled *if I succeed*. This is an all important point."

Lizzie's mother was a different story.

"The disgrace!" she wailed upon first hearing her daughter's ambitions. She shut herself in her room and became ill from so much crying, sinking into a terrible depression.

While Lizzie was visiting her older sister, Louie, in London, she received a letter from her father warning, "You will kill your mother if you go on." It was a full week before Mrs. Garrett calmed down enough to have a coherent conversation about Lizzie's plans. Their talk went on for two hours.

"But Lizzie, why don't you stay at home and act as a governess to the younger children?" her mother suggested hopefully. Lizzie said she would not find it satisfying to live at home her entire life. Her mother was mystified.

"They naturally feel very anxious about allowing me to enter upon such an untried life, and they are greatly puzzled as to the motive which can influence me," Lizzie wrote to Emily in exasperation. "I cannot make them understand how impossible it would be for me to live at home in happy idleness all my life. I believe they feel very nervous about either refusing or sanctioning it, but as long as I am very decided, there is a good hope of their coming round."

When Lizzie's cousin Sarah Freeman and her husband came for a visit, Newson brought up the idea of women physicians at dinner one evening. He was testing the waters with his immediate family to see how the idea might be received. Sarah proclaimed she was soundly opposed to such a development. Lizzie was dismayed, but Sarah failed to back up her opinion with any intelligent reasoning.

"I must say, I should prefer a woman attending my wife and daughters," Newson replied. "If I could be thoroughly satisfied that she was qualified."

"Miss Blackwell was not so strictly examined as men were," Sarah quipped with satisfaction.

"I should have expected the examiner to be more strict with her than they are usually," Newson shot back.

"If *I* had been an examiner," Lizzie's brother Edmund interjected, "*I* would have refused to examine *any* woman."

When both Newson and his daughter Alice began to speak, Newson's voice prevailed: "That would have been very mean and cowardly of you."

Newson wasn't entirely supportive of Lizzie's plans, so he

was surprised to find himself defending women doctors at the dinner table.

When it was time for Lizzie to set off in search of advice on how to proceed, he decided he didn't want his daughter roaming the streets of London alone. Only a couple of weeks after Lizzie confessed her career choice to her father, the pair found themselves walking together down Harley Street seeking the opinions of the city's leading physicians.

The street was home to approximately twenty private practices; numbers that would multiply exponentially in the coming years. By 1914, there would be nearly two hundred. Some of the doctors laughed in her face, others were frightfully rude.

"Why not be a nurse?" one of the nicer doctors politely suggested.

"Because I prefer to earn a thousand, rather than twenty pounds a year," Lizzie quickly retorted. Though they returned home with little to show for their visit, witnessing this continued opposition continued to put Newson in the role of his daughter's defendant.

When she wrote to various family members about her professional aspirations, Lizzie expressed a desire for a more engrossing pursuit:

"During the last two or three years, I have felt an increasing longing for some definite occupation, which should also bring me, in time, a position and moderate income. It is indeed far more wonderful that a healthy woman should wish for some suitable work, upon which she could spend the energy that now only causes painful restlessness and weariness."

Despite being quite clear in her letters that her mind was made up and she was not seeking any advice on the matter, aunts and cousins flooded her with liberal doses of it. They pleaded with her to abandon this highly improper scheme, couching their discrimination in concern that it would ruin Lizzie's health, fray her nerves to the point of breaking.

When Lizzie admitted to Emily that she was puzzled about

where to turn next to begin her medical training, Emily suggested she speak with the president of Dr. Blackwell's committee, Emelia Gurney. Emelia had promised Blackwell that she would assist any woman interested in pursuing medical training. Emelia's charm dazzled Lizzie, and she and her husband arranged for her to meet with William Hawes, a governor of Middlesex Hospital who happened to be an acquaintance of Blackwell's and a former business associate of Lizzie's father. Emelia and her politician husband, Russell, also hoped Hawes could be the one to convince Newson once and for all to fully support his daughter's scheme.

Hawes was obliging but shrewd when Lizzie came calling on July 7. He asked if she had any idea of the difficulties in what she was proposing.

"It is because I feel so ignorant about them that I dared not speak or think confidently of the strength of my determination," she confessed.

He suggested she should test her mettle, prove her power of endurance before she wasted any time on fighting to obtain an education. Lizzie proposed she should spend six months as a nurse at Middlesex Hospital, an arrangement Hawes could easily organize. He agreed, but on the condition that the first three months would be probationary. Lizzie expected to work in the women's ward, but Hawes had his own ideas. If she could stomach the surgical ward, he reasoned, she could most certainly handle being a physician.

It didn't matter which end of the pool Hawes threw Lizzie in, this seaside girl was determined to swim.

FOUR

More Than a Nurse

Surgery in the mid-nineteenth century was not for the faint of heart—as a practitioner or a patient—as Lizzie would soon learn. Ether had just been introduced as a surgical anesthetic in America in 1846; chloroform quickly followed in Britain in 1847. At last patients were finally, blessedly, "rendered unconscious of torture," as one clearly relieved Victorian doctor put it. Before anesthetics, patients were awake and in agony during the entire surgical procedure. They had to be held down or tied down. Surgeons had to work quickly, and speed was often favored over accuracy. In cases of cancer that were operated on, surgeons sometimes failed to clear out all of the malignant tissue. Some in the profession felt that anesthesia feminized medicine by lessening the heroics required of the surgeon.

A successful surgery also wasn't guaranteed survival. Bacteriology—indeed, the very discovery of the existence of germs—was just being born. The prevailing theory was that infection was the result of miasmas: poisonous airborne vapors. Between 1795 and 1860, only a few doctors had spoken out against miasmal theory. These dissenters believed it might be that the doctor was transferring deadly substances onto the patient. Such ideas, though scoffed at and brushed off at first, would eventually lead to the revolutionizing of medical science.

The most convincing of these examples was that of Ignaz Semmelweis. In 1847, Semmelweis began working in one of the two obstetrics wards at a teaching hospital in Vienna, Austria. He noticed the ward where midwives delivered babies had a much lower rate of childbed fever–related deaths, 2 percent, than the ward where medical students delivered babies, 13–18 percent.

Childbed, also known as puerperal fever, was an infection of the uterus. Semmelweis noticed students were heading straight from performing autopsies to deliver babies, and rightfully observed infections were arising from exposure to "cadaverous materials." After he instituted a hand-washing station of chlorinated lime solution for the students, the mortality rate in their ward fell to nearly match that of the midwives. Instead of being lauded for his life-saving revelation, Semmelweis's contemporaries mocked him, and his superiors insisted the improvement was thanks to the hospital's new ventilation system.

Alas, spic-and-span surgeons with glistening tools and brutally scoured hands was not what greeted Lizzie as she stepped into Middlesex Hospital's surgical ward for the first time on August 1, 1860. In this pre-antiseptic era, surgeons' blood-crusted black aprons, instruments, and hands were likely teeming with filth. Hospitals at the time were more often than not covered in grime. The characteristic white coat of physicians was still decades in the distance. This was the dark ages of medicine, but the enlightenment of antisepsis was flickering on the horizon.

Lizzie arrived at the hospital promptly at 8:00 a.m. every morning. During her tenure, she was living with her older sister, Louie, her sister's husband, James, and their children. By the end of her first week, she was already familiar with the cases in the two surgical wards where she was stationed.

When Emily asked for a detailed account of her day, Lizzie wrote: "I begin at once to prepare for the dressings by spreading the different ointments, preparing lint, lotion, poultices, bandages, etc. While I am doing this at a side table, the sister is going round and examining all wounds. The simpler cases she leaves entirely to me very often, but the more difficult ones, such as cancer, she dresses herself while I look on." The time this took varied constantly depending on the number and nature of the cases, but she generally had time to go upstairs and visit the patients in two medical wards before joining the house surgeon, Thomas Nunn, in his eleven o'clock rounds. A bald man with a scruffy beard and a wry sense of humor, Nunn allowed colleagues and students to call him Tommy.

"There was a small operation in the ward today, which I saw and the surgeon was very kind in explaining the case to me and making me see what he was going to do. There was only one pupil with him, but he made him stand out of my way," she told Emily. Nunn, impressed by this woman who didn't flinch in the slightest at the sight of blood, promised to take her along on his visits to the outdoor department, also known as home visitation.

After the doctor and surgeon finished their rounds, Lizzie gave patients their medicines as prescribed. Lunch was a fortifying meal of mutton chops and ale, which Lizzie ate alone in the hospital canteen. At 1:00 p.m., she returned to the surgical ward to accompany any visiting surgeons. When they were finished, she was allowed to leave. At first, she stayed until the patients had been given dinner, but quickly realized this time would be better spent studying at the museum.

"The museum reading room is such a jolly place, the air is so pleasantly warm and fresh, and I am sure that has a great effect on one's brains," she told Emily. "I am studying rheumatism just now, reading upon it at the museum (when I am tired of physiology), and watching a good many different forms of it in a medical ward."

Typically, Lizzie arrived back at home by 4:30, where she rested for half an hour, talking to Louie and James and playing with their children. After changing her clothes into something more dainty, she did algebra till teatime at seven o'clock. To close out her day, she wrote letters to friends and family by the fire or practiced Latin.

Lizzie hadn't been away from home two weeks before she started receiving melancholy letters from home. Her mother was speaking in the most morbid of terms, having decided her daughter's actions were in direct defiance of her commands. Lizzie had been forwarded an extraordinarily gloomy letter from her mother, in which she declared that Lizzie's decision to become a doctor was a source of lifelong pain to her, a living death. Soon, more letters from relatives began pouring in, urging Lizzie to return home for her mother's sake.

"I think this is quite stupid advice," Lizzie groused to Emily. "It is rather provoking that people will think so much of the difficulties, in spite of my assurances that so far from being appalling, I am enjoying the work more than I have ever done any other study or pursuit."

The nurses and doctors treated her kindly, but Lizzie was always mindful that she might invite gossip if she got too friendly with the male staff. As for her fellow students, she thought it "wise not to appear too frigid and stiff with them. If they will forget my sex and treat me as a fellow student, it is just the right kind of feeling. It does seem to be wrong in theory to treat them as one's natural enemies."

This is a tightrope that women must always walk on, to constantly have to consider: Am I being friendly enough? Am I being overly friendly? As women began entering previously men-only professions and educational spaces, these became near-constant calculations in careers and subjects across the board.

But around the senior resident medical officer, Dr. William Willis, Lizzie felt entirely at ease. The calm, straightforward manner in which he freely explained all he knew about clinical diagnosis melted away any potential awkwardness. Willis would later be the inspiration for the highly skilled and incredibly sympathetic doctor character in Joseph Conrad's semiautobiographical novel, *The Shadow-Line*. The book details Conrad's experience of captaining a ship for the first time, from Bangkok to Singapore. Before they could leave, Conrad had to call in Willis, the British Legation's physician, to tend the fevers, cholera, and dysentery his crew was suffering from.

Lizzie worked closely with Dr. Willis, joining him on rounds and asking his opinion on difficult diagnoses, learning by observing his methods and practices.

She schlepped up and down Middlesex's large stone staircases as many as twenty times a day, fetching outpatient notes, medicines, and clean linens. Lizzie quickly concluded that rich, solid-colored dresses that lacked trimmings or ornamentation like beading or braiding, and did not require frequent renewing were the most appropriate for this work.

Physicians typically wore the uniform of all professional gentlemen of the time: a white button-down shirt, black single-breasted frock coat and trousers, and a vest in a muted tone. Having no precedent for women doctors' clothing, Lizzie decided to dress similarly to the nurses she worked alongside: a button-front, tight-bodice dress, perhaps with fashionably wide bishop sleeves, and a white skirt apron.

A month into her training, she observed her first major surgery: "I did not feel at all bad, the excitement was very great but happily it took the form of quickening all my vitality instead of depressing it," she told Emily excitedly. "I was exceptionally tired after it was over, but this effect will soon cease I should think." Still, the chorus of voices telling her ladies should not enjoy or be able to endure such sights took its toll on her psyche:

"Sometimes I fear I must be dreadfully obtuse, not to feel what everyone seems to think must be so trying."

By October, she became frustrated by her unofficial position as a sort-of student, one who enjoyed all the perks of being a student at the hospital's associated school without being given any real direction or assignments and without paying for tuition or working toward a qualification. And while she found the work engrossing, her lack of knowledge of Greek often left her feeling lost and needing to look up terms. She wanted to be a fully fledged, official student. She had faced surgery—she was ready.

"It was very difficult to make way in this desultory manner," Lizzie complained to Elizabeth Blackwell, whom she also kept in correspondence with. Elizabeth was eager to hear how a woman medical student was being received in England.

Lizzie approached the hospital's treasurer and surgery lecturer asking to pay tuition. Campbell de Morgan, an imposing figure with a dark beard, told Lizzie he could not allow it, as it would mean the hospital would have to recognize her as a student. Instead, he offered to let her make a donation in order to be allowed to stay on through the winter as an amateur. He would permit her to work in the surgical wards, observe operations, and accompany the house doctors on their rounds. She made the donation and agreed to these terms.

Lizzie also enjoyed the new privilege of a small room of her own in the hospital where she could rest, read, and store her personal belongings. The compact apartment's shelves were full of old dishes. She believed she may be inhabiting a former pantry. Lizzie began pitching in with the hospital's shopping and linen washing, but one of the nurses cooked meals for her. She invited another Langham Place lady, Ellen Drewry, to come study chemistry with her in her tiny room. But Ellen's ridiculous fashion choices made Lizzie hope no one at the hospital would suspect she was associated with her.

"She has short petticoats and a close round hat and several other dreadfully ugly arrangements," she criticized.

Soon, Lizzie convinced the head nurse to allow her to take on night duty alone. After Dr. Willis made his final rounds at midnight, he would sit and chat with Lizzie.

But it didn't seem to matter how much experience she was gaining, how much responsibility she was entrusted with. When she asked de Morgan about ever getting into the hospital's medical school as a regular student: "Impossible!" he crowed. "A lady's presence at lectures would distract the other students' attention. All the London colleges will refuse to admit you. You might as well go to America at once."

In the meantime, de Morgan suggested Lizzie seek private lessons from the hospital's apothecary, Joshua Plaskitt. A young, thoughtful, and well-read medical man, Plaskitt happily agreed to this arrangement. Plaskitt had gone into medicine at his family's urging; he preferred reading Tennyson and Carlyle to medical texts. Lizzie found him an excellent teacher and thoroughly enjoyed the three or four hours she spent under his tutelage learning Latin, Greek, and materia medica every day. It was better than studying alone but not nearly as good as attending real lectures.

Willis suggested a second tutor might be of great help. Lizzie wrote to Emily to ask if she thought it would invite salacious gossip if Willis came to tutor her at Louie's house once or twice a week. Willis was about a year younger than Lizzie and unmarried. While she was waiting to hear from Emily, she consulted her father and two other friends. Weighing the risk of sullying her reputation against the potential to learn from such a kind teacher with a gift for explanation, she decided the tutoring would be worth it. Emily wrote back that it would indeed be most improper, but her letter arrived too late. Willis had arranged to come teach Lizzie anatomy and physiology three times a week for two hours at the price of one guinea[5]. Newson thought it a more than reasonable price.

It was an exciting time to be involved in the rapidly changing field of medicine, and already, Lizzie was learning of the push-pull between practitioners who clung to the old ways and those who eagerly embraced science-based innovation. Plaskitt believed medicine scarcely deserved to be called a science since it was grounded largely on empirical evidence rather than a search for "curative laws." As for Dr. Willis, he thought medicine as it was currently practiced was indeed an exact science. Lizzie said she was inclined to side with Willis.

When her three-month nursing probation period was over, she began to be treated more like a real student, even if she wasn't one. New patients were befuddled when a woman in an apron was called in to examine them; many thought their symptoms were being explained to a cook. Still, Lizzie worried her educational progress was too slow, but her two tutors were most impressed by the results of the exams they administered to her in December. She nearly had memorized the first two texts she was assigned, Barrett's *Outline of Physiology* and *Elements of Anatomy* by Jones Quain.

"The general feeling seems to be that each doctor is willing to help me privately and singly, but they are afraid to countenance the movement by helping me in their collective capacity," Lizzie complained in a long letter to Elizabeth Blackwell written on January 2, 1861. "This will, however, come in time I trust, and in the meantime it is a great thing to meet with so much individual courtesy and help."

About the work itself, she was more positive: "I feel anxious to tell you how very much I enjoy the work and study, as this is to a great extent unexpected to me. I was prepared to find the first year's preparation work tedious and wearing. That this has not been the case is mainly due to the fact of my having ac-

---

5   About £140 or $185 in today's money.

cess to the hospital practice, which acts as a continual aid and stimulus to study." She waited until March to send the letter, hoping to have better news to report to Elizabeth in the way of becoming an official fee-paying student.

When Plaskitt left the hospital to practice privately, Lizzie finally successfully petitioned the dean to allow her into the chemistry lecture. For her first class, she went to the lecture hall early and took a seat in the empty room, so as not to make a scene when entering a room full of male students. While she expected her appearance to startle them, they only showed their astonishment by an occasional grin as they came in.

Every Saturday, chemistry lecturers Redwood Taylor and V. R. Heisch orally quizzed the class on what they'd learned that week. "Last Saturday I tried to speak, but really could not," she admitted. Plaskitt advised her to get over this shyness as soon as possible in order to show she was like any other ordinary student. So the next week, she answered the first question asked, and many others. Heisch was so impressed with her knowledge, he had her stay behind in the lab after class where he showed her slides under the microscope.

The male students continued to be courteous and respectful, and Lizzie was sure they would become more comfortable around her over time. Lizzie spent all day studying or in class—an eager, dedicated scholar—so she was surprised and horrified to find so many of her fellow students merely coasting, uninterested. She reckoned about six other students were attentive and took notes, but the rest she dubbed "amazingly ignorant."

"I am very much struck with the extraordinary ignorance of some of the students. One, in his second year, did not know the healthy heart sounds. I felt so tempted to patronize him and explain them," she railed to Emily. "Mr. Taylor put some very elementary questions to one of the dunces today, and his answers tried the sanity of all the more knowing ones very much. They were several times too much even for Mr. Taylor."

After chatting with one of the doctor's clerks, she understood what was happening. He explained the students were graded on "signing up," having to simply attend lectures. Most students didn't bother to read up on the subject, and therefore lacked any basic understanding, such as the chemical symbols drawn on the blackboard.

Medicine, for many men of the time, was the profession you went into after showing no particular aptitude for anything else. Medical students had a reputation for being a rather wild, roguish bunch. Four years before Lizzie arrived, Nunn had been deputized dean of students in an effort to reduce their disorderly behavior. They often turned the dissection room into a boxing ring, preferred bars over lectures. Things had largely calmed down by the time Lizzie began her training, but she worried this was part of the reason she remained the only woman in England pursuing a medical degree.

In a letter to the *English Woman's Journal*, Lizzie expressed surprise that the movement for women doctors was progressing so slowly in England. She knew there were plenty of women who would enjoy entering the medical profession, and plenty more who wished to be tended to by female physicians. "I believe this hesitation is chiefly due to an exaggerated idea of the difficulties in the way," Lizzie wrote. She encouraged other women to join her in her quest. "We do not want to prove that rare women can do wonderful things, but that the lives of ordinary women may be more useful and more happy than they are now," Lizzie eloquently concluded. As stirring as her words were, no other women showed up to join her crusade.

Celebrated feminist author and academic Carolyn Heilbrun once aptly observed how "exceptional women are the chief imprisoners of nonexceptional women, simultaneously proving that any woman could do it and assuring, in their uniqueness among men, that no other woman will."

Soon Lizzie was allowed into the dissection room. Happily,

she found it lacking any of the ghoulish horrors her girlfriends warned may await—no corpses draped over chairs or dangling by their feet from the ceiling—just a few tables bearing bodies gently laid out and neatly covered in calico sheets. And she thought the subjects didn't really resemble people much anymore. The room, she concluded, wasn't overwhelming, and the work incredibly interesting.

First, she swapped her skirt apron for a long-sleeve smock. Then, after choosing a table facing the window, she quietly got to work. In a dissection of a foot, she was fascinated by the delicate structure of the rootlike plantar nerves that fan out from the ankle through the toes.

"I have been talking to the chemists about you," Nunn the surgeon cheerfully admitted to Lizzie when she stopped by to see him one day. "I told them that there could not be any more awkwardness in men and women working together than in them going to church together. A great deal has already been done towards undoing prejudices." Lizzie was pleased to hear that he was helping spread the word about the ease with which men and women could study together.

Independence emboldened Lizzie. She basked in her widening hospital work, reveled in each small social and educational advance she made. Sensing she was just beginning to taste the enjoyment she would experience as a real student, the more opportunities she got, the hungrier she became for more. In lamenting her lack of power at Middlesex Hospital, Lizzie told Emily that if she were given a much larger measure, she could accomplish so much more.

"It is hard to be contented with a gooseberry nature, when one sees that a peach is wanted," Lizzie complained.

Lizzie was determined to ask for permission to attend more courses when the next term began. She consulted Emelia Gurney on whether or not she thought it was immoral to employ one's feminine wiles when making such requests of men. Was flirting acceptable if it helped her achieve a desirable outcome? Should she not use her youthful looks and delicate features to help her achieve equal educational opportunities?

"I feel so mean in trying to come over to the doctors by all kinds of little feminine dodges," she admitted.

"I think they did not matter," Emelia replied. "It is often a matter of perplexity to me to know if feminine arts are lawful in a good cause. I think they have immense weight from any woman."

On the first day of the new session in May, Lizzie screwed up all of her courage and approached Dr. Henry Thompson, a tall, mumbling man with long white whiskers. She asked him to admit her to his materia medica lecture. She saw that her boldness had completely confounded him, so before he could answer, she assured him that the chemistry professors were already allowing her to attend their lectures. This seemed to ease his doubts. He said she would be welcome to attend.

Finally, de Morgan put her name on the books as a part-time student. Lizzie signed the student oath, promising, "I will not smoke in the garden or wards but will in every way comport myself as a gentleman." Now, she would receive a certificate for each lecture course she attended, but wouldn't be in the running for any of the prizes. She told the treasurer she wished to become a fully admitted student in the October term.

Many of the doctors who had been convinced she would meet with unheard of insults from fellow students now admitted to her that perhaps in some cases, the experiment may be safely tried. She told Emily she understood their hesitancy to open the school freely to women, because all it would take to ruin it was "one flirting woman," though it pained her to admit this.

Funny that she should condemn flirting when she herself admitted to doing so in certain professional settings. Perhaps she saw her own flirtations as innocent or for a greater good, while others might spend all day fluttering their eyelashes at doctors and patients for other reasons, such as trying to win a husband. On one hand, Lizzie would've loved to have a few women join her as fellow doctors-in-training, on the other, she recognized that precedent-setting required people to be above reproach in every respect. She catastrophized about women in much the same way that Elizabeth did. One "wrong" type of woman setting a terrible example had the potential to derail her whole cause.

Lizzie was also worried about how she would do on her tests since she found details and isolated facts difficult to remember. But when it was time, she did so well on her exams that she was advised not to tell the other students how high in the grade-ranking her name appeared. Even with such discretion, she could only hide her impressive intellect for so long. Her intelligence quickly became threatening to the male students. She had long since outlived their toleration; many of the students were sure she would've given up by now. Once, when a visiting doctor asked the students a question, only Lizzie knew the right answer.

That was the last straw. Embarrassed, a group of forty students met to brainstorm how to get rid of her. The group formed a committee and submitted a petition to Middlesex's administrators, requesting that Lizzie be dismissed from the school and that Middlesex "memorialize" the prohibition of women students. Some of the professors and other hospital physicians grew less and less civil to Lizzie, especially as her limited influence in the medical community grew.

"Dr. Thompson was annoyed at my notes of a case having been sent to *The Lancet*," she told her father. "I suppose he said something to the students and gave them an idea that by making this grounds for a protest they might get me removed. Considering that the case had been in the ward nearly five months one would think they might have reported it before now if they had thought of doing so. I am perfectly certain that none of them saw the real points of peculiar interest in it till I pointed them out."

Nunn said she would no longer be permitted into the dissection room without a professor present. The chemistry lecturer advised her not to attend the exam since she would be left alone with the other students to write their papers. "The students dare not be rude," Lizzie convinced herself. "I am sure and if they were, I should survive it." She refused to be frightened away.

When she heard about the petition, Lizzie composed a letter to the student committee pleading with them to withdraw their request. She told them that if her presence prevented the lecturers from giving their usual course, they had a right to object. But if the lecturers guaranteed there would be no change whatsoever in their lectures, they need not object.

The response from the committee chairman outlined a different problem. It wasn't the potential changes in course content that worried them, it was the impropriety of men and women mingling in one class while studying subjects "of a delicate nature." They refused to back down.

While she waited patiently for the hospital to decide whether or not to acquiesce to the students' petition to oust her, she had little hope. "I believe my death-warrant will be signed next Thursday," she lamented to Emily. "It is horribly vexing but I don't despair, trials are good and I very seldom have any, and it won't stop me from studying nor from finally doing my work whatever that may be. I do not feel at all crushed, though somewhat adrift."

She invited Emily to meet her at the hospital that Thursday evening, where they could have tea and then go to the Bach Society's private performance of the *Christmas Oratorio*. She tried to lose herself in the music and forget about losing all she'd worked so hard for.

When Nunn heard the school's final decision, he was too scared to tell Lizzie himself. When she finally went to ask Thompson, he was clearly nervous that she might go into hysterics upon hearing the answer. The lecturers had decided they did not like the presence of a woman in their classes and that they feared it would harm the school's reputation. She would be permitted to finish only the lectures that she had already paid for, but after that, she would have to leave. They did regret arriving at such a consensus in the case of a lady who'd displayed such an incredible union of judgment and delicacy.

If this rejection hadn't gotten to her before, it did now. "I felt horribly crushed yesterday," she cried to Emily. "It was so bad to think all the way gained during this year was to be lost in that way." Just when she was finally being allowed to participate in real classes and demonstrate how naturally she took to the material, that was when her presence was deemed unacceptable.

"You will be sorry to hear that the students have had their way," Lizzie wrote to her father. She explained that while they cited her *Lancet* publication as inappropriate, that wasn't really what they took issue with. "This special charge was only an excuse," she claimed. "They don't like to see a woman working hard and they want to snuff her out if possible. Their masculine sense of superiority is insulted by the competition which must tacitly go on."

She left herself little time for moping. Lizzie went to see the physicians at the children's hospital in town to ask permission to visit there. Between that, the final lectures, and her independent studies, she reckoned she'd have enough work to keep her busy and her mind off this setback.

After her last days at Middlesex, Lizzie spent the next few years splitting her time between London and Aldeburgh. In the former city, she enjoyed a busy life of concerts, church, garden parties, art galleries, and a lot of hard work at Langham Place. In the latter city, Lizzie practiced Greek and Latin. She applied to every London hospital, to no avail. As for the University of London, its senate was deadlocked ten to ten on the issue of allowing women students on their new charter. The chancellor, Lord Granville, broke the tie voting against it.

Just like Blackwell, Lizzie's attempts to gain entry into medical training didn't go unnoticed. *The Lancet* published the article about the commotion she'd caused: "A lady has penetrated to the core of our hospital system. How should this fair intruder be received? Is she to be welcomed as on all other occasions we should welcome a lady or should we resist the charge of parasols? We anticipate an almost unanimous condemnation of the effort to introduce young women into the classes of medical students at our hospitals."

It was a most disagreeable and vulgar article, Lizzie scoffed to Emily after reading it. A few weeks later, a notice appeared in the same journal reveling in her defeat, happily announcing that Lizzie's request for admission to the London Hospital's medical school had been unanimously declined by the lecturers.

She decided it would be best not to make any more attempts at other London hospitals just now. She would spend time in private work. That summer, back at her Aldeburgh family home, Lizzie realized how atrophied her social skills had become. Small talk had become perfectly uninteresting to her. And just as her mother had feared, the specialized knowledge she'd gained in her studies didn't do anything to improve her attractiveness to men. Lizzie liked to pretend she cared little for such things, but she wanted to get married someday.

Lizzie continued to focus her energies on securing a path to becoming a registered physician. She applied to the examining bodies in Oxford, Cambridge, Glasgow, and Edinburgh. For her name to be placed on the medical register, she would have to meet the educational qualifications and then pass a licensing exam at one of the General Medical Council–approved examining bodies. All rejected her.

The only approved body left was the Society of Apothecaries. As per its royal charter, the society could examine and license people in medicine after they completed five years as an apprentice and three years in lectures, demonstrations, and hospital practice. These qualifications could be undertaken by "all persons," the charter stated, not just men. Lizzie wrote to Plaskitt proposing that he apprentice her. She would need his name and a plan mapped out when she applied to undertake licensure through the Society. After conferring with his business associates, Plaskitt agreed. Lizzie sent off her application and waited.

On August 20, Lizzie's entire family crowded around the dining table, waiting with bated breath as she opened the response letter from the Apothecaries. They had consented to examine her once she fulfilled all of the requirements.

"Hurray!" her siblings all cheered, and hearty congratulations were offered from all at the table. She was ecstatic. It was a triumph, to be sure, but many more hurdles lay ahead, most notably, completing three years of medical schooling and finding a school that would take her.

Lizzie returned to London, again staying at her sister Louie's house. The current editor of the *English Woman's Journal*, Bessie Rayner Parkes, introduced her to Dr. John Chapman. Having exhausted all English options, Lizzie now turned her sights to becoming a student at Chapman's Scottish alma mater, St. Andrews, and sought his advice on how to make this happen. Chapman advised her to spend the winter studying Latin, Greek, history, geography, logic, and mathematics. He also provided her with introductions to attend lectures in botany at the Pharmaceutical Society, in natural history and physiology at the South Kensington Museum given by Professor T. H. Huxley, and in physics at the Royal Institution given by prominent Irish physicist John Tyndall.

At Huxley's lectures, Lizzie felt uncomfortable as the only woman in a vast sea of men. "It is a very large theatre, and one feels much more conspicuous than in a small school lecture room," she admitted. The lecture covered the differences of sex, and Lizzie had to try very hard to appear perfectly indifferent. She worried that it might injure her cause to appear either too eager or too embarrassed.

When Dr. Chapman noticed her awkwardness, he began

bringing his young daughter along with him to the lectures. As for the professor, Huxley wasn't sure about women entering the sciences, but he at least believed their intellectual inferiority was the result of nurture, not nature. "Let us have 'sweet girl graduates' by all means," he once wrote. "They will be none the less sweet for a little wisdom; and the 'golden hair' will not curl less gracefully outside the head by reason of there being brains within."

Lizzie had dinner with Ellen Drewry one October day in 1861, then together they attended an evening physiology lecture. Lizzie was pleased to find herself familiar enough with the subject to understand and enjoy it. It was an even greater surprise to realize they were not the only women in attendance that night. The Hill sisters, Octavia and Miranda, as well as Octavia's girlfriend, Sophia Jex-Blake, were also there.

Lizzie and Sophia had long moved in the same circles. Both were members of Reverend F. D. Maurice's congregation and both belonged to the same debate society. It was only a matter of time before they met.

After the lecture, the women all piled into Louie's living room, where they undertook a long, lively discussion of metaphysics, the origins of evil, and individual responsibility. The Hills were a poor family and their drawl grated on Lizzie's ears, and she was sure Louie didn't like or even understand most of what Sophia was talking about. Still, it was nice to have some intelligent women to socialize with.

Lizzie found Sophia smart but odd. "She has some peculiarities which do not quite harmonize with my own," Lizzie told her mother. But there were very few women interested in the sciences, so she was willing to overlook their mismatched personalities. "I shall be very glad to work with Miss Jex Blake for the sake of having someone to talk to; it is very hard to live such a silent life as I am tempted to do," Lizzie said.

They continued attending Huxley's lectures together, and

he eventually acknowledged their presence by beginning his lectures with "ladies and gentlemen." Little did she know, her contentious friendship with Sophia would last much longer than she expected. They would make history together.

FIVE

Young Sophia

Twenty-one-year-old Sophia Jex-Blake was big and brash, a stout, feisty educational reformer with large eyes and an even larger personality. She scoffed at conventional ideas about female propriety and often said things simply to shock people, though she remained oblivious to how chafing her personality could be. Sophia always looked deep in thought, pensive: her brow serious, her eyes sincere. She parted her long, dark hair down the middle and pulled it back in a woven nest of braids or into a wide, flat bun.

Sophia longed to become an educator and found her own women's school so she could help improve the state of women's education in Britain. Her parents didn't approve of women pursuing a career or higher education. Her father permitted her to work as a math tutor only if she did not accept a salary. But for Sophia, that wasn't enough. She was determined to work in some field that would advance the rights and educational opportunities for women. In all that she did, the more resistance she got, the harder she pushed back.

To gain her father's permission to leave her hometown of Brighton and attend Queen's College, Sophia said she had to go "into hysterics." Throwing calculated temper tantrums involving fits of screaming or dramatic melancholy was a common tactic of rich girls trying to get what they wanted from the men of the family who wielded the purse strings. These men also wielded far too much control over the lives of these adult women. Queen's was the first college in Britain where women could earn professional academic qualifications. There, Sophia took classes in arithmetic, geometry, algebra, English, French, history, natural philosophy, astronomy, theology, and church history. She was a voracious learner.

Soon, she became quite actively involved with the Langham Place feminists alongside Lizzie and Emily. Lizzie had more time for such work after being forced out of Middlesex Hospital. Ever-proper Emily found Sophia horribly abrasive and tended to avoid her. While some found Sophia too tempestuous and overbearing, those who took the time to get to know her saw that her actions came from a kind heart and good intentions.

Sophia was born in the small town of Hastings on the south coast of England in 1840 to a retired-lawyer father and a frequently ill mother. Thomas and Maria Jex-Blake were aged fifty and thirty-nine, respectively, when the exuberant Sophia bounded into their lives. A well-off family descended from landed gentry, the couple's first three children didn't survive infancy, but their last three did. Her parents were exceptionally devoted to their children after having experienced such losses. Sophia's older brother was eight and her older sister six when she was born. The family moved to nearby Brighton a few years after her birth.

Little Sophia was a bundle of energy. Her parents doted upon her like an only child since her siblings were largely away at school.

Being strict Evangelical Anglicans, all "worldly" amusements—novels, theater, dancing—were deemed sinful and forbidden in their household. Left to create her own entertainment, Sophia conjured up a fairy kingdom, the land of Sackermena, ruled by one "Grand Mogul and Despotic Emperor Grandiflora." Instead of imagining the fairies or princesses having adventures, Sophia spent most of her time concerned with her imaginary society's constitution: how lawbreakers should be punished and how the line of succession to the throne should go. From the ages of eight to ten, when she was learning how to write, Sophia filled many pages with these fantasies. She also drew large, intricate maps of the kingdom.

Her mother, Maria, had a sharp wit and remarkable sense of humor. Maria's parenting abilities were tested at every turn by Sophia. This was especially true because of Maria's undiagnosed illness, which manifested as fatigue, migraines, and fainting spells that were brought on by loud noises or emotional disturbances. Such a boisterous daughter proved too much for her to handle, and Sophia was sent to boarding school at age eight with her older sister, Caroline, often called "Carry."

"More sad and foolish behavior than yours it is difficult to imagine," her mother wrote to her soon after she arrived at school. "You behaved so ill that I doubt if I could have borne another day without being laid on a bed of sickness, and I might never have recovered. Your ever being with us again for three weeks at a time is *quite out of the question* till you have the good sense to understand (as other children of your age do) that to be happy and comfortable and to enable me in my weak state to have you at all, you must be *good*."

Knowing that she was the cause of her mother's flares of illness must have caused young Sophia great guilt and anxiety, which likely exacerbated her poor behavior. But it wasn't all guilt trips.

The frequent letters between "dearest little So" and "darling darling mother" and "darling father" over the years show dedication and increasing affection on both sides. The older siblings always believed Sophia was their parents' favorite, their special bonus baby. On the back of a hotel keeper's note, Sophia and her father scribbled this dueling verse when she was ten years old:

"My little child, You're very wild,
Could you be still, And yet not ill,
Then, little So, This I do know,
You'd be a blessing, Worth possessing."
"My dear Father, I had rather
You'd believe me, And relieve me,
When I say, As I may,
That I'll be good, As I should."

Over the next eight years, Sophia changed boarding schools six times, often being kicked out for troublesome behavior. Sophia was a fast learner. Her boredom at tedious schoolwork and agitation from not getting the regular exercise and time for play that her male peers did caused Sophia to regularly act out. Teachers deemed her headstrong, insubordinate, and regrettably unladylike.

But her fellow students saw her softer side. One schoolmate described fourteen-year-old Sophia as trustworthy, truthful, passionate, and affectionate; her biggest flaw being that she was "excessively clever and unfortunately knows it, and makes a point of showing it off upon every possible occasion."

Now, when Sophia dreamed of opening her own school for girls, perhaps she imagined creating an institution where strong-willed, highly intelligent girls could feel at home; a school where she herself could have thrived as a young girl. But her plans were dashed again when she left Queen's College prematurely over a heartache. Soon after Sophia met Lizzie, she and her girlfriend Octavia broke up. Sophia's mercurial, domineering nature had driven Octavia to call off their relationship.

Sophia had long known she preferred women to men, and Octavia was the love of her life. A beautiful woman with bewitching eyes, wide lips, and a mischievous smile, Sophia lovingly called her "Octa." They met in January 1860, when she gave Sophia a private bookkeeping lesson. Sophia describes one "most delicious day" when the couple were sitting together in Octa's bedroom. "My heart [was] beating like a hammer," Sophia recalled. Octa silently sank her head into Sophia's lap, only to raise it up again toward Sophia's face. "Then—such a kiss!"

Everything started to go downhill when Sophia moved in with Octavia, her mother, and four sisters. It's doubtful that the family was at all aware of the romantic aspect of the girls' entanglement, so that wasn't the issue. One problem was that Mrs. Hill knew Sophia's rich family looked down their noses at them. The biggest difficulty lay in dealing with the day-to-day squabbles of seven strong-willed women living together. Octavia tried to be the peacekeeper, but after a mere six months she could no longer take it and moved out. Her mother, sisters, and Sophia all wrote to Octavia incessantly, begging her to return. Octavia finally asked Sophia to move out and decided to cut all ties with her.

It was a heartbreak Sophia would never entirely get over. It proved so painful that she decided to move to Edinburgh for a clean start. Sophia had been told there were educational opportunities for women in Edinburgh, but unfortunately, the mathematics classes for ladies she attended were rudimentary at best. She eventually found private tutors that could offer her more advanced lessons in German, mathematics, and English.

Sophia must have continued writing to Octavia despite their breakup, because she received a letter from her imploring her to move on: "I wonder if it would be any comfort to you if you could know the infinite love the thought of you calls up. And yet, Sophy, this thought of me must fail you as time goes on.

My love will be ready for you when He shall bring us together again."

In her diary, Sophia eventually lamented that she'd at last faced the reality of never seeing Octa again in this life.

She tried to focus instead on her professional interests: becoming a teacher, founding a school for girls, and helping women secure access to an education that was as advanced, extensive, and rigorous as men's. Emily and Lizzie were determined that she should join their crusade to personally obtain a higher education.

"I want you to make up your mind to obtain a University degree," Lizzie urged Sophia. "You are one of the few women who could do so pretty soon…it would take most women a year and a half or two years to prepare for matriculation."

But Sophia remained skeptical of how much use a liberal arts degree would be in achieving her goal of establishing a school. She would just need training at a teacher's college. Besides, no university in the country was open to women, so pursuing a degree was essentially impossible.

Lizzie wrote to Sophia to keep her apprised of the studies she'd been undertaking. "Miss Garrett and her strength!" Sophia exclaimed in her diary. "Making me break the Tenth Commandment!"[6]

Despite all her progress, Lizzie was experiencing setbacks of her own. Only a few months after her move north, Sophia received a letter from Lizzie explaining that her applications to every medical school in London had been turned down. She asked Sophia if she would help her seek admittance to the University of Edinburgh. Having recently been on the receiving end of rejection, of the romantic sort, Sophia was all too willing to busy her mind with helping Lizzie. She told her friend she'd be welcome to come and stay with her, and that she would be more than happy to set up interviews for her around town.

On May 30, 1862, Lizzie arrived in Edinburgh and reunited

---

6   The Tenth Commandment being "Thou shalt not covet."

with Sophia. Her first appointment was the very same day with John H. Balfour, professor of botany and dean of the University of Edinburgh medical school.[7] Founded in 1726, it was the first medical school in the United Kingdom.

Lizzie stayed with Sophia for two weeks at her home in the city's bustling West End Haymarket area. As the pair went about canvassing various important citizens of Edinburgh, looking for support and advice, it was assumed that Sophia was the one interested in pursuing a medical degree. She was much taller, more animated, and, despite being four years younger than Lizzie, looked much older. Lizzie was clearly cultured and practically pretty; why should she need to pursue such a path, forsake a home and husband?

While talking about the difficulties in studying practical anatomy at one such appointment, one person—alluding to Lizzie's petiteness—said they hoped she would be able to find some "nice *little* subjects" to dissect. At this well-meaning quip, Sophia and Lizzie exchanged a knowing glance, and it was all they could do to keep their composure.

Lizzie's twenty-sixth birthday happened to fall on a day during her visit with Sophia. To celebrate, the pair embarked on a countryside expedition over a long weekend in early June. Out in the Trossachs, a natural park about sixty miles west of the city, there were steep braes, glorious wooded glens, quiet lakes, mossy rocks, and fern-covered crags to explore. Outside their bedroom windows, a waterfall roared.

When they went out hiking, Sophia sought out the steepest, most treacherous routes she could find, while Lizzie kept to the more sure-footed paths whose trees and bushes offered footholds and something sturdy to grab onto. Occasionally, they had to find an overhang to duck under to avoid getting soaked by a sudden downpour.

The last morning of their stay, they set out to ascend Craigmore,

---

7   Actress Tilda Swinton is Balfour's great-great-granddaughter!

one of the Trossachs' smaller hills at nearly 1,300 feet. When they finally reached the top, they both shouted triumphantly at the top of their lungs. It was a glorious view of the adjacent ridges and the shimmering Loch Ard below. They sat and read a prayer book for a few hours before climbing down.

Back in the city, Lizzie's father, Newson, joined them for a second round of interviews at the University of Edinburgh. In preparation for their efforts, Sophia had published multiple letters pushing the cause of women's education in *The Scotsman* and *The Daily Review*, among other papers. She also drafted a joke letter in response to her own, in which she posed as a sexist opposed to educating women. They thought publishing such a letter would be immensely fun.

Before submitting the letter, both women spent a night tossing and turning with second thoughts about the implications of such a letter. It began to seem dishonest, that such joking might reflect poorly on their cause. After a long night of considering the pros and cons of submitting such a letter, Sophia walked out of her bedroom into the sitting room and sat down at the writing table.

She turned to Lizzie. "Oh, I've annihilated the *Review* paper; it's not righteous altogether," Sophia sighed.

"No, I've been thinking in the night. I was going to advise you not to send it," Lizzie replied, immediately relieved. Perhaps they just needed to write the letter, not publish it.

Now, all they could do was wait as the University of Edinburgh deliberated upon Lizzie's fate. To see if two weeks of traipsing around the city, personally pleading with the great thinkers and influential citizens of the town to consider showing their support for admitting Lizzie to the university had made any kind of dent in people's attitudes toward women's education.

While they waited, Sophia and Lizzie received a lovely letter of encouragement from Elizabeth Blackwell. To have the support of the first woman in America to earn an MD was something quite special indeed. It invigorated and inspired them.

Finally, word arrived from the University of Edinburgh. Frustratingly, their decision was essentially a nondecision: they refused to even entertain the idea of whether or not to admit her. Still, the motion to consider the question of admitting her was dismissed by a thin margin: eighteen votes against and sixteen in favor.

"I do not know whether we are to look upon the result as a defeat or as a triumph," Sophia said, perplexed. She had quickly taken the mantle of Lizzie's cause as her own. "Very disappointing as regards immediate results, but very much as a victory for the principle, just as at London University. You see they have not refused to admit, only postponed the question indefinitely."

Lizzie was disheartened, but left no time to wallow. She had already been corresponding with the professor of medicine at the University of St. Andrews, Dr. George Day. He said Lizzie and her father would be welcome to come stay with him while she attempted to gain admittance to his university, which was fifty miles north of Edinburgh.

Sophia, meanwhile, packed up and headed to Germany in hopes of broadening her knowledge about education systems by working as an English teacher at one of the country's distinguished girls' schools. These institutions were of a much higher caliber than Britain's girls' schools: more rigorous and academically advanced. Lizzie had encouraged her to get going already on her chosen career path. "Miss Garrett was right enough when she said 'Get teaching!'" Sophia said, and so she was off.

She eventually found a temporary post filling in for an ill teacher at the Grand Ducal Institute in Mannheim. The position was unpaid, but came with room and board. It was a forty-student, two-year boarding program for fourteen-year-old girls who had completed a basic education. Sophia's room was small and spare, but she turned it into her own little paradise.

At first, she found this meaningful work incredibly invigorating, just as Lizzie had upon entering Middlesex. Her heartbreak was finally a thing of the past. In her spare time, she enjoyed reading Charlotte Brontë's novels, which occasionally brought her to tears.

"And now I have been here nearly a month, already established as if for years, in full sunshine of content. At work again! And, thank God, with such strength for it! A new sap and strength in all my veins, my heart in songs of gladness," Sophia exclaimed in her diary. "The heavy burden seems to have rolled away, the sting and bitterness quite gone; strength and power returned to my hand, colour and brightness to my life."

It brought a smile to her whole face when she wrote her mother about how energized she felt teaching. "You see idleness and listlessness is about the worst thing possible," Sophia explained, echoing the thoughts of many of her female contemporaries who similarly longed for an intellectually engaging pursuit. "Now my days are full, not only materially, but really, for it is the kind of employment that does fill and satisfy me."

As satisfying as work was, and as confident as she sounded to friends and family, Sophia occasionally wrestled with a great sense of imposter syndrome. "I seem so oppressed with a sense of the greatness, the weight of my work, and of my own miserable insufficiency for it. Oh, so weak and stupid and unfit! And it isn't humility, it's just truth," Sophia moaned, believing that while she talked a good game, she couldn't always follow through. "I'm horribly showy, always deceiving people into a belief of talents I haven't."

Maybe Sophia was coming to terms with the fact that she hadn't turned out to be as good at teaching as she'd hoped. One of her students complained about Sophia's demanding curriculum to a friend in England. Soon, the students were testing the boundaries of Sophia's patience and teaching ability. They would torment her, accusing her of crying in church and listing out all of the skills she lacked. "You cannot sing, nor play, nor dance, nor paint, nor embroider!" they would tease. "What *can* you do, Miss Blake?"

But what Sophia proved truly less than talented at was maintaining order in a classroom of twenty-five teenage girls. Though she never lost her temper at them, she could be brusque and unjust. For the most part, when her students teased her or acted up, she responded with stone-faced indifference. And besides, it was true that while she possessed a sparkling speaking voice, Sophia was a terrible singer. The girls' taunting finally abated after they saw a beautiful gown she wore to the school ball—an old bridesmaid's dress from a friend's wedding. They called it ravishing.

Some days she feared she'd chosen a path seeking her own glory, rather than a path that would glorify God. Others were simply bad days: "Cold. Therefore rather cross and grumbling. Prowling about the corridors with shoulders nearly up to my ears," she scrawled in her diary. After her eight-month teaching stint was complete, she headed home to Brighton—delayed in Germany for three weeks by a bout of scarlet fever. As her fever raged, she missed her mother and was a terrible patient.

Shortly after she arrived back home, Sophia was contacted by Reverend T.D.C. Morse of Manchester. Morse was interested in establishing a ladies' college in his town and had asked the professors at Queen's College for advice. They connected him with Sophia, saying she was highly qualified and might be interested in helping found such an institution. She jumped at the chance. Sophia spent months in Manchester drawing up intricate plans for the school, visiting other colleges to discuss what systems they used. In the end, Morse wasn't able to raise enough money to get the project on its feet and the plan was scrapped. Even though this particular college didn't make it off of the drawing board, the experience left a lasting impression on Sophia. She was one step closer to designing a school and was resolute to make it a reality.

SIX

Sophia in America

Sophia became intrigued by America's recent experiments in coeducation. For men and women to be taught together was astonishing to her. To see this work up close, she and her friend Isabel Bain sailed for Boston in May 1865. Just before leaving, Sophia attended the first meeting of the Kensington Society, where she heard Lizzie speak about the limits of parental authority. Sophia likely hadn't seen Lizzie since they stayed together in Edinburgh and was again struck by her friend's ambition. The society was a feminist discussion group established to arrange campaigns around women's rights issues like education and suffrage.

Sophia and Isabel's sea voyage was an adventurous one. "We were summoned by a cry of 'Icebergs!' and up we ran to see a bright white light on the horizon, just visible, right on our track. Soon another came in sight." What a tremendous sight this was for Sophia's first sea voyage. "On went the ship, tearing on to the icebergs, that grew whiter and larger every minute—great cliffs of white rearing themselves out of the waves that beat into spray at their base—looking so strong and grim and beautiful."

In Boston, Isabel and Sophia stayed with famed essayist and poet Ralph Waldo Emerson. He was a major player in the transcendentalist movement in America, having helped establish *The Dial* magazine that Elizabeth Blackwell greatly admired.

Tensions were high in America as the Civil War had only just ended. Sophia was surprised by how resentful people were of the Brits. Though officially neutral in the conflict, it was well known that the prime minister wished for the US to become a permanently divided nation. Thousands of Brits had lost their jobs in cotton mills after Union blockades saw raw cotton supplies from the American South dry up. In retaliation, the British repaired many Confederate ships, which went on to inflict terrible damage on Union vessels. These actions could hardly be viewed as neutral.

Emerson and his friends apparently had a lot to say on the subject. Sophia did her best to maintain her composure when such discussions arose, noting it was all she could do not to kick over the table.

A woman in their company, Elizabeth Peabody, should have been of great interest to Sophia. Peabody had established a girls' school and recently opened the first kindergarten in America. However, her fierce political views left little else to be discussed in her company.

One of Sophia's first stops in Boston was to meet with Dr. Lucy Sewall, a vocal advocate for women's rights in education and professional work. A family acquaintance of Sophia's had provided her with a letter of introduction to Lucy. She was already a medical pioneer in her own right, having graduated from the New England Female Medical College three years prior at the tender age of twenty-five.

Throughout the second half of the 1800s, more women in America were claiming medical degrees, but not from attending established medical schools as Elizabeth Blackwell had done. It was thanks to the separate medical colleges for women that began opening. First came the New England Female Medical College in 1848, established by a male homeopathic doctor who believed it was immoral for men to deliver babies. The Female Medical College of Pennsylvania soon followed in 1850, set up by a group of progressive male Quaker physicians in Philadelphia.

However, a degree from a women's medical college was seen as not on par with an MD from a traditional university. Graduates of these schools were largely categorized as among the "irregular" practitioners. In the case of the New England school, this was perhaps an apt assessment. The Female Medical College of Pennsylvania provided a more rigorous curriculum with higher quality professors, but it still lacked a hospital that allowed students to attend regular clinical lectures.

Lucy had rounded out her education with an additional year's study in Europe, training in surgery and laboratory investigations in London, Paris, Zürich, Munich, Vienna, and Edinburgh. When she returned to Boston, she became a resident physician at the New England Hospital for Women and Children. The hospital was established by Elizabeth Blackwell's protégé Marie Zakrzewska.[8]

Professional women working in careers other than teaching were a radical sight to behold, especially for an Englishwoman, so Sophia jumped at the chance to watch Lucy at work. The women were fast friends, bound by their zeal for the promotion of women's education. Sophia also found Lucy quite attractive, with her long silky hair, wide blue eyes, and a youthful face nearly as sweet as her nature.

Sophia observed and assisted Lucy in the hospital dispensary. One morning she helped her examine thirty-six patients. Some appeared with bright faces, reporting they were, "So much better, Doctor," since their last visit. As for others, Sophia could

---

8   Pronounced Zak-chef-ska.

clearly see they were in pain, "poor souls," she whispered to her diary. Lucy kindly explained each patient's treatment to them clearly and firmly. A graceful young woman with beautiful dresses, she also provided a good example of a woman who hadn't sacrificed her femininity in a male profession.

"I can't tell you the pleasure it gives one simply to see Dr. Sewall in her hospital and especially among her poor patients," Sophia wrote to her mother. "Certainly the right woman in the right place." But Lucy's bubbly personality couldn't always disguise her melancholy. "She is such a true Healer; so infinitely compassionate and sympathetic, with blue eyes sometimes quite full of sorrow for the people's pain, yet such strong firm hand and will to remedy even through pain."

Lucy was always asking Sophia and her traveling companion, Isabel, to join her in going out, to theaters or for ice cream, or playing a rousing card game called Muggins back at the hospital.

"You don't know what an immense thing it is for us to have got free admission to the Woman's Hospital life here," Sophia gushed to her mother. "We are always doing something jolly together with the students and doctors—all women, by the way."

Sophia couldn't always participate as fully as she'd like since she suffered from occasional episodes of joint pain, weakness, irregular heartbeat, and shortness of breath (possibly the consequence of a childhood infection). Unaccustomed to the heat and humidity America offered, Sophia's health problems continued their occasional flare-ups in Boston. She bounced between feelings of an overexcited puppy and a burnt-down candle. In attempting to keep up with her new friends, she was likely ignoring her body's limitations.

Lucy was quite worried about Sophia overexerting herself. She suggested Sophia use the hospital's electromagnetic machine on her face to treat her neuralgia.

These machines used electrical currents to successfully treat disorders of the nervous system and musculature: pain, weakness, nonepileptic seizures, convulsions, and cramping. Electrical baths were also a common treatment. With Michael Faraday's discovery of electromagnetic induction in 1831 came ways to better harness the potential effectiveness of such treatment. By the middle of the century, most large hospitals had a department for electromagnetic therapy.

Soon, the large tabletop apparatuses were compacted into a portable, shoebox-size medical battery. Inside the wooden box was a battery connected to a wire that was wrapped around an iron core. The core had another unconnected wire wrapped around it. When turned on, the iron core was magnetized by the direct current in the first wire. The various methods used to create a pulse in the direct current altered the core's magnetic flux, creating an alternating current along the second wire. Different makes of batteries provided either a pulsing, galvanic direct current, an alternating faradic current, or a combination of the two.

Faradization treatment was applied several times a week. General faradization was used for diseases thought to be systemic in origin. Patients would place their feet on top of one electrode platform while an electrode wand was swept across the body. Each session lasted for about ten to twenty minutes. Local faradization was applied for a few minutes to ease location-specific ailments such as migraines. Soon, medical batteries were being marketed to the public, to the exasperation of most medical professionals, who worried about untrained hands operating such devices.

After watching her for some weeks, Lucy pronounced Sophia "worn out in mind and body." She prescribed a holiday in the hills until the heat wave abated.

Sophia took a brief sojourn to West Compton, New Hampshire, near the White Mountains, then embarked on her tour of American colleges where women were welcome: Antioch and Oberlin in Ohio, Hillsdale in Michigan, the Mary Institute in Missouri. To learn about best practices in women's education, she met with women academics in all manner of fields: astronomer Maria Mitchell, retired mathematics professor Lucretia Crocker. She also stopped in at various public schools.

Sophia returned to Boston, though without Isabel, who had decided to enroll at one of the colleges they visited. Lucy offered Sophia a room to stay in at the little residence associated with the hospital and a job doing clerical and accounting work.

"I am so exceedingly content in my quaint pleasant quarters in the midst of so new a working world, that I hardly feel the need of anything beyond," Sophia reported to her mother. "I have ready to hand just as much work as I feel able for, and yet no strain on me to do it if I am not able."

"It is such a joy to me to hear of your being occupied so usefully and happily, and feeling comparatively well, though I suspect sometimes my little one is a wee overdone," her mother replied.

Sophia made a fantastic addition to the little community of hardworking women at the hospital. The day after she moved in, the student who was responsible for the hospital's drug dispensing was suddenly called away. At the same time, the hospital was dealing with an influx of particularly demanding cases. Sophia cheerily volunteered to fill the gap. A true jack-of-all-trades, she ended up acting as apothecary, general secretary, keeper of hospital case records, and even occasional chaplain. Before long, everyone had heard of this lady who was helping the doctor through "oceans of figures in hospital reports."

Sophia accompanied the doctors on their 7:00 a.m. rounds through the wards, writing down the foods and medicines each patient needed. Next, she made up all of the medicines prescribed to the inpatients and checked inventory to see what drugs needed to be ordered in the dispensary. At 10:00 a.m. on Mondays and Thursdays, when it was Lucy's shift in the dispensary, Sophia assisted, making up prescriptions as fast as Lucy could write them.

At any given time, sixty to seventy patients could be found

in the waiting room. Whenever Sophia ventured out from the back room, she was seized upon by eager patients interested to know when Dr. Sewall would be ready for them. At 1:00 p.m. when the dinner bell rang, Sophia often still hadn't finished all of her work.

"This hospital life is simply charming. So busy, so simple, so quaint and so interesting! I am entering more and more fully into it daily, and finding more and more nooks which I can fill," she told her mother. "It's a great comfort to be of some sort of use to these people who are so frightfully overworked just now." She enjoyed learning how to mix up medicines, though the prescription she made up for herself, at the doctor's direction, was "precious nasty!"

This experience in the clinic solidified for Sophia the incontrovertible need for more female physicians. Over and over again, when patients were questioned as to why they hadn't sought treatment sooner, they responded, "Oh, I could not go to a man with such a trouble, and I did not know till just now that ladies did this work."

Others exclaimed, "It's so nice to be able, at last, to ask ladies about such things!"

Week after week, Sophia watched how poor women crowded into the dispensary on the four days when lady physicians were in charge, while only a handful stopped by on the two days when a male doctor presided. Anecdotal evidence, sure, but she still felt it spoke volumes.

"I think anyone who passed a couple of mornings in this dispensary would go away pretty well convinced of the enormous advantage of women doctors," she mused.

The women who wanted to become physicians were often told that there was no demand for them. Sophia reasoned that it was likely because people didn't often think to demand what didn't exist. "I believe that there is a large amount of work actually awaiting them; that a large amount of suffering exists among women which never comes under the notice of medical men at all, and which will remain unmitigated till women are ready in sufficient numbers to attend medically to those of their own sex who need them."

Many feminine maladies were thought to be caused by the uterus itself, pregnancy and menstruation rendering women at the mercy of their reproductive system. Such theories grew out of teachings from ancient Greece, where it was believed that everyone had a creature inside them driving them to sex. For women, this creature was their uterus. The uterus didn't just want sex, it craved semen, and would only be fully satisfied when it became pregnant.

If a womb went too long without carrying a child, it became bored and listless and began wandering throughout the body. This could cause all manner of problems, the teachings went. It might restrict her breathing, leading to coughing fits, or burrow in the rib cage, prompting chest pains and heart palpitations.

The Greek word for uterus was *hystera*, so this idea eventually gave rise to the catchall condition applied to any woman whose diagnosis eluded doctors: hysteria. Before long, the term became an epithet to lob at every unwieldy woman.

By the Victorian era, a woman's entire nature—from her personality and intellect to her physical ability—was thought to be controlled by the whims of the uterus. Pathologizing of the uterus was one way to keep women out of the public sphere of professions, higher education, politics, sports, and anything else men wanted for themselves. Misogyny and sexism were now coated in a shiny veneer of "science." Having a uterus meant being prone to fits of wild hysteria, dreadful melancholy. Why, if a woman rode a train going over fifty miles per hour, her uterus would fly out of her body!

In actuality, what often caused women to fall ill frequently were the uterine problems that resulted from this faulty science, malnutrition, restrictive or heavy clothing, perpetual pregnancy, and poor working conditions. Textile workers developed brown lung disease, sewing machine operators spinal disorders, sales ladies varicose veins. Wayward movements of heavy machinery could scalp heads and mangle hands. Abusive home life also took an emotional and physical toll on women.

Sophia saw what women doctors could do for medicine, especially as it pertained to diseases of women, expressing the prescient vision that one day, when women are finally practicing medicine in large numbers, their observations and discoveries will lead to great gains in medical science.

This may not have been a widespread view, but she was not alone in her opinion. In a text published two years prior, Brighton-born physician Dr. Edward Tilt claimed, "The principal reason why the knowledge of diseases of women has so little advanced, is the hitherto undisturbed belief that one sex only is qualified by education and powers of mind to investigate and to cure what the other sex alone has to suffer." If there were women doctors, the understanding and knowledge of women-specific diseases would improve, resulting in better treatment and better health.

In her lifetime, Sophia would witness just how much the general state of women's health would improve—thanks to women physicians and scientists rethinking preconceived notions of women's inherent frailty and disease etiology. As women's rights activists pushed for safer working conditions and more practical clothing, women doctors began teaching women and girls about proper hygiene, nutrition, and exercise.

That Christmas was a merry time at the hospital. Lucy festively decorated all of the staff rooms and Sophia took holly branches around to all of the wards to ease the sting of a holiday hospital stay. They had a rush of childbirths that season, with four babies born on Christmas Eve and Christmas Day. As was

the custom, Lucy ordered a "light diet" for the new mothers—
quite the opposite of a Christmas feast.

"Well, I guess the babies were worth losing a dinner for,
weren't they?" Sophia said to the new moms jovially in an attempt to console them.

"Humph!" one of the mothers replied. "A good dinner's worth
more to poor folks!"

Sophia, taken aback by the harsh pronouncement in that moment, later reflected that this woman was actually quite sensible.
The brutal realities of poverty were coming sharply into focus
for Sophia. And they impacted the working class women more
than anyone else.

One of the more shocking things Sophia witnessed was child
abandonment. She shared with her mother when they "had two
of the babies born here found deserted in the streets the day after
their mothers were discharged." Infanticide and infant abandonment were more common in nineteenth-century America than
many people realized. Most abandoned infants were assumed to
be illegitimate, but that wasn't always the case. Poverty was the
most common cause, among the single and married alike. Unplanned pregnancies also arose from more sinister circumstances.
Women employed as domestic workers often lived in their em-
ployer's home, leaving them vulnerable to sexual abuse by their
host families. There was no recourse these women could take
if they wanted to keep their jobs and station.

Unplanned pregnancies were also on the rise as abortion became
increasingly inaccessible to women, newly considered as immoral
and expensive. When humoral theory was still being practiced,
"returning the menses" was seen as a natural process of returning
balance to the body. With the scientification of medicine came
male physicians' desire to regulate women's bodies, to medical-
ize pregnancy and other aspects of reproductive health. Women
doctors who could address these women's health concerns were
needed more than ever.

Spending so much time working in a women's hospital along-side women doctors, Sophia soon realized that medicine was capturing her heart. The flame she carried for establishing a girls' school was beginning to fade. This was, she believed, a most unexpected turn of events.

"I find myself getting desperately in love with medicine as a science and as an art, to an extent I could not have believed possible," she confided in her mother. "I always associated so much that is repulsive and nasty with it in my mind, but I find that one really loses all sense of that in close contact. I find my-self saying to myself a dozen times a day, did I not feel my life devoted to another object, I would be a doctor straightway."

She expressed an interest in staying in Boston until she could learn enough about medicine to ease her mother's chronic pain. She imagined a wonderful life practicing medicine alongside Lucy. Medicine fascinated her, and it was good work, she rea-soned. She was trying to convince herself to take this leap of commitment. "But won't Elizabeth Garrett be cross?" she won-dered. Lizzie would never have imagined her outspoken, brusque friend would want to become a doctor. What a poor example she might set!

Instead, she confided in her friend Lucy first. "If you feel you can and wish to be a doctor, you ought," Lucy told Sophia matter-of-factly.

The following summer, Sophia returned to England for a brief visit to see her parents and continue to ask for feedback about her new career plans. Sophia's mother proved surprisingly supportive, saying only that she hoped her medical education wasn't addling her brains. Her friends were supportive on the whole, but one friend told her they thought it was "indecent" for unmarried women to gain such knowledge.

"Most people are much more in favour of medicine than I ex-pected," Sophia mused. But her instinct about Lizzie was right. "Except Miss Garrett, who thinks me not specially suited." Of all the people to discourage her, after all Sophia had done to help Lizzie in her own quest for a medical education! Lizzie's rebuke surely stung, even if it was given with the intent of sparing Sophia heartbreak from failure. Lizzie thought Sophia had quite the wrong temperament for being a trailblazer in medicine.

At least she had Lucy's approval. Lucy was busy in Boston planning for Sophia's return. "I really feel quite well satisfied with the increase in my practice, and if it continues to increase for the next two years as well, we shall be able to take a fine house and live in style," Lucy wrote to Sophia. "I cannot tell you how much pleasure I get out of anticipating our housekeeping. When I am too tired to do anything, I lay on the sofa and plan and plan and think what a good time we are going to have, and am as happy as a cricket."

The nature of Sophia and Lucy's relationship is not abundantly clear; there is nothing so explicitly described between them as the passionate kiss between Sophia and Octavia. But their letters to each other show a deep caring, an incredibly intimate friendship, and a mutual interest in planning a life together. At least one historian has asserted that Lucy and Sophia did indeed form a romantic relationship. Whatever their relationship, Lucy never married.

It was becoming increasingly common for two independent women to choose to live together, referred to as a "Boston Marriage." This suited women who were interested in a life beyond marriage and child-rearing, pursuing careers of their own and enjoying financial independence. These desires may or may not have included a romantic interest in other women. Such living arrangements might have been out of love or more of a roommate situation to share costs and chores and companionship. And indeed love may also have grown among roommates.

Some married women also sought out intimate relationships with other women to fill the emotional or sexual gaps left by their husbands. Since women were excluded from having much of a public life, it stands to reason that they would be drawn together in their private seclusion. Boston Marriages and women's extramarital romantic friendships were both generally seen as acceptable until around the 1920s because they were assumed to be nonsexual.

Back in Boston and ready to start her studies in earnest, Sophia enrolled in an anatomy course at the New England Female Medical College. Quickly unsatisfied with the quality of the class, she decided to apply to study medicine at Harvard University.

"I don't mean to graduate at any Woman's College—on principle," Sophia told Lucy. She wanted her education to be just as rigorous as any man's. Lucy had attended a women's medical school, so hopefully she didn't take offense to this declaration.

Sophia was not the first woman to apply to Harvard. When Harriot Hunt, the alternative medicine practitioner in Boston, heard about Elizabeth Blackwell's acceptance at Geneva, the forty-two-year-old was inspired to dash off an application to Harvard. Despite having already spent twelve years running a thriving practice, she still would have preferred a degree to legitimize her expertise. Her admission, Harvard regretted, would be "inexpedient." The faculty feared students would leave for Yale "upon the advent of a woman student."

Two years later, Harriot tried again. This time she was given permission to purchase tickets to attend lectures. But the senior class made sure that she quickly lost that privilege with a written protest: "No woman of true delicacy would be willing in the presence of men to listen to the discussion of the subjects that come under the consideration of the student of medicine. We object to having the company of any female forced upon us." Harvard's subsequent policy forbidding women students remained in effect until 1945.

The university's terse response to Sophia's application, many years after Harriot's, explained succinctly, "There is no provision for the education of women in any department of the university."

Sophia was not one to take no for an answer. She set out canvassing Harvard professors in the hopes of convincing them to alter this lack of provision. During these meetings, Sophia found a few doctors at Massachusetts General Hospital who invited her to visit them for clinical training. She also continued to work at the women's hospital with Lucy.

In January 1868, she applied to Harvard again, this time detailing her year of clinical experience and stressing the fact that there was no school statute in place specifically preventing her admittance. The school's initial decision remained unchanged. She worried she might have to be satisfied with the poor imitation of a medical degree that women's colleges were offering.

She wasn't the only one unsatisfied with these women's schools. Elizabeth Blackwell was hard at work planning her own women's medical college just two hundred miles south of Boston in New York. Hers, she was sure, would be of a much higher caliber.

SEVEN

Facing Down Hurdles as
America's First Woman Doctor

If Elizabeth Blackwell thought her life was going to be smooth sailing once she'd achieved her goal of earning an official MD, she was sorely mistaken. She faced increasing prejudice during her attempts to craft a career as one of America's only practicing female physicians. First came the reactions to her medical degree. A letter to the editor printed in the *Boston Medical and Surgical Journal* on February 21, 1849, declared her graduation ceremony "a farce," the entrance of women into the profession something "nefarious" and clearly unearned. The letter's author pleaded with the medical profession to make her achievement, the first of its kind, be the last.

The general consensus was that by departing from women's socially acceptable sphere, Elizabeth was seeking laurels in forbidden paths, dishonoring her sex, and perverting God's laws. It was inconceivable that a woman could "go through all that we have to encounter in the study of medicine without tarnishing that delicate surface of the female mind, which can hardly be imagined even to reflect what is gross without somewhat of defilement," a Massachusetts Medical College professor sputtered. "The office of the physician and surgeon calls for those qualities which are characteristic of man."

But not everyone was opposed to the innovation. Many people pointed out that most midwives were women, and they deserved more in the way of medical education. Few were prepared to publicly argue that women could practice medicine in general, though. Most medical men conceded that women could deliver babies, but not much else.

Geneva College, where Elizabeth attended, similarly faced public scrutiny and suffered at the hands of the medical establishment for accepting a woman and allowing her to graduate. The school decided to forbid entrance to other women students to avoid additional blowback. The one and only medical school in the nation that had once admitted a woman would now no longer entertain the idea. If women wanted to learn medicine, they'd have to set up schools of their own.

Whether it was inconceivable to the medical establishment or not, Elizabeth Blackwell had done the impossible. News of the lady doctor was shocking enough that it made its way across the Atlantic to her homeland. The satirical British magazine *Punch* published a poem to mark the occasion:

"Young ladies all, of every clime
Who wholly occupy your time
In novels or in knitting,
Whose highest skill is but to play,
Sing, dance, or French to clack well,
Reflect on the example, pray,
Of excellent Miss Blackwell!"

After her remarkable graduation, Elizabeth heeded the advice of her medical mentors and set off to Paris to further her medical education. The invention of the stethoscope by René Laënnec in 1816 solidified Paris as the hotbed of medical innovation. The city became the birthplace of many medical advancements in surgery, pathology, and psychiatry, which eventually spread across the world. To train in Paris was to be at the cutting edge of medicine. Between 1820 and 1860, roughly seven hundred American doctors studied in France, including Dr. Blackwell. She brushed up on her French and was off to France in June 1849.

Elizabeth had hoped to study surgery, but found the easiest place for her to gain access was the maternity hospital La Maternité. Here, Elizabeth learned invaluable lessons in how to run a hospital for women patients. Within a few days of her arrival, she was placed in charge of six rooms at the infirmary from 8:00 a.m. to 8:00 p.m. On her days "off," she visited the nursery, went on general rounds, and checked in with patients whose cases interested her; the lectures wouldn't commence until a month after she arrived, but once they did, they took up four or five hours each day.

At La Maternité, she worked with approximately fifty women of varying ages, all studying midwifery. On their early morning rounds with the head midwife, Elizabeth describes the group as "wide awake from the hurry of their duties, but dressed mostly in haste, with little white caps and coloured handkerchiefs, and the coarser ones in short bed-gowns, their faces browned by the sun, their hands red with hard work, but all good-tempered, with a kind word always ready, and their black eyes sparkling with life." For the first time, Elizabeth was exposed to other ambitious women, similarly pursuing education in the medical sciences. Perhaps her harsh criticism of her same sex softened witnessing these women up close.

And romance nearly found her in Paris. Hippolyte Blot was a young French doctor interning at the institution. Elizabeth found him handsome, dignified, witty, and ambitious but possessing a hot temper.

Every Tuesday at one o'clock, Blot administered vaccinations to the newborn babies. Elizabeth sat next to him by the window as he used his knife to inoculate each infant. "Baby after baby is subjected to the awkward manoeuvres of the *élèves*, to their utmost dissatisfaction. The babies are very ugly in their coarse swaddling clothes," Elizabeth explained. "They are just like mummies, but they perform a terrible concert altogether."

When Elizabeth asked Blot questions about the procedure, he would focus intently on the baby, blush a deep red, and run his hand through his hair "in a very un-Frenchmanlike manner."

"I think he must be very young, or very much in awe of me, for he never ventures to give me a direct look, and seems so troubled when I address him that I very rarely disturb his life in that way," Elizabeth noted.

In addition to having students accompany him on rounds, Blot brought his microscope to the student infirmary and showed them various samples, such as the flattened squamous epithelium cells covering the skin and the hairlike ciliated epithelium that line the respiratory tract.

By August, he'd finally plucked up the courage to ask Elizabeth to teach him English. "I like him," she admitted coyly after he made this request. "I hope we may come a little more closely together."

Near the end of her stay, Elizabeth and Blot did get closer, but not in the way she hoped. On Sunday, November 4, Elizabeth was using a syringe of water to clean a newborn baby's eyes, which had been infected during childbirth by its mother's gonorrhea germs. Some of the water splattered back into Elizabeth's own eyes. Throughout the rest of the day, she had a tickly feeling like grains of sand were in her eyes. By night, they had become quite swollen, and in the morning, they were crusted shut.

Blot confirmed she had caught an ophthalmia infection from

the infant. Swift treatment was essential for recovery. Blot sent her to bed and dedicated himself to her entirely. He cauterized her eyelids, smeared belladonna ointment on them and put on plasters of powdered black mustard. He applied leeches to her temples, cold compresses and opium to her forehead. He gave her foot baths and purgatives.

Every hour, he syringed her eye. She ate only broth. Across three days, daylight gradually faded in her left eye. After the doctor delicately removed the film that had formed over her pupil, what remained was only darkness. She was permanently blinded in her left eye. Elizabeth stayed in bed with her eyes closed for three weeks until her right eye gradually began to open. Blot's careful work had saved the sight in this eye. It wouldn't be until 1881 that an effective treatment to save the eyesight of infected infants, a silver nitrate solution, was discovered.

When Elizabeth finally left Paris, she said she would miss Blot exceedingly because of the "most affectionate sympathy" between them, but stoically reminded herself that "a reformer's life is not a garden of roses." While she always clung to the hope that she might one day find the perfect partner, one of the reasons she'd entered medicine in the first place was for it to distract her from her strong attraction to men.

On her way home to New York, she stopped at the German resort where hydrotherapy was born. An increasingly popular medical treatment, the "water cure" was something Elizabeth wanted to experience for herself. Seeing how often traditional medicine failed patients had left her open to the efficacy of alternatives. In a tiny room in a massive farmhouse, she took cold baths, drank countless glasses of water, rested under wet bandages, and climbed mountains barefoot. She did not emerge a convert: wet-cloth rubdowns made her fingers numb, sitz baths made her colicky, and wet bandages interfered with her digestion. The worst part was dealing with the other guests, who, to Elizabeth's dismay, were mostly counts, barons, and princesses.

A flare-up in her diseased eye disrupted her plans and led Elizabeth back to Paris, to a surgeon she trusted. He told her the blinded eye would have to be surgically removed. While she could wear a glass eye in its place, her permanently impaired vision meant she would never be able to become a surgeon.

Instead of returning to New York, she traveled to London again for a short period of practical study at St. Bartholomew's Hospital. It was in London that Elizabeth finally found an invigorating, intelligent group of friends. Elizabeth had come to assume she was simply not a social creature since she deplored idle chatter and gossip. With few exceptions, she found the company of most women lacking in substance and stimulation. Now, she realized she just hadn't met the right people yet. Quickly, her schedule began positively bursting with social engagements involving like-minded, curious, educated, progressive, scientific types. She realized that, to her surprise, she thoroughly enjoyed social discourse.

This was when she met Langham Place feminists Bessie Rayner Parkes and Barbara Leigh Smith. Many evenings and weekends were now whiled away in their social circle. Elizabeth had stumbled upon a collection of London's brightest luminaries of their time. The group she hung out with included renowned physicist Michael Faraday, astronomer John Herschel and his wife Margaret, author and art historian Anna Jameson, and Annabella, the Lady Byron.

When Elizabeth met Barbara's cousin Florence Nightingale, the pair became fast friends. At the time, Florence was feeling stifled by the expectation that she would live idly in her parents' home waiting for a husband to whisk her away. It was a beautiful April day when the women walked around the Nightingale family's large winter estate at Embley Park together, the invigorating smell of blooming laurels encompassing them.

"Do you know what I always think when I look at that row of windows?" Florence asked Elizabeth as they strolled down the lawn, past the family's imposing drawing room. "I think how I should turn it into a hospital ward and just how I should place the beds! I should be perfectly happy working with you; I should want no other husband!"

Within a few years, Florence would become world-famous for her nursing work during the Crimean War, where she and a team of nurses greatly improved the unsanitary conditions, saving hundreds of lives. Florence's observations and suggested reforms influenced how hospitals all over the world were run.

There were a lot of similarities between Florence and Elizabeth. "They were within a few months of the same age; they both had the same sense of vocation, the strong religious feeling as the base and root of all their work, the same feeling that they had got to do, what each eventually did do, in the way of raising the standard of women's work; the same intense joy and satisfaction in her appointed task, when once she had established the right of power to do it," observed one mutual friend.

Elizabeth spent all of her last day in England with Florence. Upon parting, there were many tears. When Elizabeth later returned for her lecture tour, she hoped to get Florence's help to establish a health sanatorium in the UK, while Florence wanted Elizabeth to be the superintendent at a school for nurses she was hoping to found. Neither would concede her own dream to the other. Despite all they held in common, Florence's belief that women should be content to be nurses and not bother clawing their way into medical school to become doctors drove a wedge between the two women that their friendship never fully recovered from.

Her European adventure finally over, Elizabeth returned to New York in the damp August heat of 1851. With a degree from a proper medical school in hand, and countless hours of experience working at hospitals in America and abroad, any practice would have been lucky to have the talented Dr. Blackwell. Instead, her first attempts to find a job as a doctor were an utter failure. She applied for posts all over the city, but no one would employ her. She decided she would have to go it alone and form her own practice. But even that was easier said than done.

When she approached various New York landlords about office spaces they had advertised for rent, she was again greeted with refusals. They feared this "female physician" was an abortionist and didn't want that practice to happen on their property.

At the time, abortionists referred to themselves as female physicians despite their lack of medical training. They advertised heavily for their services, often using euphemisms to mask the true nature of their work. Practitioners offered "uterine tonics" or female washes that could "remove obstructions" and end your female trouble. The notorious Madame Restell[9] chose a more direct approach. In her first advertisement, published in the New York *Sun* on March 18, 1839, she brashly posed the question, "Is it moral for parents to increase their families, regardless of consequences to themselves, or the well being of their offspring, when a simple, easy, healthy, and certain remedy is within our control?"

Dime novelists began sensationalizing female doctors as greedy, nefarious—and more often than not, foreign—women hellbent on performing abortions for unfortunate Anglo-American women. These themes eventually made it into mainstream culture. In Edith Wharton's novel *Summer*, the young, white, and poor protagonist visits a wealthy German abortionist, who charges her a fee despite the girl changing her mind.

Elizabeth eventually found a space to live and practice in at University Place. It even had a small greenhouse attached to it. "I like the room, it has an air of pleasant gloom about it," Elizabeth declared. The landlady had rented to her despite sharing the other landlords' fears about the nefarious nature of Elizabeth's work. Instead of turning her away, the woman charged Elizabeth an exorbitant rent and often sent her patients away and failed to relay messages to her.

---

9   Real name Ann Lohman.

Progressive New York *Tribune* editor Horace Greeley ran an article lauding Elizabeth's accomplishments and celebrating the establishment of her practice. Still, patients were few and far between. Elizabeth experienced constant anxiety. She worried about making enough money to support herself, about finally gaining respect in her chosen profession. The lack of patients meant she had to ration her food and coal.

"The first seven years of New York life were years of very difficult, though steady, uphill work. Patients came very slowly to consult me," she remembered. "The difficulties and trials encountered at this early period were severe."

She was plagued by ill-natured gossip, insolent letters, and frequent "unpleasant annoyances from unprincipled men." These men often propositioned Elizabeth when she was out late at night traveling to and from her patients' homes.

Elizabeth applied to work at the large city dispensary, but was turned down. A dispensary was an outpatient clinic that provided medicines, medical care, and advice for free or for a nominal fee to the poor and working class. Many physicians hoped that by helping people when they were in need, once back on their feet, those people would become paying patients at their private practice. It was believed that poverty was a temporary state able to be overcome.

Perhaps after finding such good friends in London, her lack of social life in New York was felt more keenly. "I had no medical companionship, the profession stood aloof, and society was distrustful of the innovation. It is hard with no support but a high purpose, to live against every species of social opposition," she admitted. She confided to her little sister Emily that "medical solitude is really awful at times; I should thankfully turn to any educated woman if I could find one."

By this time, Emily herself was well on her way to following in her big sister's footsteps by becoming a physician. So far, she was following a little too closely, having been turned down by eleven medical schools. She'd been receiving private lessons from an anatomy demonstrator at the Medical College of Cincinnati. Just like Elizabeth had, she was saving money for medical school by working as a schoolteacher.

"Oh for life instead of stagnation," Emily wailed. "I long with such an intense longing for freedom, action, for life, and truth." Even seeing all the hardships her sister had to endure in becoming a physician, Emily sought the same freedom and intellectual challenge that inspired Elizabeth to become a doctor in the first place. Despite all the rejections, she continued applying to medical colleges.

Elizabeth continued regular correspondence with many of the friends she made in England and France long after returning to New York. It was one of the only things that kept her going in those dark times. Their support and encouragement sustained her while she longed for professional companionship. Elizabeth also missed the European flowers: "Take an extra whiff of the violets for me, and give my love to the daisies," she wrote to her big sister Anna, now living in Paris.[10]

That winter, Elizabeth did find one professional friend, though it would have to be another long-distance one: Ann Preston. This petite powerhouse had been studying at the newly established Female Medical College of Pennsylvania for about a year. In fact, she was one of its very first students. (And she would go on to become the first woman dean of the school.) Behind Ann's beady eyes, pinched nose, and perfectly prim facade was an energetic Quaker who put her views of tolerance to action. In addition to being skilled at caring for the ill, she was a writer and activist who fought for emancipation and helped formerly enslaved African Americans escape to safety.

She came from Philadelphia to visit Elizabeth on a particularly gloomy, snowy day. Exuding unexpected enthusiasm,

---

10   American violets being scentless and daisies unknown in the US except as cultivated exotics.

Ann explained how she was helping to grow this new women's medical school.

"That fragile lady who came to me out of the wild snow storm was an omen of success," Elizabeth declared. The jolt of Ann's optimistic energy, unique to those at the beginning of a journey, reinvigorated Elizabeth.

Despite being eight years younger than Ann, this particular brand of energy had long since faded from Elizabeth, her spirit slowly and methodically crushed over years of fighting first for an education and then to practice. Now, she was reminded that she was not alone. All of her trials and suffering would not be for naught; others were counting on her example to pave the way. It was easy to lose sight of all she'd accomplished when fighting alone, rationing coal. Ann's friendship reminded her of the bigger picture—the battle for other women to join their ranks as medical professionals.

EIGHT

Changing the Culture,
One Patient at a Time

Hoping to drum up some business at her private practice in New York and perhaps even gain some standing among her peers, Elizabeth gave a lecture in a church basement on the "Laws of Life" and physical education for girls. Attending lectures was a popular diversion for middle- and upper-class Victorian women. Elizabeth presented her holistic philosophy of tending the soul as well as the body. She believed a healthy person was one whose physical, intellectual, emotional, and spiritual needs were all being addressed. Poor health, she explained, could result from a poor diet, idleness, and lack of exercise or intellectual stimulation.

Stressing the importance of intellectual pursuits for girls flew in the face of convention, but Elizabeth's most radical prescriptions were still to come. Girls should be taught how their bodies worked, she informed the gathered crowd. They should also be encouraged to engage in vigorous physical play like running and climbing, just as their male peers were, and should postpone marriage to delay the physical strain of childbearing as long as possible. The average age at marriage was about twenty-three years old for women.

Elizabeth said she would not be satisfied until exercise was "taught to children as regularly as reading." The people in attendance at Elizabeth's lecture were mostly well-to-do Quaker women. The talk worked: many of these families became her patients. She even published the lecture due to its popularity. The first baby Elizabeth delivered was to one of the first Quaker families to employ her as their family physician.[11]

Still, her fellow physicians largely refused to consult with Elizabeth. It was nearly a year before one of them actually responded to her call. When she needed a second opinion on an elderly woman she suspected had severe pneumonia, she called in a well-known doctor who'd once taken care of her ailing father in Cincinnati. After examining the patient, the doctor ushered Elizabeth into the parlor.

"A most extraordinary case!" he exclaimed as he paced the room in agitation. "Such a one never happened to me before; I really do not know what to do."

Elizabeth was surprised and perplexed by his assessment. She thought it was a fairly clear-cut case of pneumonia; she was just looking for confirmation of her diagnosis and treatment plan. The doctor then explained that his bewilderment had nothing to do with the patient; it was entirely related to consulting with a female doctor about said patient.

Amused and relieved, Elizabeth told him to think of this merely as a friendly talk rather than an official consultation. He at last relaxed and told her what treatment he recommended. Typical remedies for pneumonia of the time included bloodletting via leeches or an incision, and cupping, where heated glasses were placed on the skin to create a vacuum and break the blood vessels under the skin. The mercury-laden concoc-

11   The baby, a girl, would go on to become a doctor herself.

tion Mars Hydrarg might also be used. Elizabeth's elderly patient went on to make a full recovery.

When Emily came to stay with Elizabeth in New York that summer, the pair hadn't seen each other in four years. Emily was nervous since their relationship had at times been fraught because of Elizabeth's bossy, competitive nature. Happily, Emily found Elizabeth had mellowed with age and was less persnickety than she remembered. Elizabeth couldn't recall a more exciting week than the one she spent reconnecting with her sister.

Again, not one to sugarcoat things, Elizabeth warned her little sister about what her future likely held once she became a woman doctor. "A blank wall of social and professional antagonism faces the woman physician that forms a situation of painful loneliness, leaving her without support, respect, or professional counsel." Whether this warning was out of a jealousy, fear of being overshadowed by her whip-smart younger sibling, or out of genuine sisterly concern, it is difficult to know. Whatever her intention, this does seem to sum up Elizabeth's experience in New York.

Emily was a handsome woman with red hair, noble features, and a low, calm voice. Tall and broad-shouldered, she cut a surprisingly striking, commanding figure. Despite her intense shyness, when Emily entered a room, all eyes were on her. You could have heard a pin drop in any room where she was speaking. When she was younger, Emily had a curious mind and conducted science experiments in her family's attic. She also cultivated a near-encyclopedic knowledge of birds and plants.

After a bit of help from newspaper editor Horace Greeley, Emily was allowed to walk the wards at Bellevue Hospital daily. Finally, in November, Emily became the first woman accepted at Rush Medical College in Chicago. In between terms, she returned to New York to assist Elizabeth and to visit Bellevue.

By the end of the summer, Elizabeth's practice was serving a steady three patients per week and she'd earned $25. Still, she wished her practice would grow more rapidly. She also wanted to do more to help the city's poor, whom she knew suffered disproportionately. So in 1853, she again applied to work at the New York dispensary. This time they were more upfront with their rejection, stating that a female doctor "would not promote the harmonious working of the institution." Once again, facing discrimination from the existing dispensaries, she decided she would establish her own.

A physician at Emily's college offered his advice on how to go about opening one. The main hurdle would be to assuage the suspicion a woman doctor's clinic would attract. He recommended she find influential men to act as trustees and consulting physicians, set up in a poor area of town, and, if enough money could be raised, provide medication for free.

She took all of his advice to heart. She found seventeen men willing to act as trustees, including Horace Greeley, and four men who consented to being consulting physicians. She also located a space to rent in a destitute part of Manhattan near Tompkins Square, an area of the East Village known as Little Germany. At least one of her new rich Quaker lady friends actively assisted in procuring medicines, a covering screen, and other necessary accoutrements.

On January 20, 1854, they filed a certificate of incorporation for the New York Dispensary for Poor Women and Children. New York's 1846 constitution had allowed for the formation of corporations by application. Included in the filing were the organization's goals to provide medical and surgical aid and medicines to women and children who couldn't otherwise afford it, to train nurses to serve the community, and to secure for its patients "the services of well-qualified female practitioners of medicine."

Elizabeth's dispensary soon after received an Act of Incorporation, permitting women physicians to be available to treat indigent women and their families. A momentous achievement indeed! No other dispensaries at the time allowed women practitioners. Elizabeth was providing not only care to the community, but creating a space for women doctors to put their medical education to good use.

Poor women immigrants who came to consult Dr. Blackwell were unconcerned about whether or not practicing medicine was a proper field for a woman. What they needed was free medical care. Three afternoons a week for two hours, Elizabeth happily provided that care—in English or German—in addition to offering advice about how to access charity services, handle drunken spouses, and find jobs. It was the perfect opportunity for Elizabeth to preach her holistic ethos of proper hygiene, diet, and exercise to the people who perhaps needed it the most.

To help with her growing workload, she had also found an assistant. "I have at last found a student in whom I can take a great deal of interest," Elizabeth excitedly told Emily of her new protégé, twenty-six-year-old Marie Zakrzewska. "There is true stuff in her, and I shall do my best to bring it out."

Born in Germany into a Polish family, as a girl Marie accompanied her mother on her rounds at a maternity hospital and spent summers reading medical textbooks and poking around the morgue. At twenty, she entered midwifery school. Lacking options for further medical education or specialization in Germany—and forced from her head-of-midwifery position by jealous colleagues—when she heard America had medical colleges for women, Marie set sail at once.

Elizabeth happily welcomed Marie's assistance at her dispensary two weeks after it opened. Despite their accomplishments and the charitable nature of the care they provided, the gossip surrounding the dispensary continued and surely convinced some women to seek care elsewhere. "These malicious stories are painful to me, for I am woman as well as physician, and both natures are wounded by these falsehoods," Elizabeth cried.

The expense of renting the space weighed on her and she became determined to purchase a house. She needed breathing room, room to do more, like offer training opportunities for women doctors and overnight beds for more serious cases. She was able to borrow enough money to buy a house near Union Square, which she initially shared with various lodgers.

Elizabeth still felt something was missing in her life. "I was very lonely and I found my mind morbidly dwelling upon ideas in a way neither good for soul or body," she admitted. "The utter loneliness of life became intolerable." Perhaps she longed for a husband, but a man who could stomach her profession as well as meet all of her high moral and intellectual expectations was much easier imagined than found. So she did the next best thing, deciding "a little human soul" that she could "develop into full maturity" would cure what ailed her. She adopted an orphan girl from the Randall's Island emigrant depot.

"Who will ever guess the restorative support which that poor little orphan has been to me?" Elizabeth declared. Seven-year-old Catherine Barry, called Kitty, brought joy, softness, and companionship into Elizabeth's life.

Kitty was a plain, obedient girl, which suited Elizabeth since she treated her as much as a housekeeper as a daughter. It wasn't unusual for children to be responsible for many chores or even for poor families to send their kids to work in factories, mills, or mines, but this was still an odd relationship: caring, but unusually formal. Elizabeth did employ a servant who also acted as a nanny to Kitty while she worked. Kitty called Elizabeth "Aunt Bessie" or "Doctor," and was incredibly surprised when she eventually met a *male* doctor.

This new maternal relationship did nothing to quiet Elizabeth's ambition for more women doctors. Elizabeth decided a hospital would be an "indispensable" part of accomplishing their work of helping women obtain generalized medical training. It would ensure women could find the rigorous clinical training she believed was required to practice medicine. The kind of training she thought most of America's female medical colleges lacked.

Included in Elizabeth's hospital plan was Emily. Her sister had been forced to leave Rush Medical College after her first year because the state medical society bullied the school into rescinding her admission. Emily was welcomed at Western Reserve College in Cleveland, and soon became the third woman in America to earn an MD from a regular college when she graduated in 1854. Nancy Talbot Clark was the first woman accepted at the college's medical school, and had become the second female MD in America when she graduated the year before Emily arrived.

After graduating, Emily again followed her sister's example and pursued advanced studies in Europe. She spent a year in Edinburgh, Scotland, followed by a year spread across hospitals and clinics in London, Paris (at La Maternité), Dresden, and Berlin.

In Edinburgh, Emily gained invaluable surgical experience as James Young Simpson's assistant in his extensive practice, which specialized in gynecological diseases and obstetrics. Appointed professor of midwifery in 1840 at the tender age of twenty-eight, Simpson went on to pioneer the use of chloroform as an anesthetic in surgery and childbirth in 1847. A magnanimous man, Simpson was short and fat with tiny feet and a large head. He derived great amusement from observing the horrified expressions on his aristocratic patients' faces as they watched a lady cross the waiting room in response to his summons, "DR. BLACKWELL!"

He was a rare supporter of women's medical education. "As this movement progresses, it is evidently a matter of utmost importance that female physicians should be fully and perfectly educated," Simpson wrote to Emily after her training had ended. "I had the fairest and best opportunity of testing the extent of your medical acquirements during the period of eight months when you studied here with me and I can have no hesitation in stating that I have rarely met with a young physician who was better acquainted with the ancient and modern languages, or more learned in the literature, science, and practical details of his profession."

Emily returned to Elizabeth's dispensary in 1856 with more training than most doctors in America could claim. Eventually, others caught on. Approximately fifteen thousand American physicians would go on to study in Germany, Switzerland, or Austria between 1870 and 1914.

In the second half of the century, Germany had begun to dethrone France as the seat of medical revolution. German researchers picked up where Parisians left off: using science to uncover the true causes and mechanisms behind disease. For the first time, clinical diagnosis could truly progress, since experimental investigations into biochemistry, physiology, pharmacology, bacteriology, and tissue pathology were yielding useful therapeutic and diagnostic data. This shift was made possible by the fact that medicine was embedded in German universities alongside other scientific disciplines, not siloed inside hospitals as it mostly was in England.

Unfortunately, the German medical revolution had not included allowing women into universities, which was why Marie left for America. Marie was excited about the prospect of helping the Blackwell sisters run a hospital. But first, she, too, would need an MD. Elizabeth helped arrange for Marie to begin studying at Emily's Cleveland alma mater. Marie's father heartily disapproved of her professional ambitions, writing that were she his *son*, he would feel nothing but satisfaction and pride, but since she was his daughter, all he could do was "grieve and weep." That rejection surely stung, but Marie didn't let it keep her from her goal.

Marie rejoined Emily and Elizabeth at the dispensary after completing her degree. On Sundays, the three lady doctors took an early ferry across the bay and spent hours walking the beautiful parks of Hoboken or Staten Island. Marie convinced Elizabeth that her plans for a vast hospital were biting off more than they could chew; they should aim smaller to start. They agreed that two dozen beds was the absolute maximum they could handle.

The three women had all succeeded in earning medical degrees at traditional universities, yet still they met great difficulties in establishing a women's hospital. A variety of objections were raised by the people they approached while fundraising. The women were told that no one would rent a house for such a purpose, that they would be subject to intense suspicion, that they wouldn't be able to control their patients, that they would never collect enough money. What most concerned some potential trustees was that the public might blame them for supporting the endeavor should an accident occur.

Despite the naysayers, the lady doctors and their backers did manage to scrape together enough money. The women found a suitable place to rent: an old-fashioned Dutch-style mansion on the corner of Bleecker and Crosby streets. In the front entrance hall, the doctors arranged a cozy waiting area complete with multiple settees on which patients and families could wait. The first floor was fashioned into a dispensary: consulting desk, examination table behind a large screen, shelving for medicines, a small table to prepare ingredients for the prescriptions. The doctors solicited pharmaceutical donations from several wholesale druggists and set to work finding affordable secondhand furniture.

After ordering twenty-four iron bedsteads for $100,[12] the women procured plenty of donated linens. They set up two wards with six beds each on the second floor. The third floor was arranged as a maternity ward, and a little room down the hall was made into a staff sitting room. The attic housed a few sleeping areas, one for interning students and the other for servants. A smaller room was set up for the resident physician and

---

12   About $3,000 in today's money.

one additional student to share. Open-grate fireplaces served as the building's heat source.

With everything finally ready, the New York Infirmary for Women and Children officially opened its doors in May 1857. On opening day, Marie said Emily seemed pleased but Elizabeth tried to conceal her happiness. This frustrated Marie, who was unaccustomed to such puritanical restraint. "They do wrong not to reward their friends by showing them a pleased countenance. They are to me a combination of contradictions. In spite of [it] all, I love them and feel sad nothing can cheer them up."

Marie stepped into the role of resident physician. Since Elizabeth couldn't perform surgery because of her partial blindness, Emily took charge of all things surgical. In addition to three servants, they also employed three nurses: one in the maternity ward and two in the general ward. The nurses' medical skills were significantly lacking, but they saw the experience as more of a training opportunity and accepted a mere $2 a week for clothing expenses. Ann Preston sent four students from the Female Medical College of Pennsylvania to train as nurses, doctors, and apothecaries between school terms.

The front of the infirmary was in what was considered to be a respectable area, but it backed up to a slum known as Five Points. Irish Catholic immigrants and formerly enslaved African Americans made up the bulk of its residents. The overpopulation and poverty that plagued this Lower Manhattan neighborhood— bound by Centre Street to the west, the Bowery to the east, Canal Street to the north, and Park Row to the south—beget high levels of violent crime, disease, and infant mortality.

Quality of life in Five Points was abysmal. Lack of knowledge about how diseases were transmitted combined with an absence of sanitation systems, overcrowded residences, and scarcity of basic healthcare, merged to make Five Points a breeding ground for illnesses of all sorts. Numerous eighteenth- and nineteenth-

century disease epidemics that swept through New York originated there.

Within a few weeks, the New York Infirmary for Women
and Children was already overcrowded, the dispensary seeing
as many as thirty patients a day. During the infirmary's first
eight months, the dispensary tended 866 patients, the hospital accepted forty-eight inpatient cases, and the doctors made a
dozen house calls—numbers that would double the following
year. Indigent patients were treated free of charge; those who
could afford it were charged $4 a week for inpatient care. In its
first year, they were already looking to enlarge their operation
due to demand for their services.

"Through a cloud of discouragement and distrust the little
medical institution worked its way," Elizabeth remarked. "The
practice of the infirmary, both medical and surgical, was conducted entirely by women; but a board of consulting physicians,
men of high standing in the profession, gave it the sanction of
their names." It wasn't just men who'd sanctioned it. Harriot
Hunt of Boston and Ann Preston of Philadelphia were both
serving on the infirmary's executive committee.

All of the lady doctors took on many more tasks than patient
care. Marie acted as superintendent, housekeeper, and instruc-
tor. She once recorded a typical day: up at 5:30 a.m. and off to
catch the public omnibus[13] to the market to order weekly provisions for the staff and patients, back by 8:00 for a breakfast
of tea, bread with butter, and hot cornmeal-mush cereal with
syrup. (On Sundays, they indulged in bacon and coffee.) After
breakfast, Marie took two of the students along with her on
her inpatient rounds while the other two students went to help
Elizabeth in the dispensary.

On this particular day, a confinement case came in—a woman
in her final weeks of pregnancy—which Marie assessed and then
instructed the nurses and students on how to handle. Next, she

---

13   An elongated horse-drawn stagecoach.

was off to the kitchen to deal with the grocery delivery she'd ordered earlier. Meal planning finalized, Marie hopped on the omnibus again and headed to the wholesale druggist, where she begged and bought what she needed to fill up the hospital pharmacy. She arrived home just in time for dinner at 1:00 p.m.: soup, meat, potatoes, and a vegetable, with fruit for dessert.

Afternoons were spent on home visits to private patients. This was the doctors' only source of income. The new confinement case kept Marie in the hospital until 5:00, so she had less than two hours to run from house to house to see her paying patients. Back for tea at 7:00: bread with butter, and a piece of cheese or fresh gingerbread. After another set of hospital rounds, Marie and the students gathered in the little hall room at 9:00 p.m. Marie sat bent over the sewing machine making towels or other needed linens. She had the students recite their day's lessons as they folded or basted her materials, then gave them a midwifery lecture. Bedtime was 11:30. Even for the heartiest women, it was a truly exhausting pace.

For Elizabeth, this was exactly what she'd hoped. She finally rejoiced in her fulfillment and independence. "How good work is—work that has a soul in it! I cannot conceive that anything can supply its want to a woman," she wrote to her friend Barbara back in London. "In all human relations the woman has to yield, to modify her individuality—even the best husband and children compel some daily sacrifice of self, but true work is perfect freedom, and full satisfaction." Barbara herself managed just fine as a writer, artist, and a wife, in addition to her work of tirelessly promoting women's rights.

Marie referred to the infirmary as a primitive establishment, an "experiment." But thanks to their studies at European institutions, the women could actually offer the city's poorest women and children incredibly cutting-edge care. Emily brought with her knowledge of Dr. Simpson's pioneering use of anesthetics in surgery. Marie's male contemporaries were shocked to learn the infirmary kept written records of every patient. Given that Marie, Elizabeth, and Emily all completed extensive practical experience in delivering babies, they could also provide maternity care far superior to their male counterparts.

Newly minted male MDs rarely had any experience with a real-life childbirth. Many young doctors arrived at a birth knowing only what they'd read in textbooks or been told by lecturers. Afterward they emerged blushing, confused, scared, and possibly scarred for life. The birthing people they attended likely experienced the same, or worse.

Victorian morals prohibited much in the way of nether-region investigation. Nudity or exposure of private areas, even to your doctor, was taboo. During a pelvic exam, doctors looked women directly in the eyes. Babies were often delivered under layers of blankets. This meant women's health problems were particularly misunderstood, underdiagnosed, and mistreated. Missing your period? Leeches would be applied to the cervix. There was even a special speculum for sliding leeches into the vagina. If that doesn't return menstruation, it's out with the ovaries! Most families included sickly women who never received proper treatment or women who endured far more pregnancies than desired. That was all going to change if the Blackwells had their way.

To keep the money flowing into their charitable institution, Marie and the Blackwells' to-do lists included constant fundraising efforts. There were bazaars, lectures, concerts, anything they could come up with to raise money. In a public appeal for funding, Elizabeth illustrated how much more they could accomplish with additional money: "We have only been able to keep a very small number of beds, but they are constantly occupied by a succession of patients, and we could fill a much larger number if we were able to support them. Our dispensary practice is constantly increasing."

Elizabeth wasn't above guilt-tripping her audience of potential donors, insinuating that Americans should be grateful these women doctors chose to grace their country with their professional presence. "We have been urged to commence this work in England, but this medical work has originated here, and we believe that it is better suited to the spirit of this than of any other country."

When actress Fanny Kemble was in town to give a series of Shakespearian readings, Elizabeth hoped she might aid their struggling infirmary by giving a public reading on its behalf. She had met Kemble once at Lady Byron's house. So Elizabeth and Marie called on Kemble at her hotel. She received them courteously and listened with interest until they mentioned that all of the physicians at their institution were women.

Upon hearing this, Kemble sprang to her feet, cast her flashing eyes upon Elizabeth and Marie, and with "the deepest tragic tones of her magnificent voice" exclaimed, "Trust a woman—as a DOCTOR!—NEVER!" It seems Kemble either took woman doctor to mean abortionist, or she represented the times with her own internalized sexism.

And when things did inevitably go wrong at the hospital, public condemnation was swift. Within an hour of one of the infirmary's patients dying shortly after giving birth, all of the woman's relations who had taken turns at her bedside appeared at the hospital with their male cousins and husbands. The men were still in their work clothes, carrying pickaxes and shovels, and demanding to be let in.

"Women physicians are inside killing women in childbirth with cold water!" they shouted.

A large crowd formed, filling the sidewalk between the hospital and Broadway. They were hooting and yelling and trying to push in the doors. Hearing the commotion, two neighborhood policemen ran up and ordered the crowd to quiet down. The policemen were quite familiar with the women's work since they often escorted the lady physicians on emergency calls to birthings or very ill women in the middle of the night.

The officers listened to the crowd's complaints, then assured them that these doctors treated their patients the best they could. "No doctor can keep people from dying some time," one policeman eloquently observed.

While the Blackwells' infirmary was the first New York hospital by women, for women, it was not the first women's hospital in the city. Dr. J. Marion Sims had opened a thirty-bed facility in a rented four-story building on Madison Avenue two years before. Sims invented the speculum and a surgical intervention for vesicovaginal fistula, a common childbirth complication that left women constantly leaking urine. These would be laudable accomplishments were it not for his barbaric research methods.

He perfected the surgery by spending four years torturing a dozen enslaved African American women in the clinic he constructed in his backyard in Alabama. He conducted brutal medical procedures on them. Without anesthesia, these women crouched on their elbows and knees, naked, while a room full of white male doctors observed. On seventeen-year-old Anarcha, Sims performed thirteen operations; eighteen-year-old Lucy shrieked in pain for the entirety of one hour-long surgery and subsequently almost died from blood poisoning. When he started treating white women, Sims used anesthesia.

The Blackwells, by contrast, treated their African American patients with respect and humanity. When working class Irish folk began rioting near the infirmary—angry that rich men could buy their way out of the military draft and worried that newly emancipated Black men would steal their jobs—the infirmary's white patients demanded the Black patients be kicked out so the institution would not be targeted. Emily and Elizabeth steadfastly refused.

The mobs attacked Black people, burned down the Colored Orphan Asylum, and destroyed public buildings, churches, and homes belonging to Black people and abolitionists. The infirmary held steady. In all, 120 people were murdered during these protests and President Lincoln had to divert several troops to quell the riots and restore order.

Emily held down the fort at the infirmary while Elizabeth took Kitty along with her on a lecture tour of England. Marie left, too, to teach obstetrics at the New England Female Medical College in Boston. Marie's initial excitement quickly melted into frustration when her request for thermometers, test tubes, and microscopes were deemed superfluous "new-fangled European notions." In fact, every attempt she made to improve the caliber of the school's instruction was shot down. Convinced the college was producing ignorant graduates ill prepared to practice medicine, Marie soon resigned.

Even with Elizabeth and Marie away, Emily was not alone at the infirmary. A steady stream of graduates from the Female Medical College of Pennsylvania were always on hand. But being surrounded by people doesn't mean you can't be lonely. Her days turned monotonous. She ate cold food in the cellar and slept as best she could in the cramped attic. Even after all she'd accomplished, her sister's foretelling of impending isolation had sadly come true. Emily received no invitations to dinners or parties. Their wealthy donors might have been willing to give money to the infirmary, but that didn't mean they wanted to be seen fraternizing with the lady doctors. Where British intellectuals found lady doctors like Elizabeth charming, quirky company, Americans saw social suicide.

While Elizabeth was abroad on her lecture tour, Emily petitioned the state to provide the hospital with funding. She secured $1,000[14] a year for the institution. What's more, by the time Elizabeth returned, Emily had done so well in running the hospital that the board of trustees had raised $50,000—enough to move into nicer premises at the corner of Eighth Street at 126

---

14   About $31,000 in today's money.

Second Avenue. It was a three-story building that would later house the Orpheum Theater.

"The master carpenters, plumbers, painters, etc. are disturbing every corner of it and will be for two weeks," Elizabeth told Barbara. "But I think we shall like it very much when we have got it in shape."

Yet despite the larger accommodations, the women continued to be inundated by more patients than they could handle. The first annual report from the new premises in 1860 counted 3,680 patients, 130 of which were inpatients at the infirmary. The rest visited the dispensary. In 1862, the doctors turned away roughly half of the pregnant women hoping to give birth at the infirmary due to lack of space.

Elizabeth wanted to do more to improve the health of the local community in between their visits to the infirmary. So her institution became one of the first hospitals in the nation to develop a community outreach and health education service. Elizabeth chose Dr. Rebecca Cole to head the initiative. She'd come to work at the infirmary after becoming the second Black woman physician in America and the first Black student to graduate from the Female Medical College of Pennsylvania.

"We established a sanitary visitor whose special duty it was to give simple, practical instruction to poor mothers on the management of infants and the preservation of the health of their families," Elizabeth reported. "Dr. Cole, who was one of our resident assistants, carried on this work with tact and care."

Rebecca took her role as tenement physician seriously, painstakingly walking mothers through the basics of household hygiene and childcare.

Soon after the move, Elizabeth grew eager to use the expansion as an opportunity to solidify their training offerings into a full-blown medical college. Student interns from the female medical colleges in Philadelphia and Boston were crowding their tiny New York establishment, so many that the doctors had to turn some of these women away, too. The hospitals near these schools did not permit women to attend clinical lectures or receive any other form of practical experience. With their connections, the Blackwells were able to help students secure additional training with other dispensaries in the city and in private classes.

Despite graciously accepting students and graduates of the women's medical schools to work and learn at the infirmary, Elizabeth held firm her belief that their educational offerings were inferior to what she had received at a traditional medical school. "I have yet to see the first decent doctor come from either of those schools," she complained.

Now, there was another women's medical college opening, and right there in New York. "I watched lately with some interest the proceedings of a little humbug of a college," she noted of the homeopathic New York Medical College for Women. "Nothing can be more shallow and unprincipled than their whole course. It was a vulgar little class of women, led by one of the commonest type of woman's right's women." This development was just the push Elizabeth needed: now, she was determined to establish her own college.

Publicly, Elizabeth was polite about America's many women's medical schools, couching such concerns as worry for the livelihoods of graduates. "Some three hundred women have attended lectures in these schools. They enter the schools with very little knowledge of the amount and kind of preparation necessary, supposing that by spending two or three winters in the prescribed studies they will be qualified to begin practice," Elizabeth declared in a speech. "It is not until they leave college, and attempt, alone and unaided, the work of practice that they realize how utterly insufficient their education is to enable them to acquire and support the standing of a physician. Most of them, discouraged, having spent all their money, abandon the profession."

Elizabeth shared her reservations concerning these American schools with Lizzie in no uncertain terms. Lizzie had just written to Elizabeth seeking advice on what to do next, now that it seemed every option was exhausted in the UK. Should she travel to America to attend one of its women's medical schools? Absolutely not, Elizabeth advised.

NINE

Lizzie Is Pushed into Private Study

Lizzie was facing a crossroads, having been ousted from the medical school in London and now running out of universities in Scotland. "I had been thinking very much what I should do next in the event of complete failure here and yesterday morning brought a letter from Miss Blackwell which helped to clear up my mind considerably," Lizzie said.

Elizabeth convinced her that seeking a medical education in America should be her very last resort, that it would be best to persevere in Britain. "Miss Blackwell's account of the female schools there confirms all my fears. She says they and their diplomas are of the worst kind."

Lizzie would follow Blackwell's advice and continue her campaign to attend school in the United Kingdom. She recognized in herself a patience and steadfastness that made her particularly suited to continue the campaign, for herself and the other women who would follow in her path.

"There is a divine and beautiful fitness in my being the one appointed to do this work. I can stand the wear and tear better than most people and with more chance of ultimate success than many," Lizzie declared. "I fear that if I gave up the post, some one less fitted for it might take it and disgrace the cause." Someone, perhaps, like Sophia. As a polite, even-tempered lady, Lizzie fancied herself the perfect person to push social boundaries. Whether right or wrong, Lizzie's narrow view of what kind of woman should lead the cause made her feel responsible to continue on. And it's true that a trailblazer must absolutely be able to withstand a barrage of wear and tear.

After striking out at the University of Edinburgh, next on Lizzie's agenda was the University of St. Andrews. Lizzie had been corresponding with Regius Professor of medicine at the school, Dr. George Day. He and his wife gave Lizzie and her father a warm welcome. A charming seaside town, St. Andrews must have reminded Lizzie of her childhood in Aldeburgh. Both towns had beautiful sandy beaches frequented by a wide variety of birds. Both were situated along the east coast of the UK, though Scotland may have been more chilly than England.

Dr. Day was hopeful about her chances of being admitted to the school, and offered his services as a tutor. Lizzie had learned the hard way not to get her hopes up too much. Day also introduced the Garretts to one of the university's principals. The one major drawback of a St. Andrews education was that there was no hospital nearby for clinical training.

This slow romancing of professors and administrators annoyed Newson. He would just as soon pay for Lizzie to go to a women's medical college in America right away, but Lizzie convinced him it would be best to keep pushing at St. Andrews.

Newson soon made the nearly five-hundred-mile trek back home to Aldeburgh. After charming everyone she could at St. Andrews, Lizzie, too, went home for the summer. She would return to the college at the beginning of the fall term and attempt to register for classes just like any other student.

"Believing as I do that women physicians of the highest order would be a great boon to many suffering women, I think my work is clear, to go on acting as pioneer towards this end, even though by doing so I spend the best years of my life in sowing that of which other students will reap the benefit," Lizzie lamented. These thoughts sound similar to the lonely martyrdom Elizabeth occasionally voiced. There was glory to be had from their sacrifices, and it was important to remind themselves— and others—of that.

Most women her age were pursuing marriage proposals, not actively turning them down. V. R. Heisch—the Middlesex professor who had excitedly kept Lizzie after class to show her his microscope slides—had continued to write to her long after she'd been forced out of the school. He eventually worked up enough courage to tell Lizzie he was in love with her and requested her hand in marriage. Lizzie was shocked and turned him down. She didn't return his feelings, but more than that, she was upset that she might never be seen in a purely professional light. She wasn't flirting and hadn't displayed any particular interest in Heisch. She was merely eager to learn more about medicine from him.

From then on, she thought even more carefully about how friendly she was with men. "I suppose I was a goose to believe in the possibility of friendship," she wrote regretfully to her mother. It was a lonely lesson to learn, that in a profession surrounded by men, she would not be able to count on most of them to see her as merely a colleague.

Back in London, a few weeks after her sister Louie gave birth to her fourth child, Lizzie was off to the Apothecaries' Hall to take the society's preliminary exam and turn in her moral character testimony and apprenticeship certification, both provided by Joshua Plaskitt. The clerk had to strike through *Mr* and *son of* when filling in her paperwork.

One of the arguments against women physicians circulating at the time in the medical journal *The Lancet* was this absence of language, the fact that "authorities on the English language have not yet found the feminine gender for the nouns physician, surgeon, lawyer, senator, etc." The writer of this particular article concluded that women must be restricted to practicing in midwifery and children's diseases, and even then they could only be effective if they remained celibate since it would be difficult for a midwife to rouse from her bed on a cold winter's night for a difficult delivery if she herself were heavily pregnant.

Lizzie returned to St. Andrews as planned in October and found a room to rent. Before setting off into the gray Scottish chill to see Dr. Day, she got up early, took a long, cold bath, and studied astronomy for two hours. Day told her she should try to matriculate for the winter term right away. Lizzie was surprised by how easy it was; she'd assumed there would be an entrance exam, and a long, drawn-out fight. But she simply walked into the school secretary's office, signed her name on the register, and paid £1,[15] and was handed a card bearing her name above the magic words *Civis Universitatis Andrewesis*. Just like that, she was a student of St. Andrews, likely its very first woman student.

Her first impressions of the people she encountered on campus did not bode well. "The students are particularly rough here, and will certainly insult me," she wrote to her sister Louie.

Alas, her easy registration was indeed too good to be true. When the university senate found out that a woman had matriculated, they sent the school secretary to return the fee. He was intensely apologetic as he placed her money on the table, but Lizzie refused to accept it, and pushed it back toward him. The secretary said he couldn't return with it still in his possession and left. Lizzie mailed it back to the university instead, saying they best honor the transaction until it was proven legally void.

Her good friend Emily made the long winter's journey to be

---

15   About £120 or $150 in today's money.

at Lizzie's side during her battle with the school. For months the university senate deliberated upon the admission of a female student. While she waited, Lizzie took Dr. Day up on his offer to tutor her. She also asked Louie if she could send her her microscope key and studs. They soon arrived, safely packaged in cotton wool. From the minute she opened the package, Lizzie was practically glued to her microscope, drinking in every detail revealed on the tongue of a limpet, the suckers of a sea urchin.

She went out to dinner with her so-called "enemies"—those that opposed her matriculation—to try to convince them to change their minds. She was shrewd; she knew money carried weight on such occasions, so she was sure to wear her finest light silk dress in an effort to appear as rich as possible. This display didn't go unnoticed.

"The chance to secure all wealthy female medical students is worth something to a small university," an editorial in *The Spectator* argued. Still, Lizzie said the ladies of the town eyed her as a social evil. Women who wished to dabble in medicine were likely deranged and certainly threatened the natural social order. Emily proved a deft weapon in humanizing Lizzie around these prickly ladies.

After Lizzie dangled the prospect of a lawsuit against the school, she received a letter from their attorney explaining that she likely didn't have a case against them. After reading it, Lizzie sank the letter deep into her petticoat pocket and told no one about it. Though Lizzie's time of need hadn't ended, Emily was called back home. Lizzie stayed on to fight alone.

When Day got busy with exams, she was left to occupy herself. During her solitary study, she had to endure the din of a temporarily full boardinghouse. At St. Andrews, candidates could present themselves for MD exams without having taken a full qualifying series of courses at the school. It was for this reason that "Scotch doctor" was a derogatory term. Lizzie watched as men of all ages and abilities were all given a chance to take the exams, while she was not.

In mid-November the decision finally came down. The university senate ruled her "alleged matriculation" null and void. Lizzie spent the night sobbing alone in her room, no doubt frustrated by all the petitioning she had done to prove she was just as qualified to study as the men.

Another disappointment came when she heard back from a friendly Edinburgh lawyer, who advised her that no, a matriculation ticket was not a legal contract. While he might be able to get her admitted to classes, she definitely had no chance of suing the university to be allowed to complete her studies and graduate.

The British Medical Journal (BMJ) spoke for the medical establishment when it announced its pleasure at such a verdict: "The female doctor question has received a blow instead of a lift at St. Andrews University. It is indeed high time that this preposterous attempt on the part of one or two highly strong-minded women to establish a race of feminine doctors should be exploded."

Feeling utterly humiliated—overwhelmed by the fame of her failure—Lizzie had an urgent need to get out of town. On a three-hour walk along the beach, she clambered over rocks and traipsed through sand, the setting winter sun gleaming off of the ocean and the cliffs. She returned to town feeling "disreputably dirty but very happy," and reported recovering her spirits with unusual speed.

Lizzie persisted in her private studies under Day, though she would have much preferred to be in classes with the other students. Day asked a fisherman to bring them every type of sea beast he could lay his hands on so Lizzie could dissect and examine each one under her microscope. She wrote to the Society of Apothecaries to ask if they'd accept these private studies in lieu of public courses, and was incredibly relieved to discover they would.

By May 1863, she had earned a certificate in Theoretical

Anatomy and Physiology from Day to add to her Middlesex certificates in Materia Medica and Chemistry, and certificate in Botany from the London Pharmaceutical Society lectures.

Having learned all she could from Day, she headed back to the bustling city of Edinburgh. The crowds, cabs, and carriages reminded her of her beloved London. She began studying under University of Edinburgh professors. Among them, world-famous physician James Young Simpson, who'd mentored Elizabeth's little sister Emily Blackwell eight years prior. He recommended his neighbor, Alexander Keiller, as a tutor for Lizzie. Keiller gave lectures on midwifery and women's diseases in addition to working at the Edinburgh Royal Maternity Hospital.

Working alongside Keiller, Lizzie would finally receive clinical midwifery experience. The hospital was the only inpatient maternity care provider in the city, unique in its willingness to care for both married and unmarried women. Despite how filthy she found the state of the hospital, she discovered she loved delivering babies.

"My dear little first born has just entered the world," Lizzie gleefully told Louie. "You cannot imagine how fond I feel of him. I wonder if one will go on feeling an immediate affection for the little creatures that come first into your hands!" Having given birth to four babies of her own, Louie likely did have an inkling of the emotions Lizzie was feeling.

The call had come at 6:20 in the morning. "Miss Garrett, here's a case and it's yours!" Lizzie had only been in bed for about an hour, as another case had kept her up all night. But when the opportunity came, "Of course I was up and dressed in a twinkling, excited with the prospect of a case 'all to myself,'" she said.

Worried about her inexperience delivering babies, Lizzie sent for the doctor, who agreed with her assessment. "He was very kind and encouraging and I was glad he stayed that night to be sure my ignorance would not do mischief," she admitted. About four hours later, a sturdy, eight-pound, twenty-two-inch boy was guided into the world by Lizzie's hands. "I did everything a doctor does usually, and found it very easy."

Afterward, she got a chance to eat breakfast and was planning to go back to bed after starting a letter to her sister, but the doctor called her in to see a postmortem examination on an infant. "It is now lunch time and so sunny that I grudge going to bed, but as we may be active tonight, I shall," she said after the postmortem, at long last getting some sleep.

The case that had kept her up the night before was another birth, but the baby had sadly been stillborn. Lizzie had assisted Dr. Thorton in the delivery. All of the doctor's efforts to revive the baby were useless. "We kept up artificial respiration for more than 20 minutes but it was no use. It is very sad to see a dear little healthy-looking child lost in that way," Lizzie said.

They believed it was the mother's fault, because she had been out dancing during the evening and had a hemorrhage, which caused the child to die. Dancing shouldn't cause harm in a healthy pregnancy, but it's possible that vigorous movement in the presence of undiagnosed complications could lead to bleeding. It's also possible the mother would have ended up hemorrhaging whether or not she went out dancing.

Mothers also died all too often; the maternal mortality rate in mid-nineteenth century England and Wales was nearly six in one thousand births. Lizzie later offered a damning indictment of inexperienced male doctors delivering babies, connecting the medical establishment's low opinion of midwifery with the high rate of maternal mortality. She argued that every medical student should be "compelled to spend six months in acquiring skill in midwifery." According to Lizzie's calculations, this simple training requirement would cause maternal mortality rates to drop by 67 percent.

By the end of July, she'd delivered a dozen babies herself and observed more than a hundred births. When the University of Edinburgh again affirmed its resistance to admitting her as a regular student, Lizzie grew despondent. After enduring so many setbacks with grace and patience, this one stung. She moved back into her big sister's home in London.

Yet again, she quickly rallied her spirits and went to work writing to various medical men, offering twenty-five guineas to anyone who would provide her with training in practical anatomy and dissection, which was required to earn the Society of Apothecaries's license. Responses ranged from polite refusal to outright hostility.

"I must decline to give you instruction in Anatomy. I have so strong a conviction that the entrance of ladies into dissecting-rooms and anatomical theatres is undesirable in every respect, and highly unbecoming, that I could not do anything to promote your end," one doctor in Aberdeen wrote back. "It is indeed necessary for the purpose of Surgery and Medicine that these matters should be studied, but fortunately it is not necessary that fair ladies should be brought into contact with such foul scenes. Ladies would make bad doctors at best."

Newson wanted to wave his magic money wand to make his daughter's problems go away, offering to spend a hefty sum to establish a female medical college right here in the UK. He'd become deeply invested in Lizzie's success, and grew increasingly incensed by the hostility and roadblocks she regularly encountered. Lizzie considered this possibility, but given what she'd been told by Elizabeth about the women's medical schools in America, she decided against this plan. It would be taking the easy way out and would concede what the medical establishment had long been saying—that women didn't belong in regular universities or medical schools.

"Something 'just as good' is not good enough," she replied to her father.

After her application to be admitted as a regular student at the London Hospital medical school was turned down for a second time, she decided to do what she had done at Middlesex.

In February, she entered the London Hospital in a nominal capacity as a nurse. The large institution boasted four hundred inpatient beds.

Nursing had evolved nearly as much as doctoring in the past century. In the mid-1700s, nurses were largely older, unrefined women. Some claimed that the transformation of the nursing profession into the honorable one we know today happened because of anesthetics. The gruesome heroic-surgeries were over, making surgeries more bearable for patients and medical professionals alike.

Lizzie told Emily it was "distressingly nervous work" at the hospital. "Standing about with nothing definite to do and the consciousness of being under a fire of criticizing eyes of nurses, patients, and students." But she had grown accustomed to being on the receiving end of gawking and glaring, and she'd already learned that the best way to discourage such behavior was to ignore it. "This stage does not last long, when the novelty goes off they look less and you feel less, thank goodness," Lizzie concluded.

Though she wasn't a student, Lizzie was able to obtain permission to attend anatomy and dissection courses at the hospital's medical school. The passionate professors made the prospect of practicing surgery intriguing, exciting even. She practiced midwifery under Dr. Nathaniel Heckford, a kindly resident obstetrician five years her junior. She earned his confidence quickly, and he often left her in charge of cases.

During one particularly trying birth, she decided an operative delivery was in order. An operative vaginal delivery likely meant use of forceps. It's possible the procedure was a cesarean section, but these were not common given that antiseptics were not around yet. It's estimated that in Paris between 1787 and 1876, no one survived a cesarean section. Lizzie called in Heckford for a second opinion, just to be sure. He agreed with

her treatment plan and let her do everything except administer
the chloroform.

"I feel seedy this morning from not having been to bed, two
cases filled up every moment from 6 last night to 10 this morning," she said of the experience. "The last was exceedingly interesting as being my first case of operative midwifery. It was
not a minor operation and I enjoyed it immensely."

Some of the London Hospital staff and students disliked a
woman forging a way into medical training under the guise of
nursing.

"A storm is going down," Heckford warned Lizzie. "I have
never seen the school in such an uproar about anything before."

"It's not my fault," Lizzie countered. "I gave them two chances
to have me as a regular student."

Before long, the school's professor of medicine, Dr. Parker,
decided Lizzie was no longer welcome. He warned all of the
doctors not to take Lizzie along with them on their rounds.
This setback cut deep.

"Snubbing is unpleasant and for a time hindering," she admitted to Emily. She knew working alone in the hospital could never
replace the teaching and guidance her male peers were receiving from the physicians. Not to mention the awkwardness that
hung in the air whenever one of her opponents entered the ward.

Despite this, she tried to remain optimistic. "The self-reliant
frame it puts me into will be good, it will force me to look
closer than I would be likely to do if I had any one to appeal to
in every difficulty," she declared.

But the possibility that she might be strong-armed out of yet
another hospital was unbearable to Lizzie. She decided to take
matters into her own hands and set up a meeting with Dr. Parker.
"I had heard of his saying nasty things and I determined to stop
it," Lizzie resolved. On the morning of April 10, 1864, she was
off to a "skirmish with the arch-enemy." It was a "horrid errand,"
Lizzie complained, to be forced to make an appointment and

traipse across town to your enemy's own home in order to defend your existence as a woman interested in learning medicine.

"My courage rose at the right moment and I was able to express myself calmly as well as strongly," she recalled later to Emily.

Parker had never actually spoken to Lizzie before. He was impressed by her persistence and eloquence. Now that he was being confronted by the educated, polite lady, he felt ashamed. He conceded that he would stop telling the doctors to ignore her, and by the end of their half-hour talk, his animosity had largely faded; he was practically pleasant.

Without any further complaints, Lizzie completed her midwifery study at the hospital in July, earning a certificate stating she attended fifty-five births. In October, she left the hospital altogether and moved back in with her sister Louie.

It was around this time, when Lizzie had more free time to socialize with Emelia Gurney or attend the occasional party, that she happened to meet Henry Fawcett at a social gathering. A political economy professor at Cambridge, Fawcett was a brilliant man with a contagious zest for life. He was incredibly tall and had been blinded in a shooting accident a few years before. Fawcett was a liberal social reformer, just like Lizzie, and he had his heart set on becoming a politician in the House of Commons.

Fawcett called on Lizzie every time he was in London, and before long he proposed to her. Her second marriage proposal! Before responding, Lizzie consulted her big sister on the matter. Louie thought the two were much too alike to make a good match and advised against it. So again, Lizzie refused. She would, in fact, go on to refuse a further four proposals of marriage from other men. Fawcett, on the other hand, would go on to marry Lizzie's younger sister Millicent.

For Lizzie to finish her prerequisite requirements for the Apothecaries' Society exam, she only needed a little more clinical experience. Since she hadn't burned her bridges when she left Middlesex Hospital, she was able to convince one of its lecturers to give her private instruction in principles and practice of medicine. Then, she reentered the hospital in a nonstudent, visiting capacity.

One day in the Middlesex pathology lab, Lizzie interjected in a discussion she overheard between the pathologist and the resident medical officer, Dr. John Ford Anderson, known by his middle name. The young Scottish doctor was jolted by this clear voice of a cultivated lady knowledgeable in medical pathology. He was so intrigued, he continued their conversation as the pair left the lab together. All the while, he was racking his brain about who this woman was. Finally, it clicked. "Are you Miss Garrett?" Ford suddenly blurted out. Clearly, her reputation had preceded her.

Lizzie didn't love being a celebrity when she was the subject of gossip or ridicule, but she didn't mind being recognized by this courteous gentleman. She replied in confirmation without the slightest hint of embarrassment and they continued chatting.

By March 1865, she had completed all of her required clinical training. All that was left was to complete classroom courses in toxicology and medical jurisprudence (forensic medicine). For these, a professor from University College London offered his tutelage services. Though it was not her first choice, a pieced-together private education was still as good a preparation as any for the medical licensing exam. It would have to be, as it was all she was allowed.

All of this private study had cost Newson a great deal—with some institutions charging Lizzie £50 for a course that men paid £5 for—but in the end he knew it was worth it to see his daughter succeed in the face of such prejudice. Her quest had brought them closer together, much closer than if Lizzie had simply left home when she got married. She needed her father still: his money, his influence, his counsel. The more he financially invested in her career, the more emotionally invested he became in her success.

That summer, Lizzie led the discussion at the first meeting of the Kensington Society on the limits of parental authority. Sophia and Barbara were among the audience. Sophia was about to leave for America. Lizzie was chosen as the inaugural speaker because she was the one in the group who had gone the farthest in pursuing a "male" profession. Her talk was of great interest to these young women, who had all found themselves wanting a different life than what their parents' expected.

After a short trip to visit some cousins, Lizzie returned to Aldeburgh to begin studying for her Society of Apothecaries licensure exam. Her home was far too loud, so she found a quiet room in one of the empty beach houses by the sea where she could spend each morning revising. Against a soothing soundtrack of gently crashing waves and hungry seabirds, she buried herself in her studies.

At last, the day arrived for all of her years of studying and training to be put to the test. At five o'clock on September 28, 1865, Lizzie entered the grand courtyard of the Apothecaries' Hall on Black Friars Lane in London. Above the door, the Apothecaries' coat of arms depicted a pair of unicorns flanking a sun-headed Apollo straddling a dragon-like serpent and holding a bow and arrow. It represented the Greek god of medicine, the bringer of help, overcoming pestilence.

The exam lasted an hour and a half and covered the practice of medicine, midwifery, and pathology. Lizzie found the test easy, but she withheld her excitement until she knew she had passed. Of the eight people who undertook it that day, she was one of only three who passed. And she had scored the highest of them all.

TEN

The Blackwells Welcome
Sophia in New York

Elizabeth forged ahead with her plans for establishing a medical college for women in New York, despite sharing Lizzie's fear that gender-separate schools would only ever be second-best. She had come to recognize the necessity of such institutions to fill the time gap between what women were ready for and what society would allow. Besides, if she was able to control the curriculum and teachings, she could make the education just as rigorous as the traditional medical colleges. In 1865, the infirmary's trustees applied to the legislature requesting a charter conferring college powers upon it.

But first, Elizabeth and Emily's infirmary would need more money if they were to create a large, permanent training program. To gather moral and financial support, they held a meeting of sympathizers at the infirmary.

With passion and determination, Elizabeth explained to the assembled crowd that their movement to see women trained as doctors "was only a revival of work in which women had always been engaged; a revival in an advanced form, suited to the age and to the enlarging capabilities of women."

In an address authored by both sisters and delivered by Elizabeth, they made the case for their school by offering a grim assessment of women doctors' current opportunities and social standing.

"Consider how women stand in this matter; how alone, how unsupported; no libraries, museums, hospitals, dispensaries, clinics; no endowments, scholarships, professorships, prizes, to stimulate and reward study; no recognized position; no societies, meetings, and professional companionship; all these things men have, none of them are open to women. One can hardly conceive a more complete isolation." The sisters were clearly speaking from their own experiences and lack of support they felt at nearly every turn. They wanted something better for the women coming to the profession after them.

They fell short of their $30,000 endowment target, but several prominent businessmen believed in their project enough to donate generous sums. They borrowed a classroom at first, then bought a property once they eventually raised $70,000.

Frustrated that her one good eye tired quickly while reading or writing, and that she could only stand to wear her glass eye for a few hours, Elizabeth found the role of school planner invigorating. Gradually, Emily and Elizabeth organized a full course of college instruction, with a few improvements on the standard, of course.

They believed the foundation of a good medical education was practical study—care and observation of the sick by their bedside. They wanted their school to be established in connection with a hospital to achieve this. Lectures should be illustrative of practical experience, not a substitute for it. In this way, they followed the English example. In England, no medical school could confer a degree if it wasn't attached to a hospital with at least one hundred beds. That's why most medical schools sprang up inside hospitals there. At St. Bartholomew's Hospital in London where Elizabeth studied, for instance, the college comprised a mere forty or fifty students who performed all of the assistant duties in a 650-bed institution that saw eighty thousand patients a year.

English students also received immersive, practical scientific study: chemistry, botany, and anatomy were experienced in laboratories, gardens, and museums. And the shortest period of study required for a physician's degree was four years, with at least ten months spent in classes each year. Their school would have lectureships for each branch of medical science, and students must attend three winter sessions of five months each, not the standard two required by most American schools, and serve as assistants in the inpatient, outpatient, and home visitation practices. Completion of a thesis would be required to graduate.

Even though such an extensive education was not required in America, Elizabeth maintained that physicians must have such training to achieve real skill in the profession.

As for the nurses' education, Elizabeth would model it on the plans drawn up by Florence Nightingale for her proposed London school. Elizabeth worried Florence's ill health would prevent her from ever realizing her London school. Florence complained of intermittent fevers, fatigue, and sciatica for thirty years after returning from the war, though she never found an official diagnosis. Even though they'd never been published, Elizabeth was well acquainted with Florence's school plans because of their friendship.

The Blackwells also established an independent examination board at their college, an innovation unknown in the United States. The board was composed of some of the most prestigious members of the profession. In addition, aspiring students would have to pass an entrance exam, a European staple that would take another ten years to become commonplace in the United States. To be admitted, women must be at least twenty-one years old, be of good moral character, and have received a good general education. Certificates of moral character could be provided by a clergyman or physician of good standing.

From a professional standpoint, such high standards would go far in helping to insulate the school from accusations of inferiority. From a business standpoint, it was a risky strategy, since requiring students to attend college for longer and to be able to pass an entrance exam would make things more challenging. Many young women would likely be unable to pass such a test or spend so much time away from the responsibilities of home and family. The Blackwells would end up turning plenty of applicants away for having insufficient basic education or for being more interested in spreading their preferred alternative forms of medicine than learning the allopathic form. Foremost in Elizabeth's mind was "cultivating a taste for science" among women.

Finally, with her own college, Elizabeth could realize her long-held pet project of rescuing hygiene from its neglected position in medical education. Perhaps with Florence in mind, she made the subject one of the principal professorial chairs, its study obligatory. The professor of hygiene would also supervise the sanitary arrangements of the hospital and head up the nurses' training program. Hygiene was the study of public health and preventative medicine, and the Blackwells' was the first medical school in the country to offer the course.

The school's overall objective, she asserted, would be to turn out physicians who would disseminate hygiene knowledge to their patients. She imagined mothers and families benefiting the most. Elizabeth had come to believe that hygiene was more important and more accessible than medicine.

Emily agreed. "I think hygiene bears the same relation to domestic and social life that mechanics does to building or engineering," she said. Mothers likely had no other means of acquiring this practical knowledge, which would help them create healthier homes and prevent many illnesses. Elizabeth used this approach as a selling point when arguing for the opening of medical education to women.

Highlighting how society as a whole might benefit from expanding women's sphere was a common framing device. Similar arguments were made on behalf of advancing voting rights to women and allowing them to hold political office. At first blush, it looks demeaning to view women's equality through the lens of how it would benefit others, but upon closer inspection, this argument might actually be a rhetorically strategic means to an end. And besides, women who chose to pursue the sciences professionally could truly serve as important examples to their daughters and other young girls.

Of course not all ailments result from poor hygiene, but for Elizabeth to recognize how much illness and suffering could be prevented by improving public health knowledge was both astute and radical. Today, Elizabeth's vision has been realized. Most family doctors now cover a number of hygiene topics with parents during well-child appointments.

In elevating hygiene, Elizabeth wished to reduce drugs to their proper place. She believed clean water, fresh air, and healthy food were more effective therapeutic agents than most pharmaceuticals. Yet for all of Elizabeth's championing of preventative medicine, she was surprisingly against vaccination. For her, this wasn't conjecture, but based on firsthand experience. After a child she was treating died, she attributed the cause of death to the vaccine she had recently administered. Smallpox was the only vaccine available during most of Elizabeth's career, but in the final decades of the 1800s, vaccines for diseases like tetanus, rabies, typhoid fever, and bubonic plague were invented. The more vaccines proliferated, the more their safety and effectiveness was discussed and debated.

Hindsight, of course, tells us Elizabeth was right to be skeptical of many of the conventional drugs used at the time, but it may well have been a step in the wrong direction to disregard science at such a pivotal moment in the discipline's history.

Surely fresh air did more good than arsenic, but so could employing newer medical diagnostics. Science had bestowed upon medicine anesthesia, vaccines, and antiseptics. Soon to follow would be X-rays and radiation. But preaching preventative health by way of a nutritious diet, exercise, and good hygiene suited Elizabeth. It remains solid advice and certainly could only stand to help the women living in the city's slums, inasmuch as they had the power and funds to implement such suggestions. It was a surprisingly progressive ethos. Doctors did not yet teach the importance of good nutrition, rest, and fresh air to their patients, and they were not taught about it in medical school.

In the midst of the Blackwells' planning, Sophia appeared. After being turned down by Harvard, Sophia reluctantly made her way to New York, where she'd heard that Elizabeth and Emily were planning a full medical college for women attached to their infirmary.

But the college was still six months away from being ready to open. In the meantime, Sophia spent a few weeks as an informal worker at the infirmary. In the mornings, Sophia had persuaded Dr. Moseley, the head demonstrator of anatomy at Bellevue Hospital, to give her and another woman student a course of private lessons in dissection and practical anatomy.

"Oh, dear, isn't it good to have some real teaching at last!" she rejoiced. Afternoons were spent at the infirmary. She was impressed with the Blackwells' work ethic and professional expertise.

"Why don't you get together a class of young Englishwomen and bring them back when our infirmary opens as a college," Elizabeth coaxed.

"Perhaps," Sophia replied coyly. After a pause, she told Elizabeth, "I had thought some of Harvard." Her dream of studying alongside male students wasn't entirely extinguished.

Elizabeth had also noticed that their spartan living conditions chafed Sophia's sensibilities. The Blackwells often kept to a frugal diet of bread, oranges, and dates. "We sleep in the garret and dine in the cellar, when we dine at all," Elizabeth once quipped. And Sophia had indeed written home to complain that, "English ladies are not given to dine in kitchens on poor kitchen fare."

But Harvard still wasn't having her, so Sophia went home to collect her things and made plans to return to the Blackwells' infirmary once their school was ready. While home that summer, Lucy came to visit Sophia at her parents' home. Sophia proudly paraded the delightful, dainty doctor around to all of her friends and relations, Lucy wearing a beautiful powder blue dress, gleefully shattering all preconceived notions about medical study making women manly. Sophia's father declared Lucy equal parts strong and tender; he was so impressed that he offered to buy her a carriage when she returned to Boston.

On Friday, October 23, Sophia appeared back in New York with her maid, Alice, and her pet setter, Turk, just in time to be among the inaugural class at the newly minted Woman's Medical College of the New York Infirmary. For a week, she traipsed up and down 137th Avenue hunting for rooms to rent. Having no luck there, she finally found a place at 222 East Tenth Street in what would later be called the East Village. It was a four-minute walk around the corner to the Blackwells' infirmary.

Fifty-five dollars a month bought her rent and gas for two back parlors on the first floor and two rooms above. She and Alice set to work making the house a home: laying down carpets, installing a stove, buying a bed, chairs, pots, and pans. But she bought as little furniture as possible. The carpets she brought from Boston, and she rented a second bed, the stove, and two tables from her landlady. Sophia squirreled away what she hoped was enough provisions to last the winter: flour, wine, two barrels of potatoes, thirty pounds of butter.

"This last week has been a pretty hard time, but now things

are falling into shape," Sophia declared. "The Blackwells are very pleasant, and, though I have no special friends here, I shall be so busy and cosy that I expect to get on capitally."

Sophia and Alice were close companions, but their rooms were situated so they could easily keep to themselves when they wanted. They were also essentially the only tenants who used the back stairs. Sophia relished living independently, with the freedom to read and study whenever she wished. The hospital life had been full of friends and revelry, but it was also highly scheduled and left her little time for reflective solitude. Sophia was excited for this next chapter, but wished she could have found a way to remain in Boston with her dearest Lucy.

She worried that Lucy would greatly miss her help and was concerned she wouldn't take care of herself, though her father's gift to Lucy was of some comfort. "I can't tell you and Daddy how thankful I am that he has given her that charming little carriage, it is such a relief to my mind to know that she will not be forced to drive herself when weary and half frozen," Sophia told her mother. She promised Lucy she'd return to Boston after finishing her degree in New York, and their life together could begin in earnest.

The college's inaugural class comprised fifteen students. The Blackwells filled the professorships only with regard to talent, paying no mind to gender. Of the eight professors at the school, only two were women. Elizabeth took the reins of hygiene while Emily taught obstetrics and diseases of women (gynecology). In addition, doctors Lucy Abbott and Eliza Chapin acted as assistant physicians, with Abbott teaching clinical midwifery. Abbott had studied at the New England Female Medical College, Chapin at the Female Medical College of Pennsylvania.

This school was the culmination of Elizabeth and Emily's life's work, and in her speech for the opening of the college on November 2, 1868, Elizabeth spoke of working toward this moment since they first established their dispensary.

"We have been facing these two perpendicular cliffs—money and skill—for fifteen years, and striving in every possible way to climb them. Little by little, however, we have laid one stone upon another, until we have gained a foundation sufficient to stand on. It is small, certainly, but solid," she declared.

Elizabeth was pleased she'd found so many men who wished to participate in the medical education of women. She was hopeful it meant mainstream acceptance of women physicians was growing. "We are so accustomed to be 'despised and rejected' that encouragement, welcome, success, seem unaccountable. But from whatever cause proceeding, the support now given to the formation of the College is warm and cordial," Elizabeth admitted.

It was true that it was becoming more publicly acceptable for women to become doctors, especially in America, where women's medical schools were increasingly common, but there were still plenty of detractors. As so often is the case, the more women pushed, the more pushback they got. An *Australian Medical Journal* article claimed medical women would never be regarded as more than mere curiosities like "dancing dogs and bearded ladies."

As far as Sophia was concerned, women had "more love of medical work, and are naturally more inclined, and more fitted for it than most men." Given the laziness or loudness of many of the male medical students Lizzie had encountered, she may well have been right.

Sophia was so excited to begin training at a real medical college, to start on a straight path toward an MD. Every morning at nine, Sophia was tasked with examining specimens in the dissecting room.

On alternating days came a midmorning anatomy and physiology lecture. Inside the small lecture room was a semicircle of two levels of risers, on top of which chairs were placed. Ladies in tiny prim hats and billowy skirts, buttons down their chest and bows at their necks, furiously scribbled notes in the note-books gently resting on their laps. In the center of the room a cadaver partially covered by a plain sheet lay on a long wooden table. The professor, Dr. Samuel Ward, stood over it, pointing out the intricacies and details of the body's inner workings. An easel behind the teacher reinforced these points with illustra-tions of whatever bodily system was being studied that day. A stool held an open textbook from which the professor could read.

Alice had lunch ready for Sophia when she came home after morning classes. Afternoon lectures commenced at two, cover-ing three subjects for an hour each. Feeling stiff and restless after having to sit for so long, Sophia immediately petitioned Emily to institute five-minute breaks between lectures so the women could stand up, open the windows, and walk up and down the corridors. Emily agreed to this excellent suggestion at once.

A full course of lectures cost $105; other fees included the matriculation fee of $5, a demonstrator's fee of $10, and a grad-uation fee of $30. First-year students studied "elementary" branches of medical science: materia medica, pharmacy, and chemistry. Sophia's class-entrance tickets to practical anatomy and principles and practice of medicine became treasured keep-sakes. The Blackwells' college also distinguished itself by offer-ing progressive classes during the students' tenure, instead of the typical repeated classes.

"The teaching is really very good and I am getting on capi-tally," Sophia proudly told her mother. "I have never worked so hard in my life and I have never been in such good health. I am absolutely well (and what a blessing that is after all these years!) I eat and walk and sleep perfectly, have no pains and aches, and the sweetest of tempers! I only wish Mother could peep in and see me in my little den, dog and Alice and all."

Elizabeth feared Sophia might be too undisciplined to com-plete their rigorous course of instruction, admitting "she must work harder than I have yet known her to do if she is to gain our diploma."

In addition to lectures, students were granted admittance to clinical lectures at various hospitals and infirmaries around the city: the Charity Hospital, the Insane Asylum, the Eye and Ear Infirmary, the Hospital for Epileptics and Paralytics, the Nursery Hospital, the Fever and Smallpox hospitals. Most notably, they could visit massive Bellevue Hospital. As many as twelve thousand patients passed through its doors each year, five hundred of which were obstetrical cases.

But women were not always warmly welcomed at Bellevue. Elizabeth heard about one particular incident involving that "unprincipled" homeopathic school, the New York Medical College for Women. They'd sent their class to attend a clinical lecture at Bellevue alongside four hundred male students. The men behaved abominably, but Elizabeth believed the women's response lacked decorum. "They did the most indiscreet, most tactless and impertinent things," she told Barbara.

According to New York Medical College for Women student Anna Manning, during their clinical studies at Bellevue, male students and doctors regularly catcalled and jeered at her and her five fellow female students. "Students of today have no idea of conditions as they were when I studied medicine," Anna later told the guests at a luncheon in her honor. "All the work at the hospital was made as repulsively unpleasant for us as possible."

As much as Sophia would have loved to be among the Blackwells' first graduating class, family matters soon interrupted her studies. On Thursday, November 12, a letter was brought to Sophia while she was studying in the dissecting room. Her mother had written to say her father was very ill. Sophia wrote back with two big kisses for her ailing daddy and cheerily imagining him getting stronger every day while her letter made its way to him.

By Monday, a note from her older sister, Carry, arrived with the grim inscription: "I believe if you could start from New

York today, you would have no prospect whatever of seeing him alive."

Sophia told Elizabeth she had to leave immediately.

"We are so sorry, my dear, not only for your great loss, but for ours," Elizabeth replied. "Please—don't let this end your hope of studying medicine."

"Don't worry," Sophia assured her through her grief. "I *will* become a doctor yet."

Sophia rushed back to England, as much as one could rush when the only transit option across the Atlantic was a ship. She arrived home on Saturday, November 28 to find her father had died ten days before she'd even received Carry's note. If she'd remained in the UK, she'd likely have been able to see her father one last time before he died. She vowed never to let such a wide ocean come between her and her family again; she would stay in the UK, despite the prepaid term of college classes she'd left behind in New York.

She wrote to Lucy during her sea voyage to let her know she no longer planned to pursue her MD in New York nor would she be returning to Boston, and to thank her for all she'd done for her. "Even now when I am going home and going under such circumstances the thought of all you have done for me and of all I owe you, comes uppermost…[all] your love and help have been given to me, and I know it is not all over now."

Lucy was crushed, but as ever, remained selflessly optimistic about what Sophia could do for the movement in her homeland. "If you don't come back to America, you won't give up the work. You will open the profession to women in England."

"But we will be together again some day, old lady, won't we?" Sophia reassured her. "Oh, dear, I am getting so tired of living and fighting and hoping! As soon as one hopes one has got a little foothold it is all knocked away from under one!"

ELEVEN

Lizzie Takes On London

Following Lizzie's incredible accomplishment of being the first UK-trained woman placed on the British medical register (Elizabeth being the first, though American-trained), *The Lancet* offered its glib congratulations. However, it surmised that, "No doubt the examiners had due regard for her sex, and omitted all those subjects of examination which would be shocking to the female mind but which are very necessary for ordinary general practice."

Lizzie had, of course, taken the exact same exam as the men. But the medical establishment had to come up with some reason for her success, some way to excuse and belittle her momentous achievement. Lizzie, the article insisted, was an exception. The author simply refused to entertain the idea that any other woman might follow her example. "We cannot accept the event as an omen of coming change." He concluded by outlining all of the posts Lizzie was unfit for because she was a woman: military, hospital, family practice, village doctor. Really, why had she even bothered?

It was unfortunately true that despite her name being on the medical register, Lizzie found no medical establishment in London willing to employ her. So in the autumn of 1865, she opened her own private practice, just as Elizabeth had. At least Lizzie didn't have to worry about having enough money to eat or heat her home since her father, Newson, paid the rent and gave her an allowance. Her mother sent weekly hampers filled with fresh produce, poultry, and baked goods from their Aldeburgh estate. Her father was positively jubilant at his daughter's hard-won success; her mother merely tolerated Lizzie's peculiar life path. In return, Lizzie wrote her parents weekly letters about her life using a goose quill pen she cut herself.

Lizzie found fine quarters in which to set up her home and private practice at 20 Upper Berkeley Street on the edge of London's medical district. The space had five floors, but no central heat or electricity. Newson supplied the practice with elegant furniture and nicely framed artwork. But what should go on the nameplate out front?

"I don't like 'Miss Garrett' on the door," Lizzie complained. It was too much "like a dressmaker." But *Dr.* wouldn't be quite appropriate yet either, since she didn't yet have an official MD. Emily also reasoned that *Dr.* might be off-putting to some.

Louie suggested *Elizabeth Garrett, L.S.A.* along with a night bell, which seemed just right. Taking her sister's advice, Lizzie's nameplate read Elizabeth Garrett, Licentiate of the Society of Apothecaries.

Lizzie employed a parlor maid who would bring patients up the stairs into the waiting room. When she was ready to see them, patients would be called down the hall to the back drawing room that she had made up as an examination room. To see her patients, she wore a beautiful brown velvet dress kissed with fine Irish lace.

A Victorian checkup would likely involve a doctor taking the patient's pulse and temperature, listening to their breathing and digestive sounds with a stethoscope, and examining a urine sample and possibly a blood sample. They would also observe the patient's overall physique—note the appearance of the eyes, the tongue, the lips, the skin—and record signs of disease and reported symptoms.

One of Lizzie's private tutors was a proponent of explaining the diagnosis to the patient, a nearly unheard of point of view at the time. That meant her patients were likely some of the first to benefit from this progressive stance. Understanding their illness and treatment could help patients understand how to better care for themselves, how to notice and report their symptoms, and how to advocate for themselves.

At first, her patients were few and far between, reluctant to consult a woman. This gave Lizzie time to attend concerts and stroll art galleries. Her quasi-celebrity status also made her the hottest dinner-party invitee in town. She once dined with John Stuart Mill and got a ride home in Kate Russell, Viscountess Amberley's carriage. Mill was a liberal member of parliament and author of several influential works on philosophy. Lady Amberley was an early advocate of women's education, voting rights, and equal pay. When word got out that Lady Amberley had given a speech on women's suffrage at the Mechanics Institute, Queen Victoria raged that she "ought to get a good whipping."

In March, Lizzie gave a lecture on physiology at her home that was attended by Amberley, philanthropist Frances Power Cobbe, and Mill's wife, Harriet, and her daughter Helen.

"Everyone cared more for it than I did," Amberley admitted, having enjoyed the company but not the content of Lizzie's speech.

Since a woman living alone was considered scandalous, Lizzie's school friend, Jane Crow, became her roommate. They lived within walking distance of Emily, Barbara, and Louie. Their proximity gave rise to many organizing opportunities. After Barbara convinced Mill to submit a petition to parliament requesting the extension of voting rights to property-owning women, the ladies got to work gathering the hundred signatures required. There, in Lizzie's London dining room, the first suffrage society in Britain was born.

While Lizzie enjoyed a busy social life, professionally she felt terribly isolated. "I was *in the fortress* as it were, but alone and likely to be for a good long time," Lizzie said. After six months of slowly growing her private practice, Lizzie, like Blackwell, decided to open a dispensary in an area of town where poor women could receive the free healthcare they desperately needed. Donations from Lizzie's acquaintances poured in to cover the costs of launching this charitable venture, nearly £150. She opened St. Mary's Dispensary for Women and Children in July 1866, located on the corner of Seymour Place in Marylebone, London, a few blocks from her home.

Every Monday, Wednesday, and Friday at 3:00 p.m., Lizzie opened her drab little dispensary. It was on the first floor of a three-story attached building. The only update she made was to whitewash the windows for privacy. A small group of men—one physician, three surgeons, and three obstetricians—acted as honorary consultants. Their approval and perceived availability would provide an air of trustworthiness and assurance that women doctors alone could not yet imbue. Lizzie also employed a male pharmacist, but asked that he take on two women assistants as paying student-apprentices.

Lizzie thrived in the busy city, even though its crowded, filthy streets were a far cry from Aldeburgh's open fields and rocky beaches. Unfortunately, the conditions of urban living meant doctors' services were in much greater demand. A thick blanket of smog hung in the air. The soot and sulfurous gases produced by domestic and industrial burning of soft coal regularly created yellowish fogs known as *pea-soupers*. Such pollution quickly led to respiratory disease, especially in the elderly and young.

Horse dung and urine caked the streets. As for human excrement, nicer homes had a privy in the back garden in the form of an outhouse. At night, you could use the chamber pot under your bed, then dump the waste into the pit in the morning. Liquid waste was left to seep into the earth while "night soil men" were employed to visit homes in the middle of the night and harvest the solids from the pit, which they would sell to farmers for fertilizer.

Thankfully, the year Lizzie opened her private practice, a new sewer system finally finished connecting most of London's neighborhoods, routing sewage to treatment plants outside the city instead of dumping it directly into the Thames. It was a project years in the making, prompted by the Great Stink of 1858. The city's population explosion was a major contributor for the need of a proper sewage system. Over the course of the nineteenth century, London's population went from less than one million to 6.5 million.

For those born in London in midcentury, life expectancy was a mere thirty-seven years. Diseases like cholera, smallpox, typhoid, and pulmonary tuberculosis (often called consumption) ravaged Victorians, cutting down many in the prime of their lives. As the de facto household caregivers, women often found themselves disproportionately affected by contagious illnesses. Infections and respiratory diseases took the most lives. Deaths from work-related injuries or exposure to toxic substances also abounded, as did those related to childbirth and domestic violence.

Poverty, overpopulation, infant and child mortality, crime, and filth abounded in the East End of London where Lizzie set up her dispensary. In his weekly magazine, *Household Words*, Charles Dickens wrote of the area in 1850: "There are foul ditches, open sewers, and defective drains, smelling most offensively...not a drop of clean water can be obtained. In some of the wells the water is perfectly black and fetid. The paint on the window-frames has become black from the action of the sulphuretted hydrogen gas. Nearly all the inhabitants look unhealthy; the women especially complain of sickness and want of appetite; their eyes are sunken, and their skin shrivelled."

In the years since Dickens's writings, living conditions hadn't improved much. In 1865, the year before Lizzie's dispensary opened, Sophia's ex-girlfriend Octavia Hill described how in the slums of Marylebone, "the plaster was dropping from the walls, on one staircase a pail was placed to catch the rain that fell through the roof. All the staircases were perfectly dark, the banisters were gone, having been used as firewood by the tenants." Octavia was advocating for housing reform by decrying the horror of London's slums. She favored low-built, cottage-style row houses with gardens instead of massive high-rise flats.

It's not surprising, then, that Lizzie's dispensary opened in the midst of a cholera outbreak. The disease is a waterborne bacterial illness transmitted via contact with the excrement of the ill—unknown facts that proved deadly in an era of unwashed hands and sewage-tainted water. Rancid food, "cold fruits" like melons, and even excessive rage were thought to cause the disease.

Doctors had plenty of misguided theories about how illness arose. Culprits included night air, sedentary habits, wet feet, and sudden temperature changes. Fevers were brought on by extreme temperatures, irregular bowels, injuries, bad air, or violent emotions. Scottish physician Dr. William Buchan had observed a connection between one's heritage and one's risk of illness when he listed "diseased parents" as among the main causes of illness in his 1848 edition of *Domestic Medicine*.

It wasn't until 1854 that a London neighborhood's cholera outbreak was convincingly traced to something in the common water supply: a well on Broad Street had been contaminated by a baby's dirty diaper, sickening hundreds of people. When the water pump handle was removed, the epidemic abated.

If not treated early, cholera can lead to dehydration and death. Desperate times called for desperate measures: cholera didn't care if you were rich or poor; patients didn't care if their doctor was a man or woman. So unlike Lizzie's slowly growing private practice, her dispensary was immediately overflowing.

During each short afternoon period, approximately eighty women per day paid a penny for her medical advice. She cared for three thousand patients that year, who between them made more than 9,300 visits to her dispensary.

Soon, she found some much-needed professional assistance. Frances Morgan, Eliza Walker Dunbar, and Louisa Atkins appeared at Lizzie's door hoping for advice on how to repeat her success in being licensed to practice medicine by the Society of Apothecaries. Lizzie invited them to come receive clinical training at her dispensary.

Once the cholera epidemic eased, most of the dispensary's patients were women and children from the nearby Lisson Grove slums. Her patients were a wretched group: rundown by poverty, exhausted by childbearing, battered by drunken husbands, bedraggled from sex work. All of these women could finally feel comfortable discussing everything that ailed them with their healthcare provider because that provider was a woman, someone they felt they could trust.

Lizzie quickly made the connection between class and health, realizing that most illnesses were often exacerbated by the unhealthy circumstances created by poverty and lack of education. She despaired that all too often, all she could offer these patients was a "liberal dose of cod-liver oil, quinine and other expensive remedies." (Quinine was used as a treatment for fevers, but only truly worked on fevers arising from malaria.)

On the other side of this coin was her private practice, which maintained a roster of prominent patients. Lady Amberley was more than happy to employ Lizzie as her personal physician. This relationship was tested when Amberley went into premature labor. Lizzie found twin baby girls presenting feet first. The first baby lived, but the second was stillborn. Amberley felt Lizzie was not sufficiently upset by the loss, but her support for women proved stronger than her personal pain and she remained Lizzie's patient.

One thing all of her patients had in common, wealthy and penniless alike, was a newfound sense of freedom in what they could reveal to a woman physician, and how much better she could understand the complex etiology behind their maladies.

Leading suffragist Josephine Butler made the two-hundred-mile trek from Liverpool to consult Lizzie. She had long experienced bouts of ill health, and was hopeful that a woman doctor might finally be able to supply some relief. From Lizzie, Butler got more detailed advice than she'd gotten from any other doctor because Lizzie "entered much more into my mental state and way of life," Josephine said. "I was able to tell her so much more than I ever could or would tell to any man. Oh if men knew what women have to endure and how every good woman has prayed for the coming of a change. I pray to God that many Miss Garretts may arise."

An avid social reformer, Josephine had recently come to prominence for her loud opposition to the Contagious Diseases Act of 1864. The act was created after the British government realized how many of its military officers were being ravaged by venereal disease. Popular wisdom maintained that women only tolerated sex, while men required regular satisfaction of their carnal urges. Prostitutes were a social necessity according to the government, and needed to be regulated.

The act stipulated that any woman suspected of prostitution could be forced to undergo invasive medical testing. If she refused, she faced prison time. Women found to be ill could be forcibly detained at a hospital for up to three months. Subsequent additions to the law saw that time increase to up to nine months and required all registered prostitutes to submit to regular exams by special police. The officers or other men with venereal disease saw no consequences whatsoever.

"By this law, a crime has been created in order that it may be severely punished," Josephine fumed. "But observe, that has been ruled to be a crime in women, which is not to be a crime in men."

Elizabeth Blackwell also disagreed with the aims of the act. She thought prostitution should be discouraged rather than regulated, and was similarly angered by its "unequal standard of sexual morality."

Nearly everyone in the women's rights movement crusaded against the act. Everyone, that is, except Lizzie. Her three years of running a dispensary led her to the conclusion that relying on people to seek treatment voluntarily would do little to stem the spread of venereal disease. She saw that women frequently failed to visit the hospital early enough after experiencing symptoms, and then didn't remain long enough after being admitted. She had to wonder if a legal mandate might indeed prove more effective at stamping out disease transmission. But she sympathized with their plight.

"Hospitals do not as a rule admit them, dispensaries cannot cure them; missions and refuges reach but few of them," Lizzie contended. "They are without their health, without character, without friends, without money. Could their position be more forlorn?"

She was also thinking of the children born to these patients, whom she saw as experiencing the pain of sexually transmitted diseases through no fault of their own. Lizzie butted heads with the Langham Place feminists when she endorsed the act; some never forgave her for what they perceived as a great betrayal. The disapproval she felt from her sister Milly proved the most distressing.

After five years, Lizzie had done much good for her community—her services appreciated by fine ladies and the most desolate alike. The dispensary books had collected a total of nine thousand patient names and recorded forty thousand visits. As for midwifery cases, 250 home deliveries had been overseen. Lizzie thrived on the excitement of the brisk walks she took between the homes of patients and the dispensary, wondering what the next case would hold. She had created a place to do the work she loved and finally felt her life's purpose achievable. But there was another part of her heart that remained untouched.

TWELVE

Sophia Storms Edinburgh

For Sophia, life back under her mother's roof in Brighton was by turns exasperatingly stifling and reassuringly simple. The well-ordered, carefree existence could be relaxing, but her mother constantly referred to her microscope slides and medical books as "nasty." Sophia wasn't one for staying still, at least, not for very long. Her desire to become a lady doctor still burned within her. By January, she was already planning trips to Cambridge, St. Andrews, Edinburgh, and other medical schools to see if she could "poke in anywhere." First, she applied to the University of London. The school told Sophia its charter had been specifically worded to exclude women. Next came the University of Edinburgh.

It was March 1869 and Sophia was nearly thirty when she headed to Edinburgh to make her case for admission. She met with David Masson, chair of Rhetoric and English Literature, who promised to provide her introductions to most of the professors in the medical school. Masson wrote to Robert Christison, chair of Materia Medica and Therapeutics at Edinburgh, and John H. Balfour, the dean of the university's medical school, on Sophia's behalf. He asked them to receive her with courtesy as she sought their opinions on being admitted to the university. She was seeking study in the summer term as a test.

Sophia was invited to breakfast with Sir James Young Simpson, professor of midwifery, and his wife, Jessie. He was quite favorable to her application to the university, and spoke very highly of his former intern Dr. Emily Blackwell. During their meal, Simpson passed Sophia the latest issue of *The BMJ*, pointing to a notice about Lizzie. "By special order of the minister" she had been admitted to the first examination for an MD in Paris, and had passed it in the presence of a crowded audience "with very great éclat."

"That woman certainly has great power of study and work, hasn't she?" Sophia declared. She would breakfast with the Simpsons again the next day to seal his approval.

Sophia had four days with near back-to-back meetings with dozens of professors and made notes of her impressions of each meeting. Some went better than others. University principal Alexander Grant and his wife, Susan, were friendly and kind. Natural history professor George Allman said he would be delighted to see her in his class. Balfour, on the other hand, questioned whether women would even be capable of dissections. Histology professor J. Hughes Bennett didn't see the need for women as doctors, but acknowledged their potential value as assistants.

For the most part, these men received her courteously, but there were exceptions. Thomas Laycock, the chair of Medicine, barked that women "had not sufficient strength for medical practice." He said most women only showed an interest in medicine so they could become abortionists. Sophia left his house in perfect agreement with him on one point, and only one: "that no woman who respected herself had better enter his class-room."

When she met with Christison, he was "uncompromising," fuming about how "the matter has been decided" against her. He was a crotchety seventy-two-year-old living legend at Edinburgh, set in his ways and used to always getting his way. Tall and trim, Christison's dark wavy hair curled around his ears and he shaved his long beard in a muttonchop style. Sophia referred to him as "the ogre."

A skilled toxicologist and forensic physician, Christison authored *A Treatise on Poisons* and *Medico-Legal Examination of Dead Bodies*. He'd earned his stripes early in his career by providing the evidence in the high profile court case of Burke and Hare. The men had killed sixteen people to make money selling bodies to an anatomy lecturer.

A misogynist and regular cocaine user, Christison believed women might make acceptable midwives, but never physicians. He lived in a world devoid of women. As a medical school professor he only taught men. In his personal life, he'd been widowed for twenty years, and his only remaining relatives were three sons and a twin brother. Utterly obsessed with poisons, Christison often took to self-experimentation. It was a practice that nearly killed him on at least one occasion. He was nefarious and ruthless, pressuring the university to shape its educational priorities around his interests and only promoting those he liked while passing over others with more experience or expertise.

If some of these attributes sound familiar it's because Arthur Conan Doyle met Christison as a young medical student. He is thought to have influenced the morally dubious traits of Sherlock Holmes, but even more so, helped inspire character traits of Holmes's arch nemesis, Moriarty.

The oppositional forces Sophia encountered at Edinburgh would be far stronger than anything Elizabeth or Lizzie ever experienced. Sure, they had their share of detractors and antagonizers, but what they faced was a cakewalk compared to what lay in store for Sophia.

Dean Balfour decided to put her admittance to a vote by the school's faculty and senate. Surprisingly, it went in her favor. She would be permitted to attend, provided she remained confined to the study of obstetrics and gynecology.

Alas, the senior assistant physician at the Edinburgh Royal Infirmary, Claud Muirhead, implored the university to rescind Sophia's admission. Muirhead was backed by a petition signed by two hundred students. William Turner also objected. All were concerned about "the difficulty and the injury to male students" resulting from professors being forced to abstain from exhaustive treatment of their subjects in the presence of a lady. It was decided male and female students would have to be taught separately, and creating separate classes for a single student would be too costly and onerous for the university. Her acceptance was overturned.

Dismayed but not deterred, Sophia spent the coming months working on her essay "Medicine as a Profession for Women," which was to be published in the upcoming anthology *Women's Work and Women's Culture*, edited by Josephine Butler. That summer, Sophia also enjoyed the distraction of a visit from Elizabeth Blackwell. Elizabeth said she had "such a refreshing time" staying with Sophia. Elizabeth was off to London next, planning to set up a private practice there.

Sophia spent hours on end in the library of the British Museum researching for her essay. The result was a comprehensive survey of prominent medical women from ancient Greece up to Elizabeth Blackwell. She was hoping to undo the erasure of women scientists throughout history. When women were told they had no scientific aptitude, there was little to point to saying otherwise unless they were inclined to do their own extensive research on the subject. Sophia wanted people to know that women had long been delivering medical care and making scientific discoveries and innovations.

Sophia points to *The Iliad* as proof of the existence of women physicians during ancient times. In it, Homer describes Agamede as a golden-haired woman with knowledge of the medicinal properties of every plant on earth. She cared for sick and injured Trojan soldiers. The translator noted that nothing was more normal at the time than women practicing the healing art of medicine.

She talks of Agnodice, Olympia of Thebes, and Aspasia, an OB-GYN in Athens and Rome. She mentions fourteenth-century Italians Dorotea Bucca and Alessandra Giliani. Giliani pioneered modern dissection and was the first person to inject anatomical specimens for preservation. She also points to sixteenth-century Spanish philosopher Oliva Sabuco de Nantes, who authored several treatises on medicine and psychology.

In her essay, Sophia demands to know "who has the right to say that [women] shall not be allowed to make their work scientific when they desire it, but shall be limited to merely the wearisome routine of nursing, while to men is reserved all intelligent knowledge of disease, and all study of the laws by which health may be preserved or restored."

Sophia called out the self-canceling arguments of medical men. Out of one side of their mouths came the proclamation that women's medical schools shouldn't be founded until it had been established that women were actually capable of studying and practicing medicine. Out of the other side they spoke of how women shouldn't study medicine alongside men, so they must have a separate medical school of their own. She laid out this hypocrisy simply: women must prove their competence in order to earn a school of their own, but could only gain the skills and knowledge to prove that competence at a school of their own. By that logic, there would never be any women doctors. Which was likely precisely the point.

To poke holes in the assertion that women should receive their medical education separately from men, Sophia looked to the idea that female patients are expected to consult male doctors without shame or unease, that male doctors are expected to shunt aside any embarrassment that may arise and treat each patient as merely another case. If doctors and patients could co-mingle, why not medical students?

"If it is indeed true that no one is fit for the profession of Medicine unless able to banish from its practice the personal idea of sex, it certainly seems as if all earnest students seeking the same knowledge for the same ends, ought to be able to pursue their studies together," Sophia reasoned.

To those who argued that women couldn't possibly be doctors because of mental deficiency, Sophia pointed out that it was actually in these people's best interests to permit women to pursue medical schooling, and see their point proven. If women truly lacked the brainpower to study medicine, the exams should triumphantly prove their point when they resulted in universal failure. But if it turned out that some of them could actually pass the exams, then surely the mental argument against their practicing medicine was null and void.

With her essay completed, Sophia returned her focus on lobbying for entrance to the University of Edinburgh. She decided that if teaching one woman wasn't worth the hassle, then all she needed was to recruit more women. Masson personally felt Sophia was being treated unfairly by the school, and related her crusade to his friend and *The Scotsman* newspaper editor, Alexander Russel. Russel covered the controversy in his column and encouraged more women to apply to the school.

Before long there were five: Sophia, Isabel Thorne, Edith Pechey, Matilda Chaplin, and Helen Evans. They were now requesting full admission to the school, not just permission to attend certain lectures. Together, the university could no longer use numbers as an excuse to refuse them entrance.

Isabel had realized the need for women doctors in the most heartbreaking of ways. A month shy of their first wedding anniversary, Isabel and her husband Joseph's first child was born prematurely. Their doctor was a former ship's surgeon, unac-

customed to treating women and children. The baby was too
weak to suck; the milk Isabel expressed often turned sour before
he could take it. The following winter, the baby developed a
cough. Leeches were applied to his throat, but he gradually lost
strength and died that October.

When Isabel heard about Lizzie's great accomplishment of
being placed on the medical register, she decided to enroll in
practical midwifery classes. "I was anxious to follow in her footsteps," Isabel explained. Before long, Isabel was writing prize-
winning essays on the subject. She even passed the Society of
Apothecaries's preliminary test. But she wouldn't be able to do
as Lizzie did and piece together private instruction to present to
the Apothecaries. The loophole Lizzie slipped through had been
immediately closed. After Lizzie passed its exam, the Society of
Apothecaries changed its rules to now only allow certificates of
instruction from recognized medical schools.

Isabel thought her only option was to study in Paris. But as
she was preparing to set off for France, she heard about the potential for women to study in Edinburgh. By the time she and
her family piled onto a train from London to Edinburgh to
join Sophia, she had four children, who all came with her: two
girls and two boys, ages ten, eight, two, and one. "They were
all suffering from whooping cough so we had the railway carriage pretty well to ourselves," Isabel joked. Joseph was living
in Shanghai at the time, where his firm was based, so she hired
a nursemaid to help her with the children, and Matilda moved
in with them, too.

Helen was born in Ireland, and like Isabel, she'd lost her first
child in infancy, and then her husband also died. Edith wasn't
sure how well she would do at medicine, but she wanted to
give it a go anyway. "Do you think anything more is requisite
to ensure success than moderate abilities and a good share of
perseverance?" she asked Sophia. "I believe I may lay claim to
these, together with a real love of the subjects of study, but as

regards any thorough knowledge of these subjects at present, I fear I am deficient in most."

Edith and Sophia moved in together, and Sophia's maid, Alice, and her dog, Turk, joined them. Their little homestead at 15 Buccleuch Place was bubbling with life. Before long, Isabel and her children had also taken up residence there. It was a brisk six-minute walk to their classes, with plenty of gardens nearby.

Edith had lush, long dark hair cascading down her proud head, and she cut a tall, classical figure. A loyal friend, her charm was disarming, her wit dazzling, and her intellect rare. She was also quite modest. All of the women passed the Edinburgh matriculation exam, but Edith earned the highest score of all 152 people taking the exam.

In the autumn of 1869, they became the first women ever to be accepted into a degree program at a British university. Five additional women signed the matriculation register: Elizabette Ken, Mary Cudell, Mary Spalding Roberts Sinclair, Elizabeth Mary Clark, and Emily Rosaline Masson (wife of professor Masson), but details about them have largely been lost to history since they did not play a key role in the ensuing fight for an education. The biographies of the first five women are preserved because they persisted beyond the first few terms and because they are the ones Sophia chose to include in her written account of the events.

"I do indeed congratulate you undergraduates with all my heart," Elizabeth Blackwell wrote to Sophia from London. "It seems to me the grandest success that women have yet achieved in England; it is the great broad principle established that conducts to every noble progress. I feel as if I must come up to Edinburgh in the course of the winter, to see and bless the class!"

The women started school in November, and there was trouble from the start. They may have forced their way into the school, but the professors and students weren't going to make getting an education easy for them. First, the university charged

them higher fees than the male students. Next, some of the professors began exploiting a university loophole that *permitted* them
to teach women, but did not *require* them to.

The school provided course materials, but left the women
to arrange their own lectures. Sophia frequently took it upon
herself to lead the women's classes, as well as tutoring them in
math. She had quite a head start on many of the other women,
having assisted Lucy at the New England Hospital for Women
and Children and studied briefly at the Blackwells' college. Essentially, they were being charged more to teach themselves the
material. And despite the content of their separate classes being
identical to the men's, the women were graded much more
harshly. Still, they undertook their two classes, physiology and
chemistry, with aplomb.

In December, Sophia and the other women read in *The Scotsman* about a riot at the Pennsylvania Hospital. Ann Preston, dean
of the Women's Medical College of Pennsylvania, had successfully petitioned for thirty of her students to attend a clinical
lecture at the hospital. When they arrived, awaiting them in
the upper tiers of the surgical amphitheater were nearly three
hundred male medical students. They began hurling spitballs,
epithets, insults, and catcalls. They jeered, hissed, stamped their
feet, and spat tobacco juice on the women's dresses. The lecturers tried to quell the boys' tantrum and proceed with describing
their cases. Despite the continued growls, stomping, and spitballs,
the lecture proceeded. Afterward, the men chased the women
into the streets while screaming indecencies and throwing stones.

"I wonder if these vulgar men have mothers or sisters whom
they respect, or who respect them?" *The Scotsman* scolded.

So far, the Edinburgh women had experienced no such animosity from their classmates. That would soon change.

Edith continued to shine academically, earning top marks
on the spring exams. In chemistry, among the 231 candidates,
Sophia placed tenth and Edith placed third in general and first

among the first-year students. Those who scored the top four
marks in the class won the coveted Hope Scholarship. But when
he announced the results, the chemistry professor said he would
be passing over Edith and awarding the scholarship to the next
man on the list. He reasoned that since their class was taught
separately, the women were not technically part of the "class."
How he could believe that, when the test was exactly the same,
would be hilarious if it wasn't so gravely unfair.

Of all the names on that list of top marks, Edith, in fact, had
the most right to the money of any of them.

Dr. Thomas Charles Hope, professor of medicine and chemistry at the University of Edinburgh from 1799 to 1843, had established a series of public lectures for ladies. He was so blown away
by their popularity that he used the proceeds—about £1,000—
to establish Hope Scholarships, which endowed students with
free admittance into the chemistry lab.

The papers were abuzz. A writer in *The Scotsman* ranted that
women had exactly the same claim to medical education as men,
so to treat them as pariahs who should be grateful for the bare
crumbs of instruction thrown their way—while reserving all of
the awards and honors for the men—was incredibly unjust. In
The Spectator, an astute observer pointed out that the lady med
students were taught separately because of the professor's delicacy, not the women's, so to make them attend separate classes
and then argue that this meant they couldn't be considered for
competition was ludicrous.

The Times took the opportunity to sing Edith's praises: she "has
done her sex a service, not only by vindicating their intellectual
ability in an open competition with men, but still more by the
temper and courtesy with which she meets her disappointments.
Miss Pechey, in the spirit of a true student, says she is abundantly
repaid for her exertions by the knowledge she has acquired; but it
is none the less hard that, having been encouraged to labour for a

coveted reward, and having fairly won it, she should be disqualified by a restriction of which no warning had been given her."

The fact that a woman could do better than most of the men sent a chill down the spines of some students and faculty. This meant that women might not be too feebleminded or physically weak to undertake studying medicine after all. The women weren't just getting by—they were excelling. Clearly, they weren't going to give up after a few months, as most of the professors had expected. They would have to make life even more difficult for them.

"The results of the class examinations aroused in our opponents a conviction that the so-called experiment was not going to fail of itself, as they had confidently hoped, but that if it was to be suppressed at all, vigorous measures must be taken for that purpose," Sophia explained.

But others saw the women's smarts as proof of their right to be there. At the next university council meeting, Masson took up the women's cause. He moved that, in view of their success, they should be allowed to attend ordinary classes so that they might be spared the expense, inconvenience, and difficulty of forming separate classes. Dean Balfour seconded the motion. Turner and Christison vigorously fought against it. The motion lost, 47 votes to 58.

Turner, Joseph Lister, and Christison seemed particularly "determined to get rid of you," Masson later told Sophia.

Lister was far more staunchly opposed to women medical students than many of his contemporaries, asserting that desegregation of the sexes would mean the death of moral standards. His contributions to antiseptic surgery are storied; his rigid views of propriety and concerted efforts to keep women out of traditional medical schools is, of course, less famous.

Lister argued that discussing medical topics in a mixed group of men and women was utterly unseemly. Men and women learning together in hospital wards—where they might jostle up against one another—was unimaginable. If women wanted to be doctors, then they must do so separately from men in study and in practice. Given that women were not welcome at traditional universities, and there were no independent women's medical schools in Britain, if women abided by these terms they would never become doctors.

Turner, Lister, and Christison had much of the medical profession on their side when they disagreed with the medical education of women. In response to the women's very public push for a British medical education, a trove of opinions on the subject were published in medical journals around 1870.

Eminent medical men filled column after column with their outrage, calling a lady doctor "traitress to her sex," declaring women helpless and deficient, and insisting they couldn't possibly work together as physicians since they "hate one another, often at first sight, with a rancour of which men can form only a faint conception." Why, "when left to their own judgement they fail." Worse still, they will never know why they've failed "until they have asked some man."

One concerned female reader even wrote in to *The Lancet*, contending "no woman in any dangerous crisis would trust herself in the hands of a woman." Women lacked "the coolness and strength of nerves" necessary to be a physician since "the constitutional variations of the female system are not to be relied upon." Further, "morally, women are not fitted to be doctors, because they cannot (even the best of them) hold their tongues." The mere thought of women attending medical classes was repugnant, the writer bristled.

In *The BMJ*, it was suggested that ladies entering the workforce would be detrimental to the interests of their sex and of society as a whole. Grave concerns were raised about what would happen to all of the poor men pushed out of their jobs by these ruthless lady doctors, going so far as to say it would "increase celibacy by reducing the emoluments of the male sex." Why the

very fabric of civilized society hinged on women being dependent upon men and not embracing their "eccentric longing for
the will-o'-the-wisp pleasures of independence."

The *Medical Mirror* rebuked *The BMJ* for its medieval notions
concerning women, yet conceded that women's "acute sensibilities" might make women ill-suited for hospitals and operating
theaters.

"Ladies are all very well in their place, and that is looking after
the latest Paris fashions and making tea at home," the *Medical
Press and Circular* demanded. The journal also made the rather
extraordinary claim that "there is an abundance of cases of disease where a physician absolutely cures, not by his pathological
knowledge, nor yet by his acquaintance with medicines but by
the prestige of his mere presence; by being able to 'put his foot
down'; in one word, by being a—man."

Who knew men could send germs packing simply with their
masculine presence? Perhaps the opposite could be true. "Dear
Goddess of Health," Emelia Gurney wrote to her friend Lizzie
that same year. "You brought in with you such a fresh current
of health and vigour that you took away my cold and I perceived
a radiance for some time afterwards."

The lady medical students didn't let all of this public hand-
wringing go unanswered. In June 1870, Sophia provided a sharp
response to the "sufficiently arrogant" *Lancet* inquiry posed by
Dr. Henry Bennet: "What right have women to claim mental
equality with men?" Bennet had published a treatise on diseases of the uterus in 1845 and invented his own speculum. One
wonders if his female patients—Queen Victoria among them—
suffered because of his belief in women's inferiority. Sophia's
reply also appeared in *The Lancet*.

"After saying that women are 'sexually, constitutionally, and
mentally unfitted for hard and incessant toil,' Dr Bennet goes on
to propose as their sole share of the medical profession its 'most
arduous, most wearing, and most unremunerative duties,'" So-

phia wrote. She surmised it was this last part that Bennet was really concerned with when it came to divvying up medical roles. He would allow women to take all of the poorly paying midwifery cases, but patients requiring costly treatment needed the superior powers of the male mind. How very chivalrous!

In the summer term, five became seven. The women welcomed two more students: Emily Bovell and Mary Anderson (sister of Ford, the resident medical officer at Middlesex Hospital with whom Lizzie worked). Their impending notoriety would see them forever remembered as the Edinburgh Seven.

When Lizzie heard about these industrious lady students, she asked her wealthy patient Lady Amberley to donate some scholarship funds to them. Amberley gave £50 for three years, and Lizzie herself funded one-third of another scholarship. Whatever initial concern Lizzie had about Sophia becoming a doctor was now set aside and her full support given to her friend.

Dean Balfour, a professor of botany, was one of the few professors who offered to teach the women a separate class. But his ill health prevented him from teaching two classes. So Sophia called on Dr. Alleyne Nicholson, who taught natural history at the university's extramural school, to see if they could join his class.

After asking his students if they were okay with the women joining them, Nicholson welcomed the women to attend his regular class. That was how, Sophia said, "the first 'mixed class' was inaugurated, and continued throughout the summer without the slightest inconvenience." The men didn't bat an eye at the women's presence. The ladies particularly enjoyed the class field trip to a dredging site on the sandy gravel banks of the Firth of Forth to study fossils.

The majority of these extramural lecturers were appalled by how the university was treating the seven women. To help their cause, they passed two resolutions in July 1870, allowing the extramural lecturers to "be free to lecture to female as well as to male students" and to ensure that "no restrictions be imposed on the lecturers as to the manner in which instruction is to be imparted to women."

Unsurprisingly, Turner flatly refused to instruct them in anatomy or even to permit his assistant to do so. It was back to the extramural professors to provide the necessary teachings. Doctors Peter Handyside and Patrick Heron Watson said they saw no problem with teaching men and women together. They told the women they could attend their regular lectures in anatomy and surgery, respectively. Handyside had even taught women before, having trained some midwives.

Anatomy students could begin coming to the dissecting room at the beginning of October, but lectures didn't start till the following month. The more studious and industrious of the students usually came at the earlier date, while the others didn't appear until November, Sophia explained. The women arrived at the earliest possible day and were assigned their own cozy corner of the dissecting room.

Human remains for dissection could be hard to come by. People who'd received the death penalty were considered fair game for slicing open in front of wide-eyed students, but there were never enough convicted criminals to meet the growing demands of medical schools and independent anatomy institutions, especially as attendance at these establishments increased. To fill this gap, anatomy professors often offered to pay for cadavers.

Dead bodies became big business. Looters snatched bodies from fresh graves to make a quick buck; corpse dealers purchased bodies from grieving, destitute families and resold them to medical schools at a profit; poorhouse owners sold off any "unclaimed" bodies to help keep their institutions running. Infants' bodies were especially prized. Some corpses were sold whole, but you could make more money by breaking them up and selling each part individually.

Dissection was seen by the elite as necessary for scientific advancement and inquiry. Before the discovery of formaldehyde's tissue-preservative properties in the 1890s, bodies might be kept fresh in spirits such as whiskey or brandy. Mercury, zinc, and other metals were also used in an attempt to prolong putrefaction. One London medical man experimenting with cadaver preservatives in the late 1830s favored using boiling water and oxide of arsenic or a mixture containing red and white lead, boiled oil, and turpentine.

The first person to attempt long-term preservation of anatomical specimens was a woman: Alessandra Giliani. She served as demonstration assistant, or prosector, to famed anatomy professor Mondino de Luzzi at the University of Bologna in the early 1300s. Giliani extracted blood from veins and arteries and then refilled them with colored liquids that solidified. Finally, she painted the structures. She developed this groundbreaking technique in order to highlight a cadaver's vascular tree without destroying it. It proved a revelation in anatomical study. Thanks to her, students could now see even the smallest of veins.

Preservation methods continued to be refined and improved over the centuries. Preservation renders the wondrous intricacies of human anatomy permanently marvelous. Techniques developed in the Victorian era saw gorgeous, treelike branches of the lungs, blood vessels, and lymphatic system emerge as resplendent, hardened structures after being injected with colored resin or wax. Bones were bleached in the seaside sun or dyed to highlight their shapes and shadows, organs suspended in jars full of wine and turpentine.

An entire body could be preserved by injecting its blood vessels and organs with balsam, oil, and resin, giving it a two-week bath in wine and dichloride of mercury, and then finishing it off with a nice coat of varnish. Such treasures would go on display in medical schools' anatomy collections, such as the one inside the Surgeons' Hall.

All through the fall, the women studied the wonders of anatomy under Handyside with surprising ease. The male students
were never uncivil and hardly engaged more than a few words
with the Seven. According to Sophia, the men were quiet,
respectful, and in every way inoffensive; they accepted the
women's presence and worked diligently beside them. And the
women didn't distract the men from their studies at all. In fact,
Dr. Handyside told Sophia "that in the course of some twenty
sessions, he had never had such quiet, earnest work as since we
entered his rooms." The women were actually a good influence on the men!

It was about this time that the women applied for permission
to study in the wards of the Royal Infirmary, but were met with
a curt refusal. The Royal Infirmary was the only hospital in Edinburgh big enough to train students. Not to be deterred, they
got professors Handyside and Watson to write letters stressing
the importance of such practical training. They also persuaded
three medical officers from the infirmary to pen letters saying
they would happily train the women if they were permitted
entry. The infirmary decided it would have to defer the vote
for another week. Eminent professor Dr. Henry Littlejohn told
Sophia that despite foreseeing the ruin it would cause to have
women doctors, he would "drink the bitter cup to its dregs"
and vote for them.

While the women were waiting on deliberations, the male
students crafted a petition to bar women from the infirmary.
They obtained five hundred signatures. A few professors warmly
applauded the men for their efforts; the women's application was
again rejected.

Now the students began to take umbrage with the women's
persistence, most likely at the goading of their professors. Several male students "became markedly offensive and insolent, and
took every opportunity of practicing the petty annoyances that
occur to thoroughly ill-bred lads—such as shutting doors in our

faces, ostentatiously crowding into the seats we usually occupied, bursting into horse-laughs and howls as we approached," Sophia recalled.

It was as if the students had organized overnight, determining how to make the women as uncomfortable on campus as possible. They received threatening letters, had smoke blown in their faces, obscenities shouted at them in the street. The women were followed down the streets, their residences vandalized.

Ever since *The Scotsman* first wrote about the discrimination Sophia faced when requesting admission to Edinburgh, women in medicine had become a hot topic in the city. It was not something discussed only among educators and medical professionals, but among the public as well. Should women be eligible for medical school in the first place? Should they be taught separately? Should they be permitted to receive practical training at hospitals? Should they be granted medical degrees and therefore be allowed to become licensed doctors? Would *you* want to be treated by a woman doctor?

The debate soon spilled over from the papers into the street. Tensions came to a head on the afternoon of Friday, November 18, 1870, two days after the infirmary decided to refuse the women entrance.

The late-autumn cold had recently descended. Scotland can be dreary at the best of times, but the colder months are especially bleak; the sun often sets before 5:00 p.m. The frosty air nipped the women's cheeks as they strode purposefully down the cobbled streets toward Surgeons' Hall, where their exam was being held.

As they neared the imposing, Grecian-style building, Sophia saw a dense mob filling up the road. Along the street and among the hall's six large exterior columns, more than two hundred men awaited the arrival of the female interlopers. These women needed to be taught a lesson, scared back into their place. The men were passing around bottles of whiskey and smoking cigarettes, howling and singing, the newspaper noted, "with more spirit than good taste." The crowd was big enough to stop traffic for upward of an hour.

As the women approached, the rowdy group shouted verbal abuse and threw wads of trash and handfuls of mud, rotten eggs, and vegetables at them. The majority of the mob was not made up of the women's fellow medical students, though a few were present. Most of them were university students from other specialties who had been summoned there by an anonymous missive circulated around the classrooms that morning.

The women continued toward the building, unfazed, when all of a sudden the men slammed the gates in their faces. Eventually, they were able to enter the building, thanks to the help of a janitor and a few sympathetic male classmates shoving the gates open with all of their might.

The male students were from then on divided: a large group against the women, and a smaller, but not insignificant group, for them. Sophia said these few friendly students were even more indignant toward the rioters than the women were, and they offered to escort them all the way into the hall to make sure they made it into the exam room unharmed.

The mayhem did not stop once they entered the hall. Much of the mob crowded in behind them. After most of the disruptive men were eventually cleared out by Handyside, the few left brought Poor Mailie, the museum curator's pet sheep who was usually grazing outside on the lawn, into the exam room. The sheep ran around the desks, scared and bleating. Handyside ordered the men out and the door shut. As for the sheep, "Let it alone," he announced. "The poor beast has more sense than those who pushed it in."

The continued clamor outside proved a constant distraction during the test. The women tried hard to concentrate as the mud on their skirts began drying into a stiff crust. Afterward, Handyside came over to Sophia and asked if she and the others

would like to exit the building through the back. She assured
him there were enough sympathetic students to act as their es-
corts out the front.

As she spoke to the professor, these kindly men gathered
around the women until they were fully encircled by these self-
appointed bodyguards. The group proceeded out the front gate,
safely past the still-howling mob. They hurried home to change
out of their mud-spattered dresses.

Throughout it all, the female students never once flinched
or retaliated. They were behaving like true scientific students.
The women's lack of reaction must have further incensed the
men, for they surely hoped to show how fragile women were:
how delicate, emotional, and easily upset they are by nature.

The sheriff would later fine just three of the disorderly students £1 each for breach of the peace.

The next day, the women arrived at school for a lecture to find
their bodyguards wielding big sticks to keep a group of angry
students at bay. The guardians tipped their hats to the women
as they approached, then quickly followed in behind them and
took their seats in the lecture hall. When the class was over, they
escorted the women home again.

Quite the opposite of being scared off, the riot newly invigorated the Seven in their cause to see women provided educational opportunities to become physicians, as well as garnering
societal acceptance in their chosen profession.

"I began the study of medicine merely from personal motives;
now I am also impelled by the desire to remove women from
the care of such young ruffians," Edith wrote in *The Scotsman*.
"I should be very sorry to any poor girl under the care of such
men as those, for instance, who the other night followed me
through the street, using medical terms to make the disgusting
purport of their language more intelligible to me. When a man
can put his scientific knowledge to such degraded use, it seems
to me he cannot sink much lower."

By coming in close contact with "such unexpected depths of moral grossness and brutality, we had burnt into our minds the strongest possible conviction that if such things were possible in the medical profession women must force their way into it," Sophia explained, "for the sake of their sisters, who might otherwise be left at the mercy of such human brutes as these."

If Sophia and her friends hadn't seen just how much of an impact they could have by initiating the reintroduction of female doctors, their eyes were now fully open. They saw the deep significance of their endeavor, recognized how much hinged on their success. It was a heavy burden to be tasked with, but realizing its wide-reaching implications helped fuel their determination like nothing before.

THIRTEEN

Emily's Turn to Shine in New York

Back in New York, eight months after Sophia had left the Blackwells' school, Elizabeth herself left. She placed Emily in charge of the infirmary and college and headed back to London, this time with designs to stay.

Elizabeth's interest in settling in London had grown during her lecture tour there. "The more I see of work in England, the more I like it," Elizabeth had confessed to Emily. Whether it was how to become a doctor, raise healthy children, or simply find engaging work as a woman, throughout Britain she found people thirsting for every facet of her knowledge. Mothers begged her for instruction in health, at least three women expressed their desire to become medical students, even "wise old physicians" asked her to break up fashionable London practices by establishing her own.

Moving three thousand miles from home was a big step for a forty-eight-year-old single mother to take, but taking on new projects and pursuing new ambitions was completely in line with her character. She had also missed the proximity to her invigorating British friends in the decade since she'd lived there.

In the months leading up to her move, Elizabeth noticed Emily appeared upset at work. She worried that Emily was no longer happy practicing medicine. But it may have been Elizabeth that Emily was having issues with, since she returned to being perfectly content in her career after Elizabeth left.

While Elizabeth may have sensed Emily's agitation at her controlling ways, she doesn't hint at any animosity toward her sister. In fact, she often spoke admiringly of her sister, that she "does grandly at the centre of this movement—towers head and shoulders above her students and exercises a certain imperiousness as head of the establishment which is not unbecoming."

What we do know is that both Dr. Blackwells were highly opinionated, particular, and exacting. They were both happy for Elizabeth's impending move and for an ocean to separate them once again.

"I am more than willing that she should assume this headship and have long assisted her in acquiring it. She fully approves of my going to Europe to reside and only wishes I could go sooner," Elizabeth said.

Emily never quite captured the public's attention in the same way Elizabeth did. Emily worked just as hard, quietly toiling away to earn her medical degree and cultivate a world-class women's college and hospital, but Elizabeth is the one who's remembered. It's hard being the second or third person to do something. Emily wasn't one to seek out the spotlight, but there's only so much time you can spend in the shade of another before the lack of sunlight begins to wear thin.

Those who knew Emily personally always recognized her talent. Sara Josephine Baker, a student at the Blackwells' medical college, believed Emily belonged "to the tradition of the great pioneers. She inspired us all with the vital feeling that we were still on trial and that, for women who meant to be physicians, no educational standards could be too high. I think not many of us realized we were going out into the world as test cases, but Dr. Blackwell did."

Back when Emily was a medical student herself, she quickly learned that given the life-and-death stakes of surgery, expertise was nonnegotiable. That went double for women. "I have seen enough of surgery to know that I cannot undertake it without being well-qualified," she wrote to Elizabeth during her first semester in Chicago. "An unsuccessful operation or two would break a young surgeon, but with a good education I think I should succeed."

From her earliest experiences of surgery, Emily displayed an almost frighteningly clinical detachment. Surgery was science. And science was spellbinding. "I went to the first severe operation, amputation of the thigh, with some nervousness but neither in that or in any other case I have seen have I felt the slightest unpleasant feeling. I believe I shall have no difficulty about that," Emily confessed to her sister. "Once engaged in observing or helping, all feeling of its being disagreeable vanishes. The blood affected me no more than so much warm water."

Observing at so many hospitals and clinics in America and Europe during her studies exposed Emily to the primitive nature of medicine at the time. She knew her sister could commiserate. "I know you look on medicine with something of contempt, and there is certainly nothing attractive in the care of miserable, forlorn sick people," Emily wrote to Elizabeth, alluding to her healthy skepticism of early allopathic treatments, and the undeniable element of drudgery in the day-to-day practice of medicine. Her thinking takes quite a dark turn from there, though. "I always feel that the best thing that could be done with a hospital were to blot it and its inmates out of existence." As horrifying as that assessment sounds, it's likely Emily meant it as a mercy, given that there was so little for doctors to offer terminally ill patients. What's more shocking is when you consider that Emily was studying in some of the most medically advanced countries, under some of the most prominent physicians in their fields. Even the best hospitals were full of misery.

During her brief time at Rush Medical College, she trained under esteemed Chicago surgeon Dr. Daniel Brainard, who also happened to be the founder of the school. She assisted him on multiple clubfoot operations, a lower jaw excision, and even held a woman down while he removed part of her diseased eye. Her professor suggested Emily purchase a better set of dissecting knives, but she settled for a knife-sharpening stone. Even this purchase felt extravagant—she bought a chipped one because it was 25 cents cheaper: $1.25—but the satisfaction of her newly razor-sharp knives made her feel "quite charmed" by the stone.

"Operations, though the showiest, are by no means the most difficult part of surgery," Emily asserted. The surgical aftercare, she observed, was even more difficult than the operation itself.

Emily shone in the role of surgeon at the New York Infirmary, and once even performed a breast tumor removal. The infirmary soon outgrew its premises yet again, so Emily transformed another, larger mansion into a hospital. Before long, they were treating upward of 7,500 patients a year.

Emily adopted a daughter of her own, an Irish infant she named Nanni. Though the baby filled her home with joy, she still longed for an intimate companion. She soon fell in love with a student at her college, Elizabeth Cushier. Their eleven-year age difference was of little consequence.

"She is a remarkable, lovely woman," Mary Putnam, a professor at their college, giddily reported to Elizabeth. "Spirited, unselfish, generous, and intelligent. I do not know what Dr. Emily would do without her. She absolutely basks in her presence; and seems as if she had been waiting for her for a lifetime."

Mary was herself a pioneer of women in medicine. She'd wanted to study science since she was a little girl, describing the overwhelming urge to cut open and examine the body of a dead rat she found when she was nine. Her training took her on a whirlwind tour of women's medical schools and hospitals. At the tender age of seventeen, she came to train at the Blackwells' New York Infirmary for Women and Children. Then Ann Preston helped her complete a degree from the Women's Medical College of Pennsylvania in a single year. When the male dean resigned in protest, Ann took over to become America's first woman dean of a medical school.

Next, Mary interned under Marie and Lucy at their Boston hospital. Mary was decidedly underwhelmed by the medical training available to women in the US, so she, too, turned her sights to France. "I have sufficient terror of New York, with its very slack interest in medical science or progress, its deficient libraries, badly organized schools and hospitals," Mary told her mother.

In Paris, Mary stayed in a guesthouse that Elizabeth had arranged for her. She spent two years auditing lectures and clinics at the world-famous University of Paris École de Médecine—also known as the Sorbonne—before finally being accepted as an official student, its first woman student. They made her enter through a separate door and sit alone during lectures.

Mary was just as fiery as Sophia when it came to defending women's right to study science and medicine. "It is perfectly evident that the opposition to women physicians has rarely been based upon any sincere conviction that women could not be instructed in medicine, but upon an intense dislike to the idea that they should be so capable," Mary railed. She would come to represent the new wave of physicians who viewed science as just as essential to the practice of medicine as compassion.

Back in New York, Mary began lecturing on materia medica and therapeutics at the Blackwells' college. She said her most crucial task would be "the creation of a scientific spirit (which at present does not exist) among women medical students." Emily and Mary had a lot of work to do if they were to improve the medical education of women in America.

In America, the movement had been mismanaged by "well-meant but ill-directed zeal," a writer mused in *The Scotsman*. Hastily forming separate medical schools for women had inadvertently created an excuse for regular colleges to continue rejecting them. And in their haste, these school founders failed to create an adequate educational program. Now, through no fault of their own, there were several ill-qualified women attempting to practice. Many students became suitably skilled by seeking additional training, but were still hindered by being associated with these other women who ostensibly held the same qualification. The experiment had failed, some might conclude, when it hadn't actually been fairly tried. The writer concluded that only when women had exactly the same opportunities as men and were judged by exactly the same standards could their abilities be compared.

Emily agreed with many of these sentiments. While she always found a fair sprinkling of women of character and intelligence among the students at her college, she wagered that the bulk of the pupils who appeared at the doors of these early women's medical schools were less than promising: "women who had failed as nurses or teachers, eccentricities of all sorts."

But Emily also recognized the necessity of the separate women's schools. Exclusion from all medical institutions was the settled policy, she explained, social and professional ostracism the norm.

"Women in medicine have been like a band of emigrants in a new country, which they could only penetrate by building their roads as they went," Emily declared. She didn't mean to insult these early women's schools or their students, only to illustrate how far they'd come. "It took courage, faith, and self-devotion in the pioneer workers in each centre," Emily said. Thanks to their hard work and vitality, many of these schools grew into influential institutions. By 1870, the census recorded 525 women doctors in America, more than every other country in the world combined.

In her book about nineteenth-century women physicians, feminist academic Susan Wells explained that for the early female entrants into the field, "medicine offered them not only the possibility of a wider sphere but the possibility of a world without spheres." These women "all felt sure that by becoming physicians they had saved their lives," by giving them purpose and providing them a space in which to use their talents and intelligence.

Upon settling in London, Elizabeth moved into Barbara's house in Blandford Square. Now, for the second time, she would enter a wide and varied circle of progressive London luminaries: philosopher and biologist Herbert Spencer, suffragist and philanthropist Rose Mary Crawshay, poet and painter Dante Rossetti, author and activist Frances Power Cobbe, and novelist Mary Ann Evans, who wrote under the pen name George Eliot. Mary Ann had remarked years earlier that Elizabeth Blackwell was "one of the women I would love from all the rest in the world to know personally." Now she would have her wish.

For work, Elizabeth rented a room in a house on York Place and hung her name on the door advertising her medical services. She soon found, however, that she had walked into a trap. "My doctor's sign was intended to conceal the dubious character of the occupier of the house," she exclaimed. Her friends came to her rescue and arranged the canceling of the lease she'd signed.

And so it was at 6 Burwood Place, a few blocks north of Hyde Park, that Elizabeth recommenced private medical practice. Her dearest Barbara was soon off to Algiers. Deprived of her social center, Elizabeth was left to her own devices to navigate London society. She quickly returned to her favored work of giving regular lectures and pushing for social reform. In 1870, she received an invitation to address the Working Women's College, where she presented "How to Keep a Household in Health." In early 1871, she was a Sunday Lecture Society featured speaker regaling a large, appreciative audience in St. George's Hall with "On the Religion of Health."

That year, Elizabeth also formed the National Health Society in her drawing room. Frances proved an agreeable cofounder and honorary secretary of the organization. Feisty Princess Louise served as their patron. With the motto "Prevention is better than cure," it aimed to begin filling the large gap in the general public's knowledge of household sanitation basics.

They gave weekly lectures to mothers' groups and working men's clubs on how to avoid spreading germs, the importance of cleaning your home, and how to cook well cheaply. Of special interest was the health of young girls. One pamphlet described the dangers to girls' health originating primarily from fashion: heavy skirts fastened around the delicate organs of the waist, pressure on the heart, lungs, and organs from unyielding bodices, and insufficiently warm dress.

It was all part of her dream of seeing society advance to a near-utopian harmony. "My long-cherished conviction of the supreme importance of the medical profession as the great conservator of health constantly deepened," Elizabeth proclaimed. "I eagerly longed to see an embodiment of Christian principles in society, which embodiment was, as yet, far from attainment."

Many of her ideas seem progressive: that girls should be taught about their bodies and about sex, that women's sexual desire could be just as strong as men's, that only those of exceptional moral fiber should be elected to government office, and that more industrial work opportunities should be created. Among her more conservative, though not uncommon beliefs were that the world should be rid of prostitution, masturbation, and artificial contraception.

As she aged, Elizabeth's ideas grew more eccentric. Her full prescription for societal perfection now included educating the "perverted" urges out of men and women, encouraging women to become police officers and to create a female priesthood, and forbidding those with chronic diseases (physical or mental) from marrying. Spending a lifetime caring for sufferers of chronic illnesses with so little to offer in the way of relief likely colored this harsh stance. But however she came to these conclusions, there is no dancing around the fact that she was now advocating eugenics.

Elizabeth found a great ally in MP James Stansfeld, who, as a fellow social reformer and respected politician, helped her and Josephine Butler achieve the repeal of the Contagious Diseases Act. Though he did not go as far as to share her insistence that the transmission of syphilis be made a criminal offense.

Elizabeth's biggest goal for her time in the UK was a lofty one: "the establishment, or opening of a thorough medical education for women, in England. As soon as the Doctorate is freely attainable by English women, I shall feel as if my public work—my own special pioneer mission—were over, but not until then."

FOURTEEN

A Lady Doctor Gets Married

Five-foot Lizzie stood alone before an imposing cast of three men draped in crimson-lined black robes and seated at a long table in a vast exam room at the Sorbonne. Behind her, the tiers of seating were bursting with male students, faculty, and onlookers excited to catch a glimpse of this renegade British woman. As the murmurs of the crowd died down, she took her seat across the table from the examiners.

She was anxious, of course, but one of the attributes that made her such a great doctor and surgeon was the calm that descended over her in stressful situations. Lizzie answered each question offered up by the examiners so quickly and correctly—and entirely in French, no less—that her audience applauded every time. Afterward, the president of the examiners, Professor Paul Broca, offered her his sincerest compliments. The crowd cheered once more.

It was March 1869, and while Sophia was badgering professors at the University of Edinburgh, Lizzie was finally on her way to an official medical degree. She'd been a registered, practicing physician in London for nearly four years now with her Society of Apothecaries license, but wanted a real MD. Now, she was one exam closer to achieving her goal.

With the proper qualifications, students could apply to take MD exams without undertaking that school's courses. Lizzie didn't feel the need to attend more lectures given all of her previous studies and experience running her own practice, so she applied just for the exams. She had turned her sights to the continent, Paris to be exact. Lizzie always knew this was a possibility. Back in 1862, she'd told Elizabeth that despite no British medical school admitting her, an MD was her preferred qualification. Even if "it should be a foreign one I believe it would command more respect than the license from the [Apothecaries] Hall alone."

Lizzie's initial application to the Sorbonne was rejected. Two other foreign women had applied at the same time, and the faculty council worried that women students might become a growing trend if they continued to accept them. Mary Putnam had been taking classes at the school since 1866, and had only just been allowed to register as a student.

Most surprisingly, the fate of these new women candidates would be determined by the empress of France. The Emperor Napoleon III was ill at the time, and so on his behalf Empress Eugénie was presiding over the Council of Ministers when they were set to make this decision. She approved the women candidates before the council even began their deliberations. "I hope these young women will find imitators, now that the way is open," the empress said.

With permission in hand, Lizzie focused all her attention on preparing for the tests. "I am giving up all society in order to keep evenings free for work, as this saves both time and energy," she determined. "It is not easy to work up for examinations amid

the distractions of practical work." She stopped accepting social invitations and no longer participated in the suffrage committee, at least temporarily. For a while, her life would only be
work and study. She planned to return home after each exam
to maintain her practice.

Word spread quickly of Lizzie's studies throughout England's
high society. One of Queen Victoria's ladies-in-waiting invited
Lizzie to visit the palace to give her a report of her work. Word
then spread around the royal family.

"Her Royal Highness, Princess Louise," the parlor maid announced nervously as she threw open Lizzie's consulting room
door one afternoon. The twenty-one-year-old princess swept in
to find a flabbergasted Lizzie atop a stepladder hanging new wall-
paper in paste-covered old work clothes. Her desk was strewn
with anatomy books and the bones of a disjointed skeleton.

As the most liberal and intellectual of Victoria's children,
Princess Louise was excited to hear all about Lizzie's achieve-
ments. Lizzie was positively starstruck with her visitor. She wore
rose-tinted glasses when it came to royalty; she hung on Louise's every word. Before leaving, Louise asked Lizzie not to tell
her mother that she'd been there since she wouldn't approve.
When Queen Victoria did eventually hear about the meeting,
she was exceptionally annoyed.

Lizzie's second MD exam came three months after the first.
This one covered surgery and pathology. Again she would face
her examiners and garner an audience, but this time there would
be more than just an oral recitation of knowledge. She would
also have to perform two operations. Of the two men who
took the exam that day, one achieved the same score category
as Lizzie, "rather good"; the other scored three levels below,
"passable." December brought the third and fourth exams: first
chemistry, zoology, botany, and natural philosophy (physics),
and then medical jurisprudence, materia medica, and hygiene.
She again earned "rather good" across the board.

January saw the test in clinical medicine, midwifery, and surgery. At one question, she began to stumble. It was in reference to eminent Irish physician Robert Graves, who first described the autoimmune disorder Graves' Disease in 1835. He also introduced timing a patient's pulse using a watch and giving feverish patients food and drink instead of withholding it. The answer to the question was on the tip of Lizzie's tongue, but she couldn't seem to coax all of it out.

"Do you not know your great men?" the examiner prodded.

"But sir, we have so many!" Lizzie replied, to the great amusement of both the audience and the examiners. She passed that exam as well.

A couple of weeks later she submitted her thesis on migraines. The subject was not necessarily a pet subject or area of specialty for her, but chosen for more practical reasons: "I had to find a subject which could be well studied without post-mortem observations, of which I can have but very few in either private or dispensary practice," Lizzie explained. "I wished also to take a large subject, one that demanded some insight into the harmony that exists between the main physiological functions."

The thesis was thirty pages long, written entirely in French. In it, she made the observation that in her patients, migraines often recurred during menstruation. She had also noticed that it was often her most intelligent patients who suffered the malady. To reduce the severity and frequency of migraines, Lizzie suggested abstaining from alcohol, eating simple and regular meals, exercise, proper bedroom ventilation, and as much fresh air as possible.

During a migraine attack, she advocated plenty of rest and hot tea. Her prescription to supplement analgesic drugs, used to treat pain, with antiemetic drugs, used to treat nausea, was an innovative drug combination that remains a prevailing treatment for migraines today. For those who suffered repeated attacks, Lizzie recommended electromagnetic treatment with a faradization machine. It was a treatment she'd used on plenty of her own patients.

She was on the cutting edge of medical discovery using this treatment. The earliest recorded uses of electrical therapy in London's hospitals happened to occur at the two establishments where both Lizzie and Elizabeth later studied. Middlesex Hospital, where Lizzie trained, had an electrotherapy machine as early as 1767, and St. Bartholomew's Hospital, where Elizabeth visited, soon followed suit.

Once she turned in her thesis, all she had to do now was wait for the summons to come before the examiners one final time.

In the meantime, Dr. Nathaniel Heckford and his wife, Sarah, needed a visiting medical officer for their new children's hospital in London's East End. And they wanted Lizzie for the job. She had studied midwifery under Dr. Heckford at Middlesex Hospital. But not everyone on the hospital board was enthusiastic for a lady doctor. The vice chair and financial adviser, James Skelton Anderson, worried the post would be far too arduous for a lady.

Lizzie appeared before the board to be questioned. Her knowledgeable responses and cool self-confidence put all of their fears to rest, and they all deemed her perfectly capable. James was so impressed that he raced out behind her to strike up a conversation.

"I caught her as she was going downstairs," James said. He told her about his sister Mary, who wished to study medicine. A dashing man, James was lanky and bearded with a thin pointy nose and smoldering eyes. James was Scottish, with a pale complexion and endearing brogue and was two years younger than Lizzie. As they talked, they realized Lizzie had already met his brother Ford at Middlesex Hospital.

Before long, the pair were working together to improve the conditions of the children's hospital. It quickly became painfully obvious that Heckford and his wife knew nothing of running a business. They splashed out on a lavish Christmas party for their hospital's young patients, complete with a rented barrel organ and Punch and Judy show, despite having only a few pounds left in their coffers. As someone who accounted for every last farthing at her own medical practice and dispensary, Lizzie was aghast at their reckless spending.

While the impoverished neighborhood found in Heckford's hospital "an ark in the midst of a dreary sea of suffering, hunger and cold," Lizzie could only see all the renovations the hospital would require. She uncovered a ladderlike staircase, ill-placed trapdoors (where goods were hoisted in), and a mongrel dog wandering freely through the filthy wards. For a start, Lizzie resolved to invoke order in the chaos of the outpatient clinic and rid the hospital of fleas and other dangerous pests and vermin, and organize the storage of drugs and the oversight of their preparation. In response to her efforts, one doctor protested that fleas were nothing to him.

It was stressful to try to help people that didn't seem to want it. "I cannot afford to waste time and strength in merely being kind to the miserable people at the Hospital," Lizzie sighed to Jamie, as she'd begun to call James. She worried that the role would divert energy from her work of building her private practice and dispensary. "It is my business to become a great physician, nothing else I could do would help women so much as this, therefore, if the hospital helps it is welcome, if it hinders away with it!"

Jamie worked at his uncle's shipping business and was an officer in the London Scottish regiment. He was already thirty-two when he met Lizzie; feared a confirmed bachelor. And yet, the pair were fast becoming more than just work friends. Letters regularly passed between Lizzie and Jamie, and soon she found herself inviting him over to dinner—always with at least her housemate present, more often making a full dinner party of it.

Even the difficult-to-impress Emily Davies declared "of all your friends I like Mr. Anderson the best!" His keen storytelling abilities, quick wit, and easygoing nature made for absorbing company, though Lizzie once chided him for his lack of observing the proper conversational etiquette of speaking to guests on both sides of him at the dinner table. Apparently, he was talking too much with one neighbor and not enough with her.

After five agonizing months of waiting to hear from the Sorbonne examiners, Lizzie finally got the summons to come before the faculty. On June 15, 1870, she appeared in a long black wool gown with starched bands (her head unadorned!). In her arms she cradled a rolled copy of her thesis. She read her thesis aloud to them and then answered a series of questions that ran the full gamut of medical and science topics: everything from how to treat pneumonia and extrauterine pregnancies to how to prepare arsenic compounds and use cod liver oil, how tears are secreted, the nature of toxic and electric fish, and how to take crime-scene footprints.

When it was finally over, Lizzie and the large crowd she had drawn were asked to leave in order to allow the faculty to deliberate. After what felt like an eternity, the double doors swung open again and a loud voice boomed, declaring her thesis "read and supported." Eleven long years since she first declared her intention to become a doctor, Lizzie could now finally officially adopt the moniker "doctor." She was the first woman to earn an MD at the Sorbonne.

The Lancet's Paris correspondent was practically giddy upon reporting the news: "All the judges, on complimenting Miss Garrett, more or less expressed liberal opinions on the subject of lady doctors. Altogether there was really an air of fête about the Faculty. On Miss Garrett's crossing the courtyard to leave the school, I observed with pleasure that almost all the students gallantly bowed to their lady confrère."

In another article, the medical journal finally conceded Lizzie's professional prowess: "Miss Garrett's abilities are so exceptionally great when tested by the standard of either sex that we will in her case put aside all controversy about women doctors and say that she is an ornament to the calling that she has embraced."

Even *The BMJ* agreed "everyone must admire the indomitable perseverance and pluck which Miss Garrett has shown." Still, neither journal applied the honorific *Dr.* to her.

Jamie was the first person to congratulate her. Many congratulatory letters came her way. One from Sophia and the rest of the Edinburgh Seven toasted her: "while congratulating you on receiving the highest honour of your profession from one of the finest medical schools in the world, we desire to express also our appreciation of the example you have afforded to others, and the honour you have reflected on all women who have chosen medicine as their profession."

All these accolades never once went to Lizzie's head. "Spite of all this *absurd bunkum*, E.G. does not, when free to be candid, think much of herself," she wrote jokingly of herself after growing flustered by the flood of praise. Jamie was helping Lizzie keep her ego in check, warning her of "too much butter," as he called praise.

"I have been pondering over your terrible hint as to the effects of butter," she replied. "I decided that so long as it was not swallowed and absorbed it could not do much harm."

Dr. Garrett was in high demand, and not just in her consulting rooms. One day in mid-October, a group of men appeared outside her house, most of them husbands and fathers of her patients, to entreat her to run for a seat on the city's newly created school board. She relished the thought of promoting her ideas on education. She believed that to promote health, children required space to play, time in the fresh air and sun, and proper bathrooms. She also wanted to advance the idea that women weren't harmed by steady work.

This was not a popular opinion at the time. Harvard physician Edward Clarke and Henry Maudsley, psychiatrist to the British aristocracy and coeditor of the *Journal of Mental Science*, believed women should forgo career and even education, believing it to be harmful to women's delicate physical states. They spread their supposedly science-based theories opposing the education of women on both sides of the Atlantic. Girls' health would be seriously injured if they were allowed to pursue education along the same lines as boys; advanced study would utterly exhaust them, damage their reproductive capacity, and even cause nervous and mental disorders.

Menstruation was believed to be a particularly perilous time to engage in arduous mental or physical activity. But what these men were actually observing was correlation, not causation: girls typically got their first periods around the same time that school began to get much harder.

Lizzie was now living proof of the opposite. In her response, she argued that experience entirely contradicted the assertion that girls become temporarily incapacitated during this period, and points out that puberty could be accompanied by weakness and behavioral regression in both girls and boys. She also highlighted the fact that most women are unbothered by their periods. "Healthy women disregard them almost completely," she wrote. Not to mention that working-class women had no choice but to keep toiling away during their time of the month. The disparity between how different classes of women were regarded—one very capable of work outside the home, the other incapable of even light activity—exposes this view to be nothing more than prejudice.

Maudsley and Clarke had it backward, Lizzie concluded, especially given the fact that they offered little-to-nothing in the way of evidence to back up their assertions. She theorized that women's nervous disorders and depression were actually the result of a *lack* of intellectual stimulation; a lack of purpose or occupation. "Thousands of young women, strong and blooming at eighteen, become gradually languid and feeble under the depressing influence of dullness," she explained.

When Lizzie ran for the school board, with Jamie organizing her campaign, she received more than double the votes of any of the other six candidates. Seen at a party a week after her election, Lizzie was described as "youthful and charming—one of the belles of the room: 'tis amusing, to see this learned and distinguished M.D. moving about in rose-colored silk and pointlace, with flowers in her hair, and receiving due homage, in both capacities, from the men." By this time, Lizzie only had eyes for one man.

In December, she told Jamie that after Christmas she planned to "live like a hermit"—only allowing herself trips to the library—in order to finish the medical textbook she had been contracted to write for Macmillan's by the May deadline. But Jamie couldn't stand to spend any more time as merely friends. When he came over for dinner on Friday, the day before Christmas Eve, he proposed marriage to her. This time, she readily accepted.

"I love you more than I thought I was made to love anyone," she confessed to him. "Life is intolerable apart."

At her age and after rejecting so many men, she may have expected marriage wasn't in the cards for her. "My horizon was suddenly changed," Lizzie observed. Emily was elated, but the same could not be said about the rest of Lizzie's friends and family. Some worried that after Lizzie married, she would leave the career she'd worked so hard for and abandon her work in the women's movement. Anyone who really knew her should've known better.

"I do hope you will not think I have meanly deserted my post," she told Milly in a bid to reassure her suffragist sister. "I think it need not prove to be so. I am sure that the woman question will never be solved in any complete way so long as marriage is thought to be incompatible with freedom and with an independent career, and I think there is a very good chance that we may be able to do something to discourage this notion."

As an unintentional public figure, Lizzie knew her marriage would be put under a microscope, debated, and discussed. People would be waiting with bated breath to see whether she could maintain her marriage and her career, looking for any little tremor to show it was impossible, to demand she was a failure at one or the other—or both. She was certain women could handle both a career and a family, and she planned on becoming living proof, explaining, "A doctor leads two lives, the professional and the private, and the boundaries between the two are never traversed."

The BMJ agreed Lizzie's marriage would be a very public test of women's capabilities: "The problem of the compatibility of marriage with female medical practice, which has been much discussed, will thus be partly tested." *The Lancet* proposed, "If she succeeds in combining the two functions of mistress of a household and medical practitioner, she will have performed a feat unprecedented in professional history."

Perhaps they forgot that working-class women had been toiling away for eons trying to care for their children while also contributing to the family finances.

One day in the underground railway, Lizzie heard two men discussing her pending nuptials. Lizzie later told Jamie that as they loudly speculated about what the lucky fellow might look like, she had half a mind to whip out his photograph and show them. Next, she heard that a doctor claiming to be a friend of Jamie's was spreading rumors about them, telling people Jamie said he "would not *allow*" Lizzie to maintain her practice after their marriage.

"Of course I don't believe it, but it is injurious that he should tell lies about us," Lizzie told Jamie. "Please stop him."

During their engagement, Lizzie wrote to her beloved Jamie nearly every day. He stopped by to see her most evenings on his way home from work. Overwhelmed by passion, Lizzie came to find these visits more than she could bear.

"I have been sitting half-tranced for nearly an hour since you left me, dearest. I am almost sure it will be better for us—for me at any rate, not to meet so very often. It is too distracting," the smitten Lizzie entreated him. "And being very much distracted and absorbed brings back a rush of doubt as to the rightness of taking such absorbing happiness."

Unexpectedly, of all Lizzie's relations, Newson was the most upset by his daughter's engagement. He'd become so proud of his ambitious, independent girl that the thought of her leaving behind the role she'd sacrificed so much to achieve made him despondent, especially after watching all she'd gone through. Jamie's family was rather uneasy about their son marrying a celebrity of sorts, but they liked her well enough. Lizzie's mother was entirely taken with her soon-to-be son-in-law, a clergyman's son! Though she was disappointed they'd opted for a nontraditional wedding ceremony.

"Fancy my being 'given away,'" Lizzie scoffed at her mother's pleadings. "Monstrous and ludicrous notion!"

They were to be married at Easter, but Lizzie wished to be rid of her paralyzing fears of her marriage interfering with her work: the best way of "exorcising the fiend," the foul "revenge inflicted by ambition," she reasoned, was to be married at once. The wedding was moved up to February. As a wedding present, Jamie gave Lizzie a carriage so she would not have to rush around London to her various appointments on foot in the muddy, mucky streets.

On her wedding day, Lizzie walked down the aisle—unaccompanied—in a gray velvet gown and matching bonnet with a pink rose pinned under the brim. From the front row, Newson bawled through nearly the entire ceremony.

The unconventional nature of the Andersons' marriage proved to be groundbreaking among well-to-do couples. Each swirled in their own separate professional circles during the workday, then came together at home to share conversation, music, and a love of books. They also enjoyed trips to the country and to the theater together. This arrangement seems perfectly normal nowadays, but was revolutionary among the upper classes in the Victorian era.

Just as had happened to Elizabeth in New York, Lizzie's London dispensary began feeling the need to expand to have inpatient facilities a few years after opening.

Many patients were too sick to come into the clinic, but their homes were too cramped and dirty for the doctors to do much for them, especially if surgery was required. Others traveled long distances from the country and could use a place to stay the night, even if their illness didn't necessarily require a hospital stay. Since opening, her patient population had shifted to include not just locals, but women from all over the city who wished to be seen by a woman doctor, especially for their gynecological complaints.

She saw an opportunity in expanding her clinic into a full-blown hospital. She envisioned well-qualified women working alongside her, gaining the trust of neighborhood patients and beyond. It would serve one of the neediest neighborhoods in London, while also creating vacancies for women in the medical profession. Only women would be hired at the hospital.

A committee was formed to find funds necessary to make this expansion possible. Its main members included Plaskitt and Emily's brother, the Reverend J. Llewelyn Davies. As rector of Christ Church in Marylebone, Davies was more than happy to offer his support for anything that would help to improve the lives of women in his impoverished neighborhood.

The Lancet declared it could "imagine nothing more injurious to poor women than to create hospitals for them from which male intellect and skill are to be excluded." (While no men would be among the regular staff, plenty of distinguished male physicians would be acting as consultants at the hospital.)

An inpatient ward with ten beds was arranged on the floor

above the dispensary. The £300 Lizzie spent on a fresh coat of paint and the installation of ventilation, running water, and drainage could only do so much to improve the gloomy, cramped space. But just like that, the dispensary transformed into the New Hospital for Women, opening in February 1872.

Patients were charged sixpence per visit, a slightly higher fee than her dispensary previously charged, but this didn't appear to be a deterrent. The neighborhood ladies still clamored for the services of a woman doctor. As a fully private institution, the hospital would need to raise £600 a year to remain in operation. People donated money as well as all kinds of goods: large blankets, towels, calico, flannel robes, wool jackets, night-gowns, flexible tubing, mattresses, a large bath, games, bedside books, eggs, preserves, flour, jelly, cake, wild game, flowers, bottles, sixteen pheasants, a barrel of grapes, a box of currants, and Christmas presents and letters for patients.

Thankfully, Lizzie had help with the expansion. Frances Morgan was back, and with an MD no less. She had returned to the dispensary in March 1871, as Lizzie's first staff assistant. Much like Elizabeth Blackwell had Marie Zakrzewska at her side, Frances became indispensable to Lizzie. Frances, along with Eliza and Louisa, hadn't been able to obtain a license to practice via the Apothecaries' Hall as Lizzie had done because of its change in rules. Instead, the women enrolled in one of the only medical schools in Europe to accept women: the University of Zürich.

Frances had completed a five-year medical degree in only three years. Afterward, she spent a year training in Paris and Düsseldorf. But having a foreign degree meant she couldn't be placed on the British medical register. If it were discovered that she was practicing medicine, there would be trouble. Those convicted of practicing medicine without their name on the register faced a fine of £20.[16]

Frances was born in Wales and well educated. As a teen she'd

---

16   About £2,500/$3,200 in today's money.

gotten pregnant, but instead of forcing her to give up the child or disowning her, her family offered the gracious act of passing the child off as Frances's little sister. She had small, close-set eyes, and long dark hair which she braided and draped in loose loops, a low halo around the back of her head. Her jaw was square, her forehead pronounced.

Frances and Lizzie each worked three shifts of two hours at the outpatient dispensary: Lizzie on Mondays and Thursdays from 1:00–3:00 p.m. and Wednesdays from 9:00–10:00 a.m.; Frances on Tuesday and Friday afternoons and Saturday mornings. They handled emergency calls on a rotation.

The medical establishment held on to the illusion that women practitioners would only be consulted for trifling ailments. Lizzie and Frances experienced quite the opposite. *The Times* reported that a visit to Lizzie's New Hospital for Women "would show that, as a matter of fact, they are trusted in cases of grave disease."

Women came in with all manner of ills. A large proportion of ailments recorded in the hospital's first few years were gynecologic. Among the most common diagnoses were uterine inflammation, fibroids, prolapse, cancer, "rheumatism of the uterus during pregnancy," vaginitis, vaginismus (pelvic floor muscle spasms), vulvar abscess, ovarian tumors, and severe period cramps. Plenty of nongynecological issues were treated as well: lung and cardiac diseases, tuberculosis, pneumonia, pleurisy, wasting palsy, gastritis, hepatitis, rheumatism, paralysis, "hysterical paraplegia," eczema, impetigo, rectal and breast cancer, anemia, "obstinate constipation," hernia, sciatica, "impending melancholia."

In the hospital's first year, 103 inpatients were served. That number grew exponentially, and by its fourth year, the hospital was treating an average of two hundred inpatients a year. On average, the women's hospital reported three or four deaths per year. These were mostly attributed to advanced cancer, cellulitis, bronchitis, and complications or infections resulting from surgery. This was well below the average mortality rate of London's other hospitals at the time, which hovered around 10 percent.

One death occurred after the removal of a cancerous tumor of the breast. The incision site became gangrenous, so more surgeries were performed to remove the diseased tissue in hopes of containing the damage. Soon, the patient developed erysipelas, a skin infection caused by group A streptococcus bacteria. This stirred grave concern among the hospital staff, as the infection quickly began spreading to other patients. These other patients eventually recovered, but it was thought necessary to empty the hospital for two months and to have it repainted and white-washed to stop further spread of the infection.

Lizzie's hospital wholeheartedly embraced Lister's newfangled antisepsis procedures. Four years prior, Joseph Lister had published a series of articles in *The Lancet* that proved a major stepping stone in cleaning up the business of surgery. His antiseptic system, based on Louis Pasteur's revolutionary assertion that airborne germs caused putrefaction, was a complicated, convoluted, and ever-evolving method of keeping wounds and incisions clean, but it did reduce mortality rates. Medical instruments were boiled, wound dressings soaked in sterilizing carbolic acid. Some surgeons used a mobile carbolic-acid spraying machine to spritz the patient during long operations.

Lizzie told her staff, "To be thoroughly aseptic as a surgeon requires the drilling of years." As the nature of germs continued to be uncovered over the century, Lister's methods made way for the thoroughly aseptic surgical conditions we know today.

In the hospital's early years, Lizzie frequently described interesting cases in the medical literature. One such inpatient was an eighteen-year-old admitted after experiencing a seizure, during which only her limbs convulsed. She was treated for rheumatic fever four years ago. A year later, she began suffering from unilateral chorea. A neurological condition, chorea manifests as jerky, involuntary movements; it's an autoimmune response that can be triggered by group A strep infection (which commonly co-occurs with rheumatic fever). The woman's arm was particularly affected by wild, unintentional flailing.

After this recent episode, her left arm and leg were left numb and her chorea more severe. Upon admittance to the women's hospital, she appeared well-nourished and was determined not to be anemic. Her digestion and uterine health were found to be normal and no heart murmur was detected. Lizzie suspected her convulsions must be the result of an embolism of one or more of the smaller cerebral vessels.

She was prescribed arsenic and potassium bromide, then discharged to continue treatment as an outpatient. Potassium bromide was discovered as a treatment for epilepsy in 1857, but it didn't work the way they thought. Epilepsy was believed to be caused by too much masturbation, and chorea blamed on hysteria. Potassium bromide was thought to quiet seizures because it dampened sexual urges. Ten grains daily became widely used as a sedative and anticonvulsant agent. It continues to be an approved antiepileptic drug in some countries.

As the century progressed, medications that actually worked—without poisoning the patients—were finally being developed. Chemists brought botanicals that had been used as herbal remedies for hundreds of years into their labs to coax out their secrets. Before long, they could extract quinine from cinchona bark to treat malaria, digitalis from foxglove to treat heart conditions, salicylic acid from willow bark (a precursor to aspirin), cocaine from coca leaves, and isolate morphine, codeine, and heroin from poppies.

Still, "not as deadly" didn't always mean safe, just as natural doesn't equal benign. Laudanum had been the go-to, cure-all drug since the seventeenth century, a reddish-brown, frightfully bitter tincture of 10 percent powdered opium suspended in alcohol. The drug was prized for its ability to ease pain without incapacitating patients. Writers and artists praised its ability to promote creativity. It was available for purchase not only at pharmacies, but at pubs, grocery stores, and barbershops. Misuse of the drug and addiction, of course, became major public health issues. By 1865, an estimated two million people were misusing opiates.

In one particularly dramatic case at the New Hospital for Women, a fifty-year-old woman presented with symptoms of ovarian dropsy, otherwise known as a fluid-filled tumor. Such symptoms include abdominal swelling and discomfort, and back pain. Frances examined her. The ovarian tumor was quite large, but her pulse was regular and her heart sounds normal. The patient looked relatively healthy, that is, she wasn't experiencing the muscle wasting and weight loss seen in most cases of advanced ovarian cancer. Frances decided the tumor should be tapped to remove some of the fluid.

"You're so cheerful and serene," Lizzie remarked to the patient as they prepped for the surgery. She must have been hopeful about the treatment, perhaps happy to be under the care of such learned, caring women. Then, without anesthesia, Frances swiftly punctured the woman's abdomen with a trocar. The tool consists of a metal cylinder within a cylinder, six inches long and half an inch in diameter.

Next, Frances slowly removed the sharpened inner tube, leaving only the outer tube in the patient's flesh. Rubber tubing was attached to the metal cylinder, allowing fluid to flow out freely into a bucket below. Frances was sure to pause the draining occasionally so as not to cause the patient to faint. The volume drained is not recorded, but ovarian cysts can hold anywhere between one and fifteen liters of fluid. After the cyst was emptied, the tube was taken out and the wound sutured. As a bandage was being applied, the patient suddenly began shifting around restlessly, then sprang upright.

"I can't breathe," she cried. Her lips and fingertips immediately turned bluish-gray as she slumped back down. For the next hour and a half, the doctors worked feverishly to revive her. The woman gasped and struggled for breath, conscious but speechless. Her heart sounds were fast and strong, but her pulse feeble. Sitting up and pitching far forward was the most comfortable position she could find, but that meant it was difficult for the doctors to keep checking her heart.

"In fact, death seemed so very imminent that our attention was engrossed with the effort to stave it off, to the exclusion even of such observations as we might possibly have made had we had leisure to think of making them," Lizzie recalled.

They surmised there must be a clot either in the right side of her heart or in her pulmonary artery. The only way to save her was to stimulate her heart to contract, flushing the clot out of the main lines of circulation. Since the patient was unable to swallow a stimulant, they instead applied a very hot flannel compress on her back, massaged mustard on her chest and legs, and vigorously rubbed her feet and hands. They waved ammonia under her nose and dipped her hands in hot water. Lizzie and Frances did all they could with little hope it would actually make any difference. "To all appearance, the woman was at the very point of death," Lizzie pointed out dramatically.

Slowly, the color began to return to the woman's extremities, and she was stable enough to swallow a few drops of stimulant. Within three hours, she was well enough to get some sleep and by the next day, she could lie down without discomfort. She would still need her ovary removed soon.

Lizzie published fascinating cases such as this and opinion papers in medical journals with great frequency, covering an impressive breadth of topics:

- "A Case of Contraction of the Lower Extremities, with Muscular Wasting and Commencing Atrophy of the Optic Nerves"
- "Clot in the Heart and Cerebral Embolism"

- "Sex in Education"
- "Medical Education of Women"

This is one of the many ways women physicians contributed to improving medicine. They helped normalize case reports documented in medical journals. These columns had previously been used as a way for doctors to show off by sharing only the most extreme, grotesque, and freakish cases. Women doctors showed that it was more impactful to share case notes from more run-of-the-mill patients and maladies. Such insight would be far more useful for fellow practitioners, especially when the patients were women and when the doctor successfully employed a unique treatment.

Lizzie's hospital and her family were growing. In 1873, the pregnant Lizzie performed a wide array of surgeries: removing fibroids and ovarian tumors, fixing prolapsed uteruses, mammary abscesses, imperforate hymens, and vaginal fistulas. More and more, she was proving how adept she was as a surgeon. It was another slap in the face to the naysayers, who claimed pregnancy would interfere with women's medical capabilities.

But Lizzie's skills were truly tested when an ovariotomy was needed by a patient.

An ovariotomy was first performed in 1816, but its extremely high mortality rate made it a controversial surgery that most surgeons didn't dare attempt. It was so dangerous, in fact, that Lizzie's hospital's management committee actually forbade her from performing her first ovariotomy on its premises.

So determined was she to do it, she rented a room in a private home and had it cleaned, whitewashed, and disinfected. Jamie footed the bill to make it possible. Lizzie successfully performed the surgery with a nurse by her side and under the watchful eye of Dr. Thomas Smith of St. Bartholomew's Hospital. Having proved herself, her Women's Hospital permitted the second ovariotomy to take place within its walls. In each case, the patient recovered perfectly. Lizzie was the first female surgeon to ever successfully perform this particular surgery. But another, more important milestone was about to be had.

On July 28, 1873, at the age of thirty-seven, Lizzie gave birth to her first child. A darling daughter, whom they named Louisa. Lizzie was overjoyed that the child was a girl. The top floor of their home was converted into nursery rooms and a nanny and wet nurse hired, as was the custom for most middle- and upper-class families. Now, Lizzie was a wife, surgeon, and mother. She loved her daughter deeply and managed to find plenty of time with her despite this extra help and her many professional undertakings.

The same year, she was elected to the British Medical Association (BMA). She resigned from her post at the children's hospital to give her the much-needed time to join this association. And even though Lizzie was somewhat of a celebrity, it would be two years before all of the members realized there was a woman in their midst.

In June of the following year, her New Hospital for Women expanded again, taking out a fourteen-year lease on 222 and 224 Marylebone Road. She spent £780 on repairs, new furniture, and installing baths. Their previous premises were too small to house all of the patients who needed a bed, and the hospital staff felt uncomfortably crowded.

When a journalist visited the hospital to write a feature about it for *The Queen*[17] magazine, they were immediately impressed by its orderliness and pervasive feminine vibe. They watched intently as the house surgeon prepped for an operation. "As we looked at the patient and her surroundings, the thought could not but come before us, if we had something similar to undergo, how the suffering would be lightened by the fact that only women were present."

Lizzie seemed to be living proof of a woman's ability to "have

---

17   This was a precursor to Harper's Bazaar.

it all." Her family never felt neglected, and neither did her work. But mothering did not come naturally to Lizzie.

Noise bothered her, and she had a difficult time communicating with children and engaging in their play. But, according to Louisa, "love overcame these difficulties. She tolerated a baby banging two spoons together as she wrote and was a devoted wife and wise mother."

Despite having a nanny, little Louisa wasn't shut inside all day. She often accompanied Lizzie on visits in the carriage and regularly romped around the wards of the New Hospital for Women, her dense bangs and a long blue sash bouncing from patient to patient. A blurring of the stark lines Lizzie hoped to construct between her public and private lives, sure, but it was also a great opportunity to show her daughter a world where women worked as doctors. (Louisa grew up to become a surgeon herself.)

Through it all, Lizzie was always mindful that every appearance she made in public made a statement about women doctors as a whole. Her reputation would shape the belief about women's capabilities and the opportunities other women would receive. Lizzie understood this all too well.

"Now put on your smartest evening gown, my dear," she once told a hospital colleague. "I want you to come with me to a reception, and show them that a woman house surgeon can look pretty and be charming."

FIFTEEN

The Campaign in Edinburgh Ends

The Surgeons' Hall riot that Sophia and the other Edinburgh Seven endured proved a turning point in swaying public opinion about women doctors. To be the first of anything is to have your every move ruthlessly scrutinized, a fact all of these women were painfully aware of. Had any of the Edinburgh Seven fought back during the riots, they would have faced even further ridicule as lacking femininity, or worse, lacking the composure required to be a doctor. Even as the mud and insults rained down, they knew they had to stand there and take it to prove their scientific chops, to prove it would take much more than that to rattle them.

They also knew they couldn't appear disgusted or shocked by any medical procedure in front of men. Back when she was a student at Geneva Medical College, Elizabeth had prescribed herself an incredibly restricted diet, "so rigid as almost to trench upon starvation," her older sister Anna claimed. She did this to make sure she didn't accidentally flush or visibly change color to suggest she was embarrassed by the teachings.

These women were playing the long game: they knew if they were ever to achieve their goal of being seen as equal to men—and therefore deserving of the same opportunities—they had to behave perfectly, even under a downpour of profanity, trash, and the odd loose sheep.

While public opinion was turning in favor of the women students, male students still complained, claiming that studying wouldn't be possible with women present, since scientific education delved into "spicy" and indelicate areas.

Professors likewise echoed this concern, one telling his class, "There, gentlemen, I have minutely described to you those interesting incidents which it would have been impossible for me to notice if women were present; and I hope that we may be long spared the annoyance which their presence here would inflict upon us." This was followed by a thunder of applause from his students, which all too well shows the prejudice the women were facing inside the classroom.

But the majority of papers condemned their undignified and unbecoming behavior at the riots. One *Scotsman* article claimed the incident would see medical students become synonymous with all that was cowardly and degrading. Another mocked the men's temper tantrum: "A new obstacle has been thrown in the way of women acquiring a knowledge of the medical profession. The special obstacle at present is injury to the delicacy of mind of the male students. This delicacy, if real, must be a serious drawback to the proper exercise of their profession."

Sophia began receiving a flood of letters from people expressing solidarity and sorrow at how badly she and her fellow women students had been treated. She also heard from a few ladies who worked in the medical field who were especially shocked since their experiences had been so different.

A woman who trained as a surgical nurse at London's Middlesex Hospital wrote to Sophia, sharing her surprise. "Part of my time was spent in study in the female and part in the male wards; and I never found either students or patients see anything at all exceptional in my presence in the latter. I never saw any difficulty in this arrangement, nor had any reason to suppose that the students did."

Elizabeth was also surprised that Sophia's journey hadn't been as smooth as her own clinical training in London. She worked at St. Bartholomew's Hospital from 1850–51 and said she was received by the medical faculty with a friendly courtesy she would always be grateful for. When it came to men and women studying together, Elizabeth observed that "a small select number of women may join an ordinary school with little difficulty, and there is even less trouble in arranging hospital visiting than class-room instruction." But perhaps seven women at once was more than the medical establishment could stomach.

Hearing of such genial experiences likely did little but rub salt in Sophia's wounds. She was happy to hear that mixed-sex study was an achievable goal, of course, but why should her group endure such harassment? The surgical nurse was likely overlooked because she was training for the acceptable female role of nurse, of doctor's *assistant*, rather than aiming to be the doctor or surgeon. In Elizabeth's case, she likely posed less of a threat as a lone woman who already had a medical degree.

How quickly and easily she'd gathered a decent-size group of women interested in medical education must have been alarming to the medical school. It represented an impending sea change in the status quo. The more women doctors that existed and flourished, such as Elizabeth and Lizzie, the more women could see their own future as medical professionals.

The abuse the Edinburgh Seven endured from their fellow students only escalated. The male students now took every opportunity to sling mud and trash at the women whenever they saw them in the street. They surely felt emboldened by the support of many of the faculty members, most notably that of esteemed professors Christison and Lister.

One male medical student wrote to Edith, "I venture to hint my belief that the real cause of the riots is the way some of the professors run you down in their lectures. They never lose a chance of stirring up hatred against you. For all I know they may have more knowledge of the riotous conspiracy than most people fancy."

If Sophia was currently but a burr in Christison's saddle, she was about to become a full-blown nemesis. On January 2, 1871, a public meeting of the infirmary's contributors was held to elect its board of managers. Sophia knew the new managers would be the ones to decide whether or not women would be allowed to enter the infirmary, so she went to the meeting to push for her preferred candidates: those who were amenable to women doctors. The meeting was typically held in the Edinburgh Council Chambers, but the Surgeons' Hall riot had sparked an unusual amount of public interest in those in charge of medicine and medical training in the city. They needed a bigger space, so the meeting shifted to the spacious St. Giles Cathedral.

During the course of the meeting, Sophia ended up calling out Christison's teaching assistant, Mr. Craig, as the drunken, foulmouthed ringleader of the Surgeons' Hall riot.

It was a raucous meeting. Sophia started from the beginning, briefly detailing the women's trouble in gaining admittance into the university, then described how, up until they sought entrance to the infirmary, the male students had been accepting of their presence. It was their desire to gain clinical experience on the wards of the infirmary that infuriated the students, she explained. Those who had been quiet and courteous became impertinent and offensive, culminating in the riot.

"It is true that other students, who were too manly to dance as puppets on such ignoble strings, came indignantly to our rescue, but it is evident that some new influence had been at work. I will not say that the rioters were acting under orders, but this disgraceful scene would never have happened had it not been clearly understood that our opponents needed a weapon at the Infirmary," Sophia proclaimed. "I know that Dr. Christison's class assistant was one of the leading rioters."

At this accusation, hissing broke out in the cathedral, which was answered by calls for order. Craig wasn't present at this meeting, but Christison was.

Sophia continued, speaking loudly over the murmur. "And the foul language he used could only be excused on the supposition I heard that he was intoxicated. I do not say that Dr. Christison knew of or sanctioned his presence, but I do say that I think he would not have been there had he thought the doctor would have strongly objected to his presence."

"I must appeal to you, my Lord," Christison screeched, thrown into a rage by Sophia's remarks. "I think the language used regarding my assistant is language that no one is entitled to use at such an assembly as this, where a gentleman is not present to defend himself, and to say whether it be true or not. I do not know whether it is true or not, but I know my assistant is a thorough gentleman, otherwise he never would have been my assistant; and I appeal to you again, my Lord, whether language such as this is to be allowed in the mouth of any person. I am perfectly sure there is not one gentleman in the whole assembly who would have used such language in regard to an absentee."

"If Dr. Christison *prefers*—" Sophia retorted coolly, but Christison interrupted her before she could finish.

"I wish nothing but that this foul language shall be put an end to," the red-faced doctor sputtered.

"I do not know what the foul language is," the lord provost interjected. "She merely said that in her *opinion*—"

Again, Christison interrupted, finishing the lord's sentence. "In her *opinion* the gentleman was intoxicated."

"I did not say he was intoxicated," Sophia corrected. "I said that I was *told* he was."

"Withdraw the word 'intoxicated,'" the provost instructed.

"I said it was the only excuse for his conduct," Sophia reiterated. "If Dr. Christison prefers that I should say he used the language when sober, I will withdraw the other supposition." At this quip, the church filled with roars of laughter.

Susan B. Anthony and Elizabeth Cady Stanton's weekly feminist periodical *The Revolution* covered this gathering all the way from America and concluded that "if anything can batter down the old fogyism of Edinburgh University, it will be the artillery of wit and ridicule Mrs. Jex Blake has at command."

Craig subsequently sued Sophia for defamation. Such civil suits were relatively common practice since the thirteenth century, though not likely filed against many women, and it created quite the stir. The courtroom was packed with onlookers hoping to catch a glimpse of this strange beast that was a female medical student. "Plainly dressed in black, with white round her neck and wrists, she presented the appearance of a tall and well formed, handsome and determined woman, with dark hair and eyes. She was perfectly cool and collected, and her manner was a great contrast to the nervousness of Dr. Christison."

When Isabel appeared as a witness in support of Sophia, the papers reported their disappointment upon finding this other female medical student neither odd nor eccentric. "Sedate, quiet and ladylike-looking, and dressed in an unobtrusive fashion, and yet fairly within the pale of orthodoxy, Mrs. Thorne confused the minds of many." But their confusion was not just about her dress and demeanor. "Why was she married? That female medical students should dare to be good-looking, dare to be married, dare to be dressed in good taste, is, of course, an unpardonable crime."

Craig won the case. But of the £1,000 in restitution he was seeking, the judge awarded him one farthing (¼ of a penny). This was surely meant as a slap in the face since in his closing statement, Craig's lawyer declared a nominal sum would be more of an insult than a victory. The papers lauded Sophia's quick-witted talent for self-defense and even went so far as to proclaim her performance vindicated her sex's pursuit of higher education. Sophia was triumphant. She fed on the public support that surged to defend her after each setback. And in this case the public also donated more than enough money to cover her legal expenses.

Back at the university, the chivalrous students continued to appear at school every day to protect the women as they made their way to and from classes, until finally the protestors let up. Sophia then asked the volunteer guard to discontinue their kindly escort services. Things went far more smoothly at the end-of-term exams in March.

The presidents of the Royal Colleges of Physicians and Surgeons typically came to present the prizes for the school's top students, but this year, after learning women were among the recipients, they declined to appear. Bucking tradition, it seemed, was less unprincipled than bestowing academic honors on the likes of women. There would be no ceremony that year; the prizes were merely mailed to the winners. This was entirely unprecedented.

A writer in Edinburgh's *Daily Review* made the astute observation that while only 23 percent of the male students earned a place on the school's prize list, 100 percent of the female students did: "Those who wantonly throw obstacles in the way of this gallant little band [are] wanting not only in the spirit of chivalry, but of fair play."

In June, Sophia appealed to the University Senatus, pointing out that as it stood now, the women students would be unable to take all of the classes they needed to graduate. The school would have to take action in order for them to complete their studies. The university maintained that they must be taught separately in its regular classes. Students were only permitted to take four classes in the extramural school toward their degrees. All of the courses the Seven had taken up till that point had been with extramural professors, as they were the only ones willing to accommodate the separate classrooms. Sophia explained that the university would either need to employ additional professors in the regular school to teach them since the current professors largely refused to hold separate classes for them, or it would need to relax its limits on extramural classes.

After seeking a legal opinion, the Senatus announced its response at its next monthly meeting: "the University must still be regarded as an institution devoted exclusively to the education of male students....males alone have any right to demand the privilege of Studentship." Even people who had been "permitted to matriculate" did not necessarily have the right to claim the position of student, it concluded.

Now, the presidents of the Royal Colleges of Physicians and Surgeons took a more direct approach. They notified the extramural lecturers that after the summer term, women students studying for medical degrees would no longer be permitted entry into the Surgeons' Hall. The professors could still teach the women students, just not in this building. Some interpreted this additional barrier as an act of cowardice, fear of the competition medical women might pose if they earned a degree.

"The medical profession seem to think that they have only to get behind these devoted students, and shout 'boo!' loud enough to frighten them out of their five wits. They might surely have known Miss Jex-Blake better by this time," a writer in the *Glasgow Herald* noted. "Are the Edinburgh Medical Faculty really afraid of the competition of the ladies?"

The more publicity the women received, the more women outside the university rallied behind them. More than simply supporting the ladies' efforts, many were beginning to question how fit these men were to practice medicine, given their unseemly outbursts.

At a meeting to again consider whether or not the women should be allowed into the wards of the Edinburgh Infirmary, a frail, elderly local woman addressed the audience, saying she spoke on behalf of 1,300 of the city's women: "If the students studying at present in the Infirmary cannot contemplate with equanimity the presence of ladies as fellow students, how is it possible that they can possess either the scientific spirit, or the personal purity of mind, which alone would justify their presence in the female wards during the most delicate operations on, and examinations of, female patients?"

At this remark, a group of rowdy students hissed and laughed. One of them announced that Sophia had told him she stopped her studies in America because of the poor character of the female med students there. When Sophia stood up to protest, the men began yelling and throwing peas at her. Despite their behavior, she emphatically denied ever saying such a thing.

Even though the Edinburgh Infirmary continued to deny the women entry, the publicity of their fight led several physicians around town to invite them to come learn by tending poor patients at their outpatient clinics. "We availed ourselves of every other opportunity for observation that presented itself," Isabel said. The doors opened for them at the Royal Dispensary, Chalmer's Hospital, and the Poorhouse Infirmary.

More than ready to be out of the spotlight, Sophia got to enjoy a brief moment of personal bliss when Lucy Sewall sailed across the Atlantic to spend the month of September 1871 with her. The pair visited a friend who was dying of tuberculosis, attended a British Association for the Advancement of Science meeting, and then headed back north to a rustic farmhouse inn—complete with a ghost-in-residence—in Perthshire, Scotland. The outing and companionship was a welcome reprieve. Lucy and Sophia never lost their desire to form a professional partnership.

"Lucy, I do *so* wish you would stay with us here for a few years. You would be a sort of Queen among us—and would do quite infinite good to everybody concerned—ladies, poor women, students, and all," Sophia pleaded. "People are getting wild for women doctors here—and you might make almost any income, and do quite incalculable good by living here."

Going wild for women doctors was a bold assertion, given there were so many who argued against them, and did so on the grounds of lack of demand. But the truth was that many women had long wished for female doctors to consult, but it wasn't exactly something that was openly discussed. Until now. Seeing the women at Edinburgh being treated so horridly simply for attempting to study medicine was just the conversation opener that was needed. It was high time the public woke up to the reality of how women's health had suffered from the lack of women doctors. Soon, stories began pouring out of the woodwork.

"A Woman" wrote to the *Manchester Examiner and Times*: "I can count almost by dozens the cases which have come under my personal observation of health ruined, and life's pleasures and usefulness alike lost with it, because young girls (and sometimes older women, too) will not submit to receive from a man, however respected, the personal examination and treatment necessary for their restoration." Whether this woman was a nurse or was just speaking of the lives of friends and family is unclear, but she voiced a feeling shared by many others.

In *The Scotsman*, a self-described Englishwoman who had a terrible experience being treated by an eminent Edinburgh doctor spoke of the "anguish of mind suffered silently by women in such circumstances is not to be described. It is surely time for men to cease to speak of what women feel in this matter. It is impossible for them to know what women will never tell them. What women need is, that some of their own sex should have the power of qualifying themselves to act as their advisers."

Women had been experiencing less-than-stellar healthcare from men (or purposefully avoiding it) for some time. What made these public declarations exhilarating was that women were finally talking about it.

Another letter in the *Daily Review* described an impromptu

interaction during a shopping excursion: "I happened to be speaking to a young shopwoman—a total stranger to me—and in the course of conversation advised her to seek medical advice, when she replied, with a sudden gush of tears in her eyes, that she had been in the [Edinburgh] Infirmary for a fortnight, and had during that time suffered so much from the constant presence of crowds of male students during certain inevitable but most unpleasant examinations, that, as she herself forcibly expressed it, 'it almost drove me mad.'"

Of course, women should be free to practice medicine in any department or specialty, on patients of any gender. That so many of the first women doctors chose to open hospitals for women and children was not necessarily a reflection of the belief that they should treat only these groups, but more likely a reaction to the uniquely poor or rough medical treatment women received at the time.

If Sophia foresaw women going wild for women doctors in Edinburgh, Lucy had already experienced that rush in New England. Since its opening in 1862, her Boston women's hospital had undergone an expansion in an effort to keep up with demand, and was preparing to undergo another. What began as a ten-bed endeavor was about to transform into a fifty-five-bed purpose-built institution on a nine-acre property in the suburbs, its annual number of inpatients doubling from 118 to 244; the number of patients seen at its dispensary doubling to nearly three thousand. At least half of its patients traveled from beyond the Boston area just to consult lady doctors.

Alas, Lucy needed to return home. On her long sea voyage back to America, she wrote to Sophia: "I have been thinking last night that if you and I could ever practise together, we ought to do better than either alone, for you have many qualities in which I am wanting. When I lie awake nights and think of you wanting me to help you in Edinburgh, it seems as if I must break off from all my ties, and come back to you at once; but then my New

England conscience wakes up and tells me that my life must be duty and not pleasure, and I try to be contented with doing the work that God gives me."

A week after she returned home to Boston, Lucy wrote to her dearest Sophia again—her bubble of passion had finally subsided. "Last night for the first time since I left, I dreamed of having patients instead of dreaming of you." It was yet another partnership in Sophia's life that would never be.

Reluctantly, Sophia turned her sights away from planning a future with Lucy and back toward her problems of achieving a medical education in Edinburgh.

Upon regrouping to decide their next move, the women agreed that forcing the university to guarantee they would eventually be allowed to graduate could be put on hold. Their more pressing concern was that they be allowed to take the first professional exam that October. Medical students had to sit for all four professional exams during their four years of medical school. The five women who had met all of the requirements for the test subjects—chemistry, botany, and natural history—sent in their application and fee to take the first professional exam. They were the original five women to matriculate.

Ten days before the exam, they got a letter from Dean Balfour, stating that their application and fees had been received in error; without permission from the Senatus, they could not attend the exam. Sophia spent the day running around the city trying to fix the problem in time. She consulted her lawyer. Her lawyer told her to consult Lord Advocate and Sheriff Patrick Fraser. Fraser saw her in right away and assured her the dean's actions were illegal. He quickly composed a note to that effect.

Back at her lawyer's office with note in hand, Sophia's lawyer drew up a letter threatening to sue Dean Balfour for damages should he choose not to reverse his decision. Sophia proceeded to hand-deliver the letter to him. Facing legal repercussions, he backed off immediately.

When their results on the exam came in, only four of them passed. Sophia herself had failed! Utterly mortified, she knew in her heart that she hadn't done enough to prepare. Still, she worried it was fuel their opposition could easily point to as proof of women's mental inferiority. And let it slide, her opponents did not.

"It is a little amusing, indeed, that one of the Ladies who had rendered herself most conspicuous, should after all have failed under the test of examination," said a writer in *The Times*.

"Poets have always sung the blessings of obscurity. Those who sit on pinnacles are seen from afar, and no screen intervenes between them and curious eyes," *The Lancet* smugly said of Sophia after her failure for what they saw as a distastefully limelight-seeking crusade. "Medical students who have lately endured the pangs of a plucking must rejoice that they are not so well known to the public as is the champion of women's rights, Miss Jex Blake."

Sophia made a big stink about the examiners grading her more harshly because of all the trouble she was causing them, but an independent review she sought out confirmed she likely did not do well enough to earn a passing grade. Truly, there had been so little time for Sophia to study, what with challenging the university's relentless attempts to provide the women with a lesser education, if any education at all. She'd also received several invitations to speak at women's rights events, which took up a good amount of time.

Sophia was also dealing with a falling-out with Josephine Butler, who was livid with her for siding with Lizzie on the issue of the Contagious Diseases Act. Butler was counting on the high-profile, expert support of both these medical women to bolster her campaign against it. To be snubbed by both of them was a major blow. "We are on opposite sides on one of the most vital questions of the day," Butler lamented. She couldn't believe "medical ladies have no sympathy" with the way women were cruelly being targeted by the act.

Sophia had her own battles in Edinburgh to contend with. At a University Council meeting at the end of October 1871, Dr. Alexander Wood moved that the school must grant these women the facilities and tuition to complete their studies. To support his motion, he presented a petition signed by nine thousand women. The petition was orchestrated by a woman who'd witnessed the Surgeons' Hall riot. Even *The Lancet* agreed, "Edinburgh stands convicted of having acted unfairly towards seven ladies whom she first accepted as pupils, and then stopped half-way in their career."

It was a close vote, 107 against and 97 for, but the women did not prevail. Sophia claimed—in the pages of *The Scotsman* no less—that had it not been for Professor Christison, the past two years would have been smooth sailing for them instead of constant roadblocks and nasty students. Whether or not he was the primary opponent against their cause, it's clear Sophia viewed him that way.

The vote against them was a big blow, and now concerned about their prospects, Sophia ventured to ask the university what it had in mind when it came to graduation. Would the university make the efforts necessary to allow them to finish their degrees? She wrote to the University Court in November to find out. It had been two years since the women's admission, during which time they had completed half of the courses required for graduation. The court would have to act to enable them to complete their studies.

The following January, the court finally responded, claiming that graduation was not essential to medical education. If the women abandoned their talk of graduation, the school would give them "certificates of proficiency." Should they accept these terms, the court would arrange for them to receive the instruction required to complete their studies. The school would not agree to count any classes they took as qualifying toward a degree.

Sophia said the university "would not stir a finger in any way whatever to enable us to become legally qualified doctors, though they might, if we spent a good many years of labour and a quite unlimited sum of money in obtaining our education, give us at the end these wonderful Certificates of Proficiency, which would be worth exactly—Nothing!"

She told them since no "certificates" were recognized by the Medical Act—meaning they wouldn't be qualified to practice medicine anywhere in the UK—any such documents "would therefore be perfectly useless to us."

Sophia and the other six women brought a legal action against the school demanding that they be awarded their degrees. They believed suing the school was their last hope. Elizabeth told Sophia, in no uncertain terms, that taking legal action against the university was ill-advised. The money wasted on a lawsuit would be much better spent in other ways, she urged.

But just as their case was being prepared, they received good news. A lawsuit would not be necessary; things had gone in their favor. The lord ordinary's decision was that withholding regular degrees from fully accomplished female students and giving them certificates of proficiency instead was incompetent and unjust: "a mere mockery." Though he could not compel the university to admit women into the ordinary classes, he believed the University Court could use its powers to recognize their work in extramural classes as counting toward their degree.

Sophia was elated at this victory, but her rejoicing was tempered because she knew that the university wouldn't let things go that easily. *What is their next move?* she must have wondered. Soon she found out. The university was preparing its appeal to a higher court.

Yet, there was something else that was about to derail the movement—romance. Opponents of the Edinburgh Seven were eager to prove that women shouldn't be doctors because marriage and families would surely prove too much of a distraction.

First, Claud Marshall came and swept Lizzie's new sister-in-law Mary off her feet. She dropped out of the university as a result.

Next, their supportive *Scotsman* editor Alexander Russel had fallen for one of the Seven.

"Oh, sit down a minute," Russel implored Sophia as she got up to leave his office, thinking their business had concluded. "So your class is thinning?"

"Yes," Sophia admitted dolorously. "We've lost one."

"And I hear you're going to lose another!" Russel said.

"Oh, no," she protested. "I hope not."

"But I think so," Russel replied mischievously.

"Do you?" Sophia asked cautiously, her brow furrowed. "Well, have you heard who?"

"Ms. Evans."

"Oh, no, I don't believe it," Sophia sputtered.

"Well, she told me so herself," Russel said proudly.

"Did she? Who on earth to?" she asked.

At this, an awful shade of red began to creep across Russel's face, all the way up to the top of his bald crown.

"Have you no idea?" he said.

"No…" she fibbed as the truth sank in.

"Really no idea?" he pushed.

"How should I?" she insisted.

"Well, she asked me to tell you about it, does that give you an idea?" he said, growing perturbed by her obtuseness.

"Mr. R," she declared, finally giving in to his little game. "You don't mean to say it's you?"

His redness deepened. "Yes, I do."

"Well! I hope your treachery will go between you and your sleep!" Sophia said.

"Now don't you be hard upon her! Will you go and see her?" Russel asked.

"No, certainly not. The most she can expect is that I don't send a policeman after her," she joked.

"And brand her with D?" Russel suggested. Like you would an army deserter.

"Yes," Sophia snapped. "You may tell her I won't do that, and that's the utmost she can expect!" As she left, she added, "Well, I think you're an uncommonly lucky man, but I do hope your conscience will prevent you sleeping!"

Within two months, Matilda wed her cousin, Edinburgh professor William Edward Ayrton. Through the winter term, the Edinburgh Seven lost three original members to marriage. (Matilda and Mary would eventually complete their medical degrees in Paris.)

"I do hope you and Miss Pechey will remain firm to the end," Agnes McLaren urged Sophia, "for really three marriages within six months is quite alarming."

Agnes was an active suffrage campaigner in Edinburgh and the daughter of the city's parliamentary representative. She was also a vocal champion of their cause and a frequent visitor at Buccleuch Place. The group dubbed her "St. Agnes." She and four other women, Annie Clark, Elizabeth Ireland Walker, Sophy Jane Massingberd Mundy, and Bose Anna Shedlock, had recently decided to matriculate. And the previous summer term saw the group joined by Annie Reay Barker, Anna Dahms, and Jane Russell Rorison (all three of whom eventually became successful medical practitioners). So despite the group's losses to marriage, there were still plenty of women seeking medical schooling at Edinburgh. (Annie and Agnes also become doctors, but we hear more about them later when they rejoin the group in London.)

For Agnes, studying medicine wasn't about feeling called to heal or a fascination for science, but about independence. "If I felt I had a vocation for medicine, it would make me bolder, but you know that I cannot honestly plead that. On the contrary, I have very grave doubts of my capacity for it," Agnes admitted. "No, the attractions to me would be a definite sphere, and an independent one."

That April, Sophia was invited to speak at a suffrage event in London at St. George's Hall. "Don't have any libel cases," Edith teased Sophia while she was preparing her lecture. "How I wish I could be in the gallery to make faces at you and throw peas!"

She gave a speech on women in medicine to a packed audience, eager to hear the leader of the Edinburgh Seven speak. Seated on the platform alongside her were Elizabeth and Lizzie, the two people most instrumental in her ongoing journey toward a medical degree.

Her speech was long and admittedly rather dry. She briefly explained how Elizabeth and Lizzie pursued their medical degrees before giving a detailed account of her own trials at Edinburgh. The audience was somewhat disappointed that Sophia was not as fiery and impassioned on the podium as they'd been led to expect. Her speech may have been more subdued than her audience imagined, however she did find an opportunity to publicly call out her nemesis by name.

"The whole opposition to the medical education of women has in Edinburgh, been dictated by one man and his immediate followers," Sophia proclaimed. "It is hardly necessary to say that that man is Sir Robert Christison, whose great age and long tenure of office naturally give him unusual weight, both in the University and among the medical men of Edinburgh."

No peas were thrown, and the lecture was printed later that year as "Medical Education of Women" along with an earlier essay by Sophia. She had lovingly dedicated it to Dr. Lucy Sewall.

Over the summer, the lady students fanned out for training. Edith found a post at a London Lying-in Hospital, Emily Bovell and newly married Matilda headed to Paris, and newcomers Jane and Anna were warmly received by Marie and Lucy at their Boston hospital.

"I have seen now Dr. Sewall use forceps three times, and it is impossible to see anything prettier. She uses any sort of instrument beautifully," Jane wrote to Edith from Boston. "I think well-done surgery is fascinating, and I never saw anyone handle an instrument so easily and so securely. I should feel safe whatever she was going to do to me or mine."

By the end of the summer, Sophia was showing signs of burnout. It had, after all, been a long, hard journey. Between lectures, writing letters, and making personal visits to advocate for their cause, Sophia's workdays regularly lasted twelve hours.

"Oh Lucy, I'm so tired of it all," she moaned. "I am getting more and more doubtful whether I myself shall ever finish my education. I think when once the fight is won I shall creep away into some wood and lie and sleep for a year."

That winter, the Edinburgh Royal Infirmary's board of managers finally passed a motion to allow the women students entry, so long as they did so separately from the men students. Another Balfour, not the dean, but Dr. George W. Balfour, dedicated one hour a day, three days a week to teaching them in the medical ward. Balfour was a magnanimous man who specialized in heart and circulatory diseases. Then on Sunday mornings, they shadowed Dr. Watson in the surgical ward. The women's clinical training would be limited to only the patients on these two wards.

"There were no attendances on casualties or out-patients, no pathological demonstrations, no surgical dresserships, no special departments of any kind," Isabel lamented. "We had to be content with what our kind friends could give."

The next term was anything but dull. In their extramural course on medical jurisprudence (forensic medicine), Professor Littlejohn regaled them with one gory story after another. The murder trial of accused poisoner Madeleine Smith, the burial of a foot on Inchcolm Island, the case of suffocation with a piece of tripe. Saturdays were reserved for field trips: Craigentinny sewage farm, a cattle slaughterhouse, a speedy climb up Liberton Hill to view the filter beds with Littlejohn lecturing to his breathless students as they struggled to keep up.

As Edinburgh's first medical officer of health, Littlejohn

oversaw key public health advancements in the city: improving drainage and water supply, widening streets, and addressing overcrowded housing units. Most notably, Sir Littlejohn is considered one of the inspirations for the character Sherlock Holmes. Littlejohn was legendary at the University of Edinburgh. Whenever he entered the lecture hall, his students broke into wild applause. He spent forty-two years teaching, and according to his obituary, his lectures had never been surpassed in their vividness, raciness, and memorability. "With humor which was contagious, with wit which was sparkling, with gestures which were intensely dramatic, and with an immense collection of extraordinary anecdotes, Littlejohn held his students spellbound whilst in his class," it read.

He taught students how to give testimony in court cases: how to describe injuries, interpret bloodstain evidence, and analyze footprints. "Never confide professional matters in your wife," he recommended. He also had a lot to say about women's bodies: "a vaginal examination may cause a sudden death."

"The unimpregnated uterus is the slowest organ to decompose." Firearms are "not used by women as they do not understand them."

One wonders what the ladies, as the first women to take this class, thought upon hearing these outlandish ideas.

Slowly but surely, the remaining women completed all of the courses required to graduate in the University of Edinburgh extramural school: clinical medicine, midwifery, materia medica, and pathology. Sophia earned honors in these last three courses. Their work in the medical and surgical wards at the infirmary also continued—thanks to the "unfailing kindness" of doctors Patrick Watson and George Balfour—until they finished the required two years of clinical training.

Despite completing all the prerequisites for graduating, the Edinburgh Seven were not feeling hopeful. They were still waiting on the justices to decide the verdict of their degrees. "I think we have no chance, the influence of the medical men being so much against us," Edith lamented.

One spark of hope was that all of their publicity was finally leading politicians to take notice of their plight. Liberal Member of Parliament David Wedderburn announced his plans to introduce a bill to grant Scottish universities the power to educate and confer degrees upon women in medicine. Sophia set about drumming up more support for such a bill by writing to and meeting with various government officials.

The Home Secretary, one of the top government officials in the UK, thought it would be best to expand the bill to include not just Scottish universities and medical degrees, but all UK universities and every subject: "Though it may not be very agreeable to my constituents I should have no objection to introduce an enabling bill giving all Universities the power if they please to confer medical degrees or indeed any other degrees on women."

This Enabling Bill survived a change in government and was reintroduced by conservative Member of Parliament Russell Gurney (Emelia's husband) and his liberal Member of Parliament counterpart. It was hoped the bill would be harmless enough not to provoke opposition. After all, it didn't *require* schools to admit or educate women, it just clarified they indeed had the power to do so. But petitions against it rolled in. Even among those who believed the Edinburgh Seven had been treated unfairly, there were worries that since university programs were created with men in mind, they might not be suitable for women.

Sophia's nemesis Christison attacked the bill, saying professors would resist teaching ladies. "It is not easy to compel a man to do that which he hates, or force him to that which he feels may kill him." (And they say women are the melodramatic ones!) At the same time that Christison was working hard to squash this bill and stifle women's equality, the prime minister recommended that the queen bestow a baronetcy upon him for his contributions to medicine.

The second reading of the bill was slated for April, but was deferred so that the politicians could have more time to ponder its implications. The bill was finally discussed in June. Again it was delayed. The women didn't have time to wait and see if the wheels of politics would ever turn in their favor.

Not known to sit idly by, the band of women had already begun to inquire about gaining admission to other institutions. With their transcripts positively bursting, applying to take the MD exams should have been a mere formality. Still, they struggled.

The women visited Birmingham, St. Andrews, the University of Durham, and various centers in Ireland. Durham decided they could not consent to admitting women to the school, even just to sit the examinations. St. Andrews appeared more hopeful. At least four professors were on their side. Alas, the doors were again only cracked, and would not fully open to them.

Isabel attempted to secure a path to the medical register outside of a degree: appealing to the Royal Colleges of Physicians and Surgeons and the Apothecaries Societies of London and Ireland. The women did their best to see that no stone was left unturned. But their determination and restraint was beginning to waver in the face of medical men constantly questioning their abilities.

"Since I saw you I have indeed suffered many things of many physicians, and my temper is no better but rather worse," Edith complained to Sophia. "If I could only have spoken my mind when they talked their conceited bosh about their infinite superiority, and said, 'Do you know what a poor fool you are making of yourself?'; but to sit still, smiling benignantly, when men, commonplace enough, goodness knows, in everything but their uncommon stupidity, boasted of their mental capacity!" It was a frustrating place to be—dependent on the decision of men to deem them worthy or not of sitting for an exam.

The Prince of Wales's personal physician, Dr. Thomas King

Chambers, urged the women to forget about the medical degree and "practise boldly as unregistered practitioners who are
ready to submit to examination when called upon," after finishing their education. It was a startling piece of advice that the
women took under consideration.

Lucy warned Sophia against taking such a path. "I was very
much troubled by your last letter for the idea of your beginning
to practise without a diploma seems to me such a mistake," Lucy
cautioned. "It appears to me that by practising illegally in that
way, you will be giving up all you have been fighting for, and
will be opening a way that some women who have not studied
thoroughly may use; and there will be no way of your showing
the public the difference between your qualifications."

The Edinburgh Seven wouldn't be left guessing for long. The
justices soon handed down their decision: the University of Edinburgh had overstepped its bounds when it allowed the women
to matriculate in the first place. Their admission was rendered
illegal; they would not be allowed to graduate. Without a medical degree from a British university, they couldn't be placed on
the medical register, they couldn't legally practice medicine.

They'd taken every class they could, often organizing their own
classes, faced harassment from their fellow students, and had roadblocks erected in their path at every turn. Despite all of their years
of studies and struggle, they would not be allowed to graduate.

There was no reason to remain in Edinburgh. "At the end of
March 1874, the medical classes in Edinburgh were given up,"
Sophia declared, deflated.

"We had therefore been attracted to Edinburgh, paid heavy
fees, and had lost over four years' time by the action of the University," Isabel said, summing up their sad state of affairs. The
male-dominated medical institution may have won this battle—
but the war to see women's path to the MD cleared was only
just beginning.

SIXTEEN

Finding a Way Forward

After such a public setback, disagreements bubbled within the movement about what their next steps should be, about which path would lead to their goal of equal educational and professional opportunities in medicine for women. The spotlight placed on all of these "first women" was the crux of many internal disagreements, since it fueled the immense pressure they all felt to get it right the first time. The problem, of course, was they each had different ideas about what getting it right meant.

Since the Edinburgh Seven were unsuccessful at obtaining a degree, Lizzie believed that meant the entire exercise had been a disastrous failure. She feared Sophia may have actually set the movement back. Her "want of judgement and want of temper" had done a great deal of harm, Lizzie scolded.

Sophia was more optimistic. She saw Edinburgh as a lost battle paving the way to a winnable war. "There was no 'failure'... It was the seed sown in tears in Edinburgh that was reaped in joy elsewhere." Given the old-fashioned attitudes of most medical men and the immature state of public opinion, Sophia said waging a battle such as theirs had been vital. This option was much quicker and more effective, she claimed, than if they'd waited around for a policy to be passed allowing women students before entering college.

Indeed it was no small thing to bring the public's attention to the question of women becoming doctors. Now, it was being widely discussed, giving women an opportunity to loudly profess a need for women doctors and to argue against any doubts of women not being competent enough to obtain a degree and care for patients.

Unlike her predecessors, Sophia wasn't afraid to take big risks or be publicly humiliated if it meant getting results more quickly. Her impulsive, outgoing nature was in direct contrast to the demure, feminine Lizzie and the eccentric, introspective Elizabeth. They both favored a slow and steady chipping away at barriers and attitudes, and didn't approve of Sophia's confrontational tactics.

Lizzie saw Sophia rocking the boat to its breaking point. After witnessing what happened in Edinburgh, she now believed women should go abroad instead of fighting with British institutions to allow their admittance, just as she had done.

Lizzie made these feelings known in *The Times* of London: "The real solution of the difficulty will, I believe, be found in Englishwomen seeking abroad that which at present is denied to them in their own country. By going to Paris, female students can get, without further difficulty or contention, at a very small cost, a first-class medical education," though she conceded there was one small problem. Even with an esteemed degree like women could receive in Paris, the women would be unable to legally practice in the United Kingdom. Her license from the Apothecaries' Hall allowed her to legally practice, but it had changed its rules after Lizzie earned her license to prevent other women from following her example.

But in Lizzie's opinion, this was not an obstacle that couldn't slowly be overcome. If they could point to a considerable number of women who'd earned MDs in France, then quietly build up reputations as trustworthy and valuable members of the profession in England, surely the government would eventually see they deserved to be allowed onto the registry. This proposition was sure to take quite a long time, though. Lizzie didn't seem to care about how long things took as long as they were done properly.

About three weeks after Lizzie's article was published, *The Times* published Sophia's rebuttal: "I can imagine few things that would please our opponents better than to see one English-woman after another driven out of her own country to obtain medical education abroad, both because they know that, on her return after years of labour, she can claim no legal recognition whatever, and because they are equally certain that, so long as no means of education are provided at home, only a very small number of women will ever seek admission to the profession."

Sophia recognized that attending foreign medical schools, for exams or a full medical education, was not a viable solution for every woman, or even most women, since it unfairly excluded those who lacked the funds to undertake travel and lodging abroad. She went so far as to say that those who took the easy way out by going abroad were traitors to the movement. "I most firmly believe that every woman who consents to be thus exiled does more harm than can easily be calculated to the general cause of medical women in this country."

Though fighting for the same rights and opportunities for women, Sophia and Lizzie could not have had more different views or personalities. Sophia was a fiery, impetuous trouble-maker, and Lizzie a calculating, self-effacing lady. Lizzie loathed being the subject of gossip, but she underestimated the importance of publicity on the path toward social change. Sophia knew any publicity could be good publicity. Her boldness thrust the topic of women doctors into headlines across the globe. Sophia's larger-than-life personality was a gift to journalists.

Lizzie was content to quietly tunnel her way alone underground to gain access to the fortress of medical education. Only after achieving individual success through the tiny pinhole she'd managed to carve out did she turn her sights to opening up the profession to other women.

Sophia knew strength lay in numbers. She gathered comrades at the outset and set about blasting a hole through the front gates. Unfortunately, the establishment was well-armed and ready for such a noisy invasion, so at the end of the battle, not one of the seven women could claim the right to a medical degree.

One physician who assisted the women in their early movement asserted, "Mrs. Garrett Anderson is a fine instance of an individual success, but Miss Jex-Blake fights the battle, not for herself, but for all."

Opposition is an underrated motivator. Liberal Member of British Parliament James Stansfeld observed how all of the obstinate resistance to the women's movement only helped fuel their cause. "Opponents, when the time has come, are not merely dragged at the chariot wheels of progress—they help to turn them. The strongest forces, whichever way it seems to work, does most to aid. The forces of greatest concentration here have been, in my view, on the one hand the Edinburgh University led by Sir Robert Christison, on the other the women claimants led by Sophia Jex-Blake." Which force would be the strongest was yet to be determined.

Stansfeld had taken a great interest in the women's medical movement after seeing Sophia speak at a women's suffrage event back in 1871. In his opinion, he saw the campaign for women in medicine starting with Sophia, when she first applied to the University of Edinburgh in 1869. He explained, "I have not dated the movement from Mrs Garrett Anderson's personally successful attempt, because its immediate consequence was the closing of the door through which she had forced her way. Her honourable place appears to me to be that of a forerunner of the movement."

The same debate that Elizabeth Blackwell wrestled with in America was happening again in Great Britain. Since no institution would open its doors to women, should they create their own women's medical school? Being accepted alongside their male peers in established colleges and hospitals was always the ultimate goal. These schools were well funded and enjoyed high-caliber professors, well-appointed laboratories, specimen-filled museums, and unfettered access to large hospitals. Most of the women in the movement realized that such acceptance would take so long that separate schools were an important, if hopefully temporary, solution.

In *The BMJ*, one doctor wondered why no one had attempted to open a women's medical school in the UK yet. There must not be a big enough demand of women wanting to study medicine to make it a worthwhile pursuit, they concluded. How wrong they were about the interest.

Sophia's views on the subject of gender-separate education had been evolving. Before Edinburgh, she enjoyed a blissful naivete, believing that if men and women studied together, "no serious difficulty need ever occur, except in cases of really exceptional coarseness of character on one side or the other." She assumed that there might be a few days of embarrassment as the students became accustomed to mixed company. But that eventually the novelty would wear off, "the embarrassment will disappear in the interest of a common study."

Her hopeful prediction didn't come true, of course. After Edinburgh, she changed her tune. Experiencing firsthand the nastiness mixed-gender education could bring, Sophia now advocated for women to have their own separate schools. This would at least be a better temporary solution than expecting every woman interested in pursuing medicine to travel to continental Europe.

"I had honestly supposed that ladies need fear no discomfort in an ordinary medical class, as 'the majority of the students would always be gentlemen.' I regret that on this point I have been compelled somewhat to modify my opinion," Sophia admitted. The problem was never the women, of course. It was the men. Some boys were simply unfit to be admitted to a mixed class. Sophia now saw that separate education was necessary, but still dreamed of gender integration.

"I hope, even in my life-time, to see the day when such regulations are no longer required," she opined. Though Sophia's faith in humanity understandably took a hit, it would never be entirely diminished. She truly believed mixed classes were the way to go. "I have very little doubt that this will ultimately be the usual arrangement as civilization advances," she concluded.

Sophia wrote to Dr. Francis Anstie of Westminster Hospital for advice. He had become a fan and supporter of Sophia during her fight at Edinburgh. Florence Nightingale regarded Anstie as one of the greatest "workhouse doctors" out there. In addition to his work in reforming the workhouse infirmaries that treated the poor, Anstie also campaigned against overcrowding in London. Florence admired Anstie's passion for standing up for the rights of the less fortunate, and many letters passed between them.

Whether Anstie could convince his colleagues to begin accepting women students at his hospital's medical school was altogether another matter.

"I think it very unlikely that any proposition would be entertained with regard to surrendering our position as teachers of male students," Anstie admitted. "I fear there is no way, except by the ladies raising enough money to found a school for themselves. I think your best course would be to take some premises in London, and build a thoroughly good school, fit for first-class teaching of the theoretical courses. But the difficulties about clinical teaching seem very great."

Sophia returned home to Brighton, to rest and decide on her next course of action. She arranged an apprenticeship with her old teacher, Mr. Salzmann.

Quickly tiring of being away from a city where she could fight for real training, Sophia soon left her home again. She was off again to London, to continue crusading.

SEVENTEEN

Societies and Controversies

As for Lizzie, she was about to embark on a trip to Edinburgh, where the battle of the Edinburgh Seven remained fresh in everyone's mind. She'd received an invitation to read one of her papers at the British Medical Association's annual meeting in Edinburgh. "I do hope it will be useful in a solid way to the cause," Lizzie said about this high-profile opportunity. Perhaps she could offer herself as a sterling example of a woman doctor. She had never encountered hostility at her branch meetings, and so was unprepared for what awaited her in Scotland.

When Lizzie and her sister-in-law Mary arrived, they were told all of the student tickets had already been distributed. Mary would not be allowed to attend. The conference president, none other than Christison himself, gave what Lizzie called a "horribly dull and long" speech more about gender politics than medicine. "A liberty" had been taken in admitting a female member, and allowing her to read a paper at a national meeting, Christison declared. With Mary not allowed to attend, Lizzie was the only woman in the audience.

"Storms are brewing here," she wrote home to Jamie from the meeting, wishing his wise counsel was closer at hand. She so wanted to publicly defend herself against such ridiculous vitriol she received from Christison, but to do so grated against her sensibilities. "Don't think I am unhappy, dearest," she assured Jamie. "Someone must do it and with all my inner joys, you and the dear babies and my work, I can stand it better than most people could. If I can do my duty the defeat will be but one more step towards final victory."

At intermission, Lizzie beseeched the secretary to give Mary a ticket, and he eventually gave in. But just a short while later, he wrote to let Lizzie know he'd overstepped in issuing the ticket and would appreciate it if Mary did not use it. But they had been out at lunch and never gotten his note. Mary and Lizzie spent all afternoon listening to paper presentations and discussions. By this time, her New Hospital colleague Frances had arrived in preparation to deliver her own research. In the presence of two women doctors, the atmosphere at the meeting grew increasingly hostile.

Lizzie started to wonder if they would even be allowed to read their papers.

The next morning, Lizzie hiked up Arthur's Seat alone, practicing her speech. When she returned, she was told that while she was gone they decided she would not be allowed to give her paper. Fuming, Lizzie stormed over to the heads of the BMA's obstetrical section, Drs. Keiller and Duncan, and said, "If you would say to me that any one of your number has read my paper and thought it not worth producing, I will at once acquiesce, but I do not think it ought to be stopped in deference to prejudice."

They said they would take her words into consideration and let her know their decision.

Later that afternoon, she received word that she had been put on the schedule to read her paper the following day. Frances did not fare as well. When it was discovered she was not on the medical register because her degree was from Zürich, her election to the BMA was deemed "irregular." Hundreds of men in the same position were reelected that year, but Frances was not.

The next day word had spread, and medical men piled in to see Lizzie deliver her paper on menstrual cramps. "We have had a great triumph!" she exclaimed to Jamie. "The paper was very well received, heard by an immense audience and a vote of thanks passed. The room was crammed and everyone shook hands afterwards."

It must have been especially rewarding for Lizzie to deliver a paper in the obstetrical section at the BMA meeting since her application to the Obstetrical Society had been turned down the previous year. When she was proposed as a fellow, her application was even signed by many eminent physicians—a few were society members themselves. Had her admission been all they were considering, she likely would have been admitted. But the group took the opportunity to consider the admission of women in general to their society.

Their bylaws allowed any registered medical practitioner to be put forth as a "candidate" for membership, but all subsequent references substituted "gentleman" for "candidate." It was a perfect opportunity to claim this language meant no women could ever be candidates.

The men of the Obstetrical Society had whiled away their afternoon debating the merits of allowing girls into their clubhouse. "Pleased as we are to meet ladies upon other occasions, would be anything but pleased to meet them here," proclaimed Dr. Charles Taylor. The introduction of a lady would cause "unquestionable damage to the Society," Dr. Wiltshire demanded. "If we are interested in the Society, and in obstetrics, the best thing we can do is exclude women altogether."

Even Dr. Aveling, who had signed Lizzie's nomination, objected to the general admission of women. Knowing her personally, he didn't believe she would interfere with their regular goings-on. Lizzie would have made a fine addition; she was a competent and knowledgeable physician. It was an imagined stampede of women stealing their jobs—tiny brains and inferior muscles and all—that had them shaking in their boots.

One fellow spoke out in favor of women's admission. Dr. Galton suggested that obstetric medicine might be advanced by the admission of women, it was their duty not to exclude them. Despite believing women unfit for the profession, Galton said qualified women practitioners were in a unique position to make obstetric observations and bring interesting cases before the society. He proposed women should be admitted.

When voting time came, only four men were in favor of the motion. Women would not be allowed a seat at the table. Afterward, Wiltshire expressed his fear that the issue might be brought up again in the future. The president reassured him the matter was settled for the moment.

The irony of their prejudice may have been lost on all those in the room, but it did not escape *The Scotsman*. The paper toasted them for "deciding that no woman could ever be allowed to join in discussion concerning the treatment and relief of those sufferings which women alone have to endure."

After hearing about the details of the meeting and their decision to exclude her from the society, Lizzie wrote a letter to *The BMJ*. She decided that defending herself was necessary as one of the speakers was reported to have claimed her name was smuggled on to the medical register. Lizzie was livid at this implication, after all the additional steps she had to take, the path she had to forge alone, to make the register.

"'Smuggling' implies dishonesty, or at least as much dishonesty as is involved in creeping or stealing in, slily or insidiously. It would, I submit, be incorrect to describe the method I pursued in getting upon the Register in these terms," Lizzie proclaimed. Still, she remained hopeful that they would eventually see the light: "I cherish the hope that, in the not far distant future, a wider construction of the bye-laws of the Society will be acceptable to its members." Lizzie was looking forward to the day when women were no longer denied the advantages of society membership in any profession.

Now, at the BMA's annual meeting, she was coming face-to-face with the very men who had excluded her from the Obstetrical Society.

Edinburgh professor Joseph Lister was absolutely furious that a woman had been allowed to become a member of the BMA. He demanded that the organization's constitution, which permitted anyone on the medical register to be admitted, must be interpreted within the context it was written. To him, that meant "the idea of any woman being likely to become a registered medical practitioner was far from the minds of the founders and original members of the Association." Lister argued that terms like "person" should be interpreted as *male* person. Just like the Obstetrical Society, he was trying to interpret the by-laws to forcibly leave out women.

At a subsequent BMA meeting, the topic of continuing to allow women entry was raised again. Lizzie planned to "lift the question onto a higher plane and to appeal to the best part of their minds." She stood up and declared that the group should think more of itself than as a mere men's club, that barring women would run counter to the spirit of scientific inquiry they claimed to support.

"We have heard a good deal of this Association being described as a 'club' for social purposes. But the object of the Association is twofold: 1. The promotion of medical science; and 2. The promotion of the interests of the profession. No one can venture to say that medical science will be promoted by excluding a body of honest and painstaking workers, who will bring to the study of many important problems some experience of their own essentially different from that of male practitioners," Lizzie demanded.

She argued that allowing women doctors to practice outside the bounds of the association's professional codes and agreements was actually not in the group's best interests. Including them would give the association more control, not less. "Let your prejudices melt away," she concluded. Loud cheering erupted in the BMA meeting hall.

But the charm of one woman did little to budge their principles. The motion to exclude women was passed by a majority vote. In deference to Lizzie's popularity and professional standing, the ruling was not made retroactive. By being grandfathered in, she became the only female member of the BMA until the ruling was repealed in 1892.

Soon, Lizzie had other concerns to keep her occupied. Her hospital was embroiled in a controversy over surgery. Lizzie believed a surgeon's most important skills weren't related to manual dexterity, but rather in the art of knowing how to heal a malady, whether with surgery, or, if possible, without it. In practice, she wasn't always so restrained.

"I had a very big operation yesterday and so far all promises very well with the patient," Lizzie told her sister Milly. "It is one which has only been done a few times in England—not at all often anywhere, and the mortality has been very high. So if mine recovers it will be quoted for a long time—I fancy too that the tumour in my case was larger than any yet. It was a much overgrown spleen." Still aware of how her performance impacted the wider view of medical women, she added, "I tell you this for the *sake of the cause*."

Perhaps Lizzie thought these surgeries were worth the gamble, both medically and professionally. Perhaps she was more focused on the potential for professional notoriety than she was on the best interests of her patients. The more daring the surgery, the more severe the case, the more noteworthiness she and her scientific sisterhood could claim—so long as it proved successful.

She once excised a tumor so large that she sent it to the Museum of the College of Surgeons for display. She boasted to her husband about how well the patient's recovery was going, but in fact they later died. Lizzie was playing a dangerous game, caught between surgical ambition and operative success.

Frances became so concerned about Lizzie's overzealousness and lack of skill in surgery that she resigned from her position at the New Hospital for Women. This turned out to be the first in a series of such resignations at the hospital. Consultant surgeon W. A. Meredith left because he "found that the record of Mrs Anderson's operations at which he had been present showed too high a percentage of failures."

Louisa Atkins quickly followed. Louisa had interned with Lizzie in the early days of her hospital, then earned her MD in Zürich, Switzerland. After a few years as house surgeon at the Birmingham and Midland Hospital for Women, Louisa returned to London and to a job at Lizzie's hospital. Having worked as a surgeon, she knew her stuff. Now, she'd decided Lizzie's judgments were off.

"I could not justify it to my conscience to allow any patient of mine to be operated under the present system," Louisa reported to the hospital committee. She strongly believed that Lizzie's abdominal surgeries "will be injurious to the patients, to the cause of medical women and to the Hospital itself." But the committee had no intention of censuring or even admonishing Lizzie.

Six weeks later, Louisa told them she'd "witnessed another operation performed by Mrs Anderson which did not in the least modify my opinion that she is not competent to undertake such operations singlehanded." Still, they did nothing. Louisa resigned in protest along with Mary Dowson, the hospital's pathologist and chloroformist.

In case the hospital's contributors started raising questions about the safety of the institution, the committee made a point to describe operations in its minutes. In one such case, "Mrs Anderson reported that she had performed a serious operation (which could not have been postponed without injury to the patient). Mr Imlach, a specialist of Liverpool, was present at the operation and wrote the following opinion: 'Have just witnessed as difficult an abdominal section as any surgeon could have to perform, and think that in technical skill and promptness I have never seen anything much more perfect.'"

Imlach was a puzzling choice of spokesperson since he himself was known among the profession as someone who occasionally performed potentially unnecessary surgeries.

Lizzie stood fast in her belief that every surgery she undertook was absolutely essential to the patient's recovery. She was glad that her hospital committee was on her side in the matter, and the episode didn't seem to leave a mark on her reputation.

As the next frontier in medicine, surgery was an increasingly hot-button issue. Now that more effective anesthesia was used, surgeons could attempt more invasive procedures. Abdominal surgeries were no longer off-limits. The first successful hysterectomy was performed in 1853. And development of sterile conditions for surgery greatly reduced the odds of patients succumbing to post-op infections. Some, however, thought things were moving too fast.

Elizabeth, despite once desiring to become a surgeon herself, agreed that it was becoming an increasingly audacious practice. "I consider the loss of a natural internal organ a very grave mutilation of the human body." She feared the long-term impact on patients of such surgeries were going unrecorded, and believed that if such data were collected, the results would be damning against surgical intervention.

"When you shudder at 'mutilations,' it seems to me you can never have handled a degenerated ovary or suppurating Fallopian tube, or you would admit that the mutilation had been effected by the ignorance or neglect of a series of physicians before the surgeon intervened. There is no such special sanctity about the ovary!" Mary Putnam argued with Elizabeth.

Lizzie clearly concurred with Mary. Shirking the responsibility of an operation when the situation called for it, Lizzie believed, was sheer cowardice.

Elizabeth used the surgical controversy at Lizzie's hospital as an opportunity to publicly separate herself from such butchery. She feared Lizzie was tainting the image of women physicians; she didn't want them gaining a reputation as scalpel-happy. She also felt speaking out against what she considered superfluous surgeries was more important than avoiding calling attention to disagreements within the movement.

"The temptations to operate upon women are great and peculiar and it is not to be wondered at that the first note of alarm has been sounded in connection with a hospital for women," Elizabeth asserted in the *Hastings Daily Chronicle*. "We shall never have our hospitals thoroughly entitled to public confidence until the older members of the medical profession openly take up arms against the younger members, who are converting houses of charity into butchers' shops."

Elizabeth wasn't alone in her hesitancy of surgery's growing domain. John Erichsen, an eminent surgeon who spent twelve years as a consultant at Lizzie's hospital, once explained his own reservations about the increasingly experimental nature of surgery at a BMA meeting: "The uterus and the spleen, the stomach, the pylorus and the colon, have each and all been subjected to the scalpel of the surgeon; with what success has yet to be determined; and it is for you to decide whether these operations constitute real and solid advances in our art, or whether they are rather to be regarded as bold and skillful experiments on the endurance and reparative power of the human frame—whether, in fact, they are surgical triumphs or operative audacities."

In these arguments, there was an element of the old school

butting up against the new. Medicine as an intuitive, moralistic practice versus an empirical, secular science; the lofty pursuit of prevention versus the realistic necessity of intervention. While some hills were worth dying on, the medical women would have to find a way to work together if they wanted to see women doctors get the training and acceptance they deserved.

EIGHTEEN

A Place All Their Own in London

In mid-1874, Sophia took matters into her own hands. She decided to take Anstie's advice and open her own women's medical school. If successful, she could finally realize her lifelong dream of founding a school for women, and women in the UK could finally earn a medical degree in their own nation without begging and pleading with professors and enduring the hostility of male students. It was a decision that would change the course of British medicine.

She may not have had a degree of her own, but she didn't really need one to organize a school; only her professors would need to be experts in their field. Besides, Sophia was so close to an MD she could practically taste it. She decided her school's council would be made up of only registered practitioners. And there were two people she greatly desired to have associated with it. They were the only two women currently on the British medical register, and both were currently practicing in London: Elizabeth and Lizzie.

Elizabeth was immediately amenable. While Sophia had been busy fighting the University of Edinburgh, Elizabeth had become a consulting physician at Lizzie's hospital (before the surgical controversy). Sadly, by the end of 1872, Elizabeth had to cut down her work because she became ill with gallbladder disease. She told Barbara she'd endured thirteen attacks of agonizing pain and vomiting over just a few months. The many doctors she consulted offered little in the way of a diagnosis or cure, but morphine helped take the edge off. Kitty was a great help to her mother in these times, dutifully nursing Elizabeth, but she also noticed how difficult it was for doctors to admit that they were ill.

Elizabeth was convinced that London pollution was to blame for causing or at least exacerbating her illness, so she, her sister Marian, and Kitty traveled through Switzerland and then settled in Rome for a year. Their return to London saw Elizabeth's return to practice.

She had to make enough money to fund the six-month trip back home to America that she'd promised Kitty she could take alone that spring. Kitty was now in her late twenties and eager to see her homeland. After leaving her daughter on the boat, Elizabeth couldn't stop thinking about her "little voyager" whose "poor little tearful face I was obliged to leave amongst strangers— a leave taking which gave me a sharp pang, and brought up my own tears." As recurring bouts of illness overtook Elizabeth, work became increasingly difficult. She longed for the kind of work she'd most enjoyed in New York—planning a medical school. Sophia's request couldn't have come at a better time.

Elizabeth felt her experience and influence would be beneficial, provided she could wrest some control of the organization away from such young, impetuous hands as Sophia's. Besides, organizational planning and teaching might be easier, more reliable work than trying to manage a private medical practice with occasional gallbladder attacks. And it would be exciting to be part of the establishment of yet another women's medical college.

"I feel much interest in this school as a true though small beginning and shall do all I can to help it on," Elizabeth said with determination. Having Sophia take the lead, according to Elizabeth, would provide her with the opportunity she had been looking for since she came to London: to help forge the path to a medical education for women in England without too much personal responsibility. She was annoyed, and a bit concerned, that Lizzie had refused to help so far.

Elizabeth was drawn to these two women for different reasons. She admired Sophia's tenacity and Lizzie's persistence. She thought of herself as a mentor to both women, having inspired, counseled, and assisted them during their fight for training. Her criticisms of Sophia were clear, but Elizabeth didn't wear rose-colored glasses to assess Lizzie, either. When Barbara once wrote to Elizabeth of a sour interaction she'd had with Lizzie, she replied: "I am very sorry to hear of Mrs. Garrett's harshness, though I am not surprised for I always saw an element of hardness in her character which was dangerous." As a practitioner of the older school who prioritized bedside manner, Elizabeth must've bristled at Lizzie's cool, standoffish demeanor.

Lizzie's involvement with Sophia's plans would take much more cajoling. The time was "not ripe" to establish a women's medical school, Lizzie believed. (She later called herself timid for this assertion.) Sophia wrote to ask her to sit on the school council, explaining that leading medical men had already consented to join the teaching staff, and she was sure medical examiners would see it as a properly equipped medical school. Why, the school's plans were practically complete. Sophia was completely confident the school would be a success.

Lizzie hesitated. She was even more guarded than Elizabeth when it came to Sophia, even though the two had been close years earlier. She had her own reputation to consider. For the past nine years, she'd slowly developed her independent practice and women's hospital. Lizzie was living proof that a woman could be a diligent, skillful physician. Her reputation among the profession and her patients was hard-won, enviable; she couldn't throw that all away by associating herself with a venture that may fail. Lizzie's narrow view of progress for women didn't have any room for failure, for herself or others.

And to Lizzie, Sophia's work in Edinburgh was a failure. Sophia's future partner explained how Lizzie "looked through the wrong end of the telescope at Sophia." Lizzie failed to realize "how that same impulsiveness (mistakes and all)" was what made their movement widely popular among the public and how the blunt opposition and pushback she faced in Edinburgh would have happened sooner or later. The bigger question was if Lizzie could get past her perfectionist ideals and embrace Sophia's plans for a medical school.

There was one thing that could ease Lizzie's reservations about associating herself with the school: Sophia's name not appearing on any materials relating to the women's medical college, despite her spearheading the project. The public saw her as a provocative pioneer, but among most of the medical community she was an infamous rabble-rouser. Wise Dr. Anstie was the one who convinced Sophia that her lack of a medical degree meant she shouldn't be named in the school prospectus. Sophia was a smart girl. That these fears were actually because of her negative notoriety likely did not escape her.

Elizabeth agreed it was a good omen that Sophia agreed to keep her name off of any school documents. "She is in such odium with the profession that her name would have damaged the chances of the school, and this voluntary suppression of herself makes me hope that we may retain her energy and avoid her tactlessness."

Sophia knew what Lizzie thought of her, but she still wanted her to be involved. For all of their differences, one thing the pair had in common was indefatigable candor. Sophia knew that Lizzie saw Edinburgh as a defeat, and was frustrated by the lack of respect from her so-called friend.

"If I kept a record of all the people who bring me cock and bull stories about you," Sophia wrote to Lizzie, "and assure me that you are 'greatly injuring the cause,' I might fill as many pages with quotations as you have patience to read, but, beyond defending you on a good many occasions, I have never thought it needful to take much notice of such incidents." Sophia continued, "Nor do I much care to know whether or not certain individuals have confided to you that they lay at my door 'the failure at Edinburgh.' It can serve no purpose whatever to go into this sort of gossip."

Sophia was growing weary of such infighting and of constantly having to defend herself. But Sophia was also humble enough to know when personal glory should take a back seat to the greater purpose. She tried to reassure Lizzie with the rest of her letter, stating if it was decided that her name would likely injure the school's chances of success, she would cheerfully stand aside and let Isabel or Edith take the reins. "I think it of very great importance, both for your credit and ours, that there should be no appearance of split in the camp."

Lizzie had only one night to mull Sophia's invitation to sit on the school council as the meeting of the school-planning committee was the next morning. If she refused, it would reflect poorly on the movement by making it known that there was a split between these women. If she accepted, she'd have to put aside her misgivings about Sophia and work together to ensure the school's success.

At Anstie's house the next day, a heavily pregnant Lizzie appeared. Against her better judgment, she agreed to be involved. Edith was also there. They all agreed to found a school to educate women in medicine in a way that would enable them to pass examinations and place their names on the medical register.

Anstie was named dean, and a provisional council of twenty-one registered medical practitioners assembled. Among them was *BMJ* editor Ernest Hart, biologist Thomas Huxley, Lizzie, and Elizabeth. The school was lucky to have Anstie for such a prominent position. He was well respected and well connected in the profession. A few weeks after the meeting, Lizzie gave birth to her second child. It was another daughter, whom she and Jamie named Margaret.

Elizabeth was still in France during the meeting, though was anxious to be back in England soon. She claimed she and Lizzie "thought it better to accept the offer in order to see if we can possibly exert a controlling [influence]." Four days after that first meeting, Elizabeth was back in London and having dinner with Sophia to commence planning.

Isabel was also in France during the meeting. Upon her return a few weeks later, she sought to discourage Sophia from the enormous step of founding an independent school. But as soon as she saw how much had already been accomplished in so little time, she changed her mind and happily agreed to start helping raise funds. James Stansfeld, the liberal member of parliament, served as honorary treasurer. Sophia and Isabel, as well as Dr. King Chambers and Arthur Norton of St. Mary's Hospital, were named the four trustees. Sophia, unofficially, also acted as organizing secretary.

The school's curriculum would cover four areas: the study of healthy function, the study of disease, the machinery for investigation or cure, and the art of healing. Anatomy taught the structure of a human body, chemistry its organic and inorganic elemental makeup, physiology its structure at work. Learning the processes of disease would hopefully mean spending as much time as possible in hospital wards, outpatient clinics, and post-mortem examinations, in addition to lectures on surgery and pathology. Students should search the wards for cases illustrating each disease covered in their lectures and make observations, so as to fully understand them.

The early years of hospital training were often the most difficult part of med school. Students may not understand or follow everything they're hearing at first, but anything they could glean there would help make their lectures and readings infinitely more vivid. To aid in overcoming this learning curve, students shouldn't wait until the end of their three years of classroom studies to begin clinical studies.

During their third year, students should master the tools of the trade, or the "machinery": stethoscope, thermometer, ophthalmoscope, laryngoscope, and sphygmograph. Nearly all of these tools had only recently been invented, most around the mid-1850s, revolutionizing the process of diagnosis.

Most of these tools remain in use today in streamlined forms. The sphygmograph was a precursor to the blood pressure cuff. Strapped to the wrist, it was a system of levers attached to a scale pan upon which weights were placed to estimate the pressure required to stop the radial artery's blood flow. It was one of the first noninvasive tools to assess blood pressure and was redesigned in 1863 to be portable.

These tools should be practiced on healthy people before students attempted to use them in diagnosing or treating sick people, Lizzie asserted; it would waste students' time and risk injury to the patient not to abide by this rule. Students should practice on each other. Also included in the machinery category were the microscope, gynecological and operative midwifery instruments, surgical appliances and dressings, electrical therapies, and medications. The fourth year, students would focus on applying what they'd learned. This was an incredibly thorough education plan, but to achieve it, they would first need to find a hospital where students could train.

Sophia and Lizzie were now seeing a lot of each other, but

that didn't mean they were getting along. "Friendship was out of the question; co-operation uneasy," Lizzie's daughter later said.

Thoughtful, tactful, and diligent, Isabel unofficially acted as intermediary between Sophia and Lizzie. She admired and got along well with both women, so she helped talk them down when tensions got high. Now a month away from her fortieth birthday, Isabel was two years older than Lizzie and six years older than Sophia. She'd also raised two children who were now teenagers, and her other two kids were now school-age. (Her son Atwood and her daughter May would both become surgeons.)

Arthur Norton, like Anstie, had become friends with Sophia after she rose to fame in Edinburgh. He was also a consultant at Lizzie's hospital. Both Norton and Elizabeth commented on how it was Sophia's great energy that propelled the school's rapid establishment.

"I have just been saying that no one but you could have done all that work," Agnes gushed to Sophia. "But indeed there is almost nothing that you don't do better than everyone else."

Sophia brimmed with optimism at a time when, with such slender funds, none whatsoever should have existed. Thirteen people had each donated £100, among them were Sophia and her mother, and Isabel, her husband, and her brother-in-law. Lucy Sewall donated £10. This initial amount would cover a property lease. The councillors emptied their pockets to scrape together what they needed to cover the rest of the expenses.

When fellow boat-rocker Mary Putnam Jacobi heard about the progress Sophia had made in setting up a school, she wrote jealously from America: "You have fortunately been able to interest a much larger and better class of people than have ever bestirred themselves in the matter here. You at least have had the advantage attaching to a conspicuous battle with real and dignified forces engaged on each side; whereas here, this question, as so many others, has rather dribbled into the sand."

Mary, who'd recently married trailblazing pediatrician Abra-

ham Jacobi, had been trying to drum up interest in her new organization, the Association for the Advancement of the Medical
Education of Women. The women's medical schools in America
were graduating plenty of lady doctors, but prejudice was still slow
to dissipate. No woman had yet been allowed into the American
Medical Association, and few established universities admitted
women. Mary grew weary of the constant flow of sexist pushback
she encountered. Her frustration was palpable when she wrote:
"The continually renewed discussion concerning the sphere, capacities, rights, functions, duties, and allowable occupations of
women seems rather ridiculous. We may justly ask why women
require so much more discussion than men; the argument is largely
superfluous, and the sermon often impertinent."

A few days before the opening of the London School of Medicine for Women, Elizabeth told Barbara she was very busy in
the delicate work of reorganizing the school plans and securing
proper safeguards against the "headlong energies of its most active member." Elizabeth complained that she'd shouldered this
work of Sophia-proofing the school on her own, since Lizzie
was so busy. "We shall always have a bit of trouble with Miss
J.B. but things look rather promising for getting sufficient controlling force to keep her cleverness and energy in their proper
place. But all are working harmoniously," Elizabeth assured.

Lizzie proposed that she should be the Diseases of Women
(gynecology) chair at Sophia's school, but Sophia said no. Men
should occupy the chairs at first to seal the school's reputation,
she explained. That would have been a reasonable response, except that Sophia then turned around and asked Elizabeth to be
chair of Hygiene. Elizabeth should have jumped at the chance,
given it was her favorite subject, but she felt she must decline
out of solidarity with Lizzie.

Sophia allowed Lizzie to be lecturer of Midwifery. A few
months later, Elizabeth was named chair of Diseases of Women,
"chiefly because we did not wish that specialty to fall into the

hands of men and it seemed it rested with me to rescue," Elizabeth explained to Barbara. Of the thirteen original lecturers, all but Lizzie were recognized by the Colleges of Physicians and Surgeons. This prestige was an important point in establishing the school's reputation.

But involvement with the school proved to be a challenge for some of the men who received scorn from their day jobs.

One of the school council members, Dr. William Broadbent, said there was quite an uproar among the committee members at his hospital, St. Mary's: "We had a grand battle on the question of the connection of some of our lecturers with the medical school for women. The majority of the Committee were against the ladies medical school, and we were asked to reconsider our connection with it."

Broadbent himself wasn't slated to be a lecturer, but Norton, King Chambers, Walter Butler Cheadle, and George Critchett, who all worked at St. Mary's, were. The committee at St. Mary's did not like so many of its physicians being associated with a women's institution. Critchett and Norton already served as consultants at Lizzie's hospital. Apparently being an occasional consultant to a women-run hospital was acceptable, but to be teaching at an institution aimed at creating more women doctors was a step too far.

Because of all this pressure, "much courage was required for a medical man to declare himself a friend of the movement," Isabel explained.

In all of this planning, the school was still without a physical location. They had nearly finished putting together their staff of lecturers before finding a place for the school to exist. In September, after an exhaustive search, Sophia finally found suitable premises: a "very old-fashioned house" in Brunswick Square.

The building had many spacious rooms on the ground floor, apartments reimagined as lecture halls tucked underneath a broad veranda. Upstairs was a series of rooms that Sophia said would do nicely as a museum, a library, and a reading room. Out front was a long walled garden of an unusually large size for the city center. The house was southeast of Marylebone; about two and a half miles from Lizzie's hospital.

This curious old house was "in a central position, within easy reach of museums and libraries, but retired from the roar and bustle of noisy thoroughfares, a range of spacious rooms stretches along front towards a green sward of an old-fashioned garden," one newspaper reported. Perfect for deep concentration and rigorous studying.

On September 15, Sophia wrote excitedly in her diary that they had signed the lease and were officially in possession of 30 Henrietta Street. In her elation, she rigged up some beds and slept there that night. Her dream to open a school was at last becoming a reality—MD or no!

Less than a month later, on October 12, 1874, the London School of Medicine for Women opened, to little fanfare. Yet according to Isabel, it would become the "Mother School of all British Medical Women."

Elizabeth was already feeling flummoxed and terribly underappreciated by the time the planning finished and the schooling commenced. "I have been having an anxious and busy time about the College—all alone—for Mrs. Anderson only comes back tomorrow; and of course our 'active member' does not appreciate the really valuable service I render the college," Elizabeth sulked to Barbara on opening day.

Unfortunately, Anstie, who had been one of their biggest champions, didn't see the school's opening. He'd died tragically of blood poisoning in September. "Of all the people connected with the school at that time, he seemed the most vital and important," Lizzie's daughter lamented. He was only forty-one years old, and left behind a wife and three young children. He likely contracted the infection while conducting a postmortem, accidentally puncturing his finger. The postmortem was done to better understand a disease that was ravaging children at an orphanage. He was a well-beloved colleague and friend, and would be greatly missed.

Norton heroically took over as dean and would prove to be a tenacious replacement. The day after the opening, Norton wrote to fourteen examining bodies requesting the school be placed on the list of recognized medical institutions. All declined.

In the school prospectus advertisement, class fees were listed as £8 each; fees for the full three-year curriculum were £80 if paid in full. If paid in installments, the full fees were: £40 the first year, £30 the second year, £15 the third. Sophia was listed as a trustee. The inaugural class counted fourteen students, including Sophia, Isabel, Edith, Agnes, Annie Clark, and Lizzie's sister-in-law Mary from the Edinburgh gang.

Poor sweet Mary. She had been left a pregnant widow only a few months after her wedding, and then her baby died soon after birth. But here she was, pressing forward in her quest to become a doctor. In total, all but two students had attended classes in Edinburgh (some just auditing extramural courses). On Mondays, Wednesdays, and Fridays at 2:30 p.m., they all crowded into the little room at the left of the garden entrance for their chemistry class. The school's curriculum was beyond adequate: their zoology, mental pathology, and ophthalmic surgery courses were not offered by most medical schools as they weren't required by examining boards.

Though the school didn't have enough money to offer simultaneous lectures, it could provide a full course of instruction over three years. Now that the planning phase was over and the work of running the school had commenced, the provisional council handed over the reins to a governing body. Sitting on it were Charles Darwin, Professor Huxley, the Dowager Lady Stanley of Alderley, the Earl of Shaftesbury, and Lizzie's little sister Milly.

The London School of Medicine for Women was met with derision by much of the medical profession. An article in *The*

Lancet, published five days after the school opened, noted that none of its lecturers were "distinguished as teachers of the first rank." The author also expressed shock that the school was offering every medical course, since the point of women doctors was surely only to tend women's diseases: "The lady students must apply themselves to the study of the unpleasant and, for them, disgusting details of practical anatomy." Imagine!

"I know of nothing in medical education especially distasteful to female students," Lizzie once remarked. "Everyone expects to dislike dissecting, but as a matter of fact no one does—it is found to be extremely interesting."

The article concluded that Sophia's school, and women doctors in general, were headed for "annihilation," since "the sentiment of English men and of English matrons is decidedly opposed to the institution of medical women."

There was one tangible problem the article brought up: the school was not attached to a large hospital where students could perform their practical and clinical studies. Without a hospital, the school would not be recognized by the examining bodies. Try as they might, no local hospital would open their door to female students. Lizzie's hospital was ready and willing, but only had twenty-six beds, not the minimum requirement of one hundred. Negotiations with the London Hospital eventually broke down. The Royal Free Hospital flat out refused, despite currently having no other university association. Elizabeth and Lizzie continued to fret.

Lizzie knew that without hospital wards to learn in or an agreement with an examining institution, the school wouldn't survive for long. Such a public failure, and so early on, would be quite a blemish on her otherwise remarkable reputation. The school had three choices:

1. Establish a new hospital (requiring an initial outlay of £16,000 and an annual income of £5,000).

2. Move to a provincial town where hospital access could be
   secured.
3. Close.

They couldn't have another scenario where women students
spent time and money for an education that led to nothing. Lizzie
believed it would be unconscionable to invite new students until
they could guarantee a complete education that would qualify
them to sit for an MD exam.

Sophia got to work with her connections in Edinburgh. She
reached out to the small committee that had sprung up to help
the Seven gather petition signatures and execute public funding
appeals. They pressured the Royal Infirmary there to fully open
its wards to women. This meant that her school's students could
attend all of their classes in London, then head to Edinburgh to
gain all of the hospital practice required by the examining boards.
It wasn't the best solution, but a decent temporary fix that would
provide some reassurance for its students.

By the end of the summer session, there were twenty-three
students. At the school's first prize-giving ceremony, Sophia
thanked the members of the Edinburgh committee in the audience for their help in securing access to the infirmary there.
"With such friends and such help as we can boast, I doubt not
that the question of examination and registration would be
solved with equal success," she declared.

When it was Lizzie's turn to speak, she addressed the students.
She urged them not to despair at the examining boards' refusal
to admit them, and assured them that they could have a successful practice if they applied themselves diligently and made
themselves competent practitioners.

First prizes in Anatomy, Physiology, and Chemistry were all
awarded to Edith Shove, clearly a standout student. In subsequent session exams, she earned the highest marks in Compara-
tive Anatomy, Botany, Surgery, Forensic Medicine, Ophthalmic
Surgery, and Pathology. The ceremony was covered the next

day in *The Times, Morning Post, Morning Advertiser, Standard, Telegraph, The Hour,* and the *Daily News.*

At the start of the school's second year, five new students appeared. Classes were given in anatomy, physiology, and practice of medicine. But things were looking bleak once again. They were no closer to providing the necessary local clinical training than when the school opened, and students started leaving. The school's closure felt imminent.

A delegation from the London school went off to plead with the government to intervene on their behalf. Into the Duke of Richmond's office crowded Lizzie, Sophia, Norton, Stansfeld, King Chambers, and Lord Aberdare. Lizzie pointed out that they were not asking for special privileges, only for the removal of the special obstructions that had been strategically placed in their path. Their plea was ignored, and it was decided that the school would have to close after the next winter session.

The government did do one thing, however—it called upon the General Medical Council to consider the topic of female practitioners carving a path to registration at its next meeting in June 1875. And so, roughly twenty men spent half of the meeting's allotted six days debating the "woman question." Here again, we find some of the enemies of the Edinburgh Seven in a position to make decisions about the existence of women doctors: Dr. Andrew Wood and Professor Turner.

"No amount of special pleading or ingenious argument can break down the physiological barrier which separates the two sexes from each other," Turner railed in the meeting. "The physical framework of a woman is inferior in its capacity and power." Women's smaller brains implied "a smaller capacity for concentration of thought, for intellectual capacity, and for prolonged exertion, either mental or bodily," he reasoned. Further, "the preponderance of the emotional qualities in woman's nature ill adapts her for the performance of the profession of medicine."

A fellow council member reminded Turner that the brain-to-body size ratio is the same in women as it is in men. One witty observer later noted that "according to Turner's reasoning the best students of medicine would be elephants and whales!"

Dr. Wood explained he had long opposed women in medicine and received a considerable amount of flak for it. He had seconded the motion to bar Sophia and the other women from attending the University of Edinburgh back in October 1869. When the warmhearted Sir James Simpson introduced them, Sophia says she "asked Dr. Wood to favour me with five minutes' conversation, to which his reply was that he would rather not, and turned on his heel."

Wood agreed with Turner about women's physical inferiority: "Fancy a woman called to reduce the dislocation of a hip-joint! Could a woman do that?" Wood reckoned he was actually doing these poor women a favor by endeavoring to ensure they could never practice medicine: "I am the most honest friend of these women, when I say to them: 'Do not enter a profession which I know is not suited to you.' I think we have had a little experience in Edinburgh as to the evil that happens from leading women into a wrong position. Some of our professors led these women upon the ice."

He also claims that if people knew what medicine entailed, they would not be calling for women to participate. "They do not know all the repulsiveness of the dissecting-room. They do not know the bloody scenes of the operation-room." His diatribe continued at length, describing a woman's sphere—why, "she has the bearing and suckling of children" in her domain!—and whining about why women chose *his* profession to force their way into first instead of law or clergy.

Dr. Humphry chimed in to remind the group that the question under consideration is not whether women should be encouraged to study medicine, but whether they should be excluded from it. Thankfully, Christison had retired from the council two years prior. It's a pity no one chimed in to suggest that perhaps these men had no idea what it was like to be a sick woman dealing with rough, dismissive male doctors.

The council's final decision was to officially adopt the opinion that though the study and practice of medicine presented special difficulties to women, they were not prepared to say women ought to be excluded from the profession. They recommended that men and women should take the same medical registry licensing exams. If examining bodies refused to accept women candidates, a separate qualification of "licensed practitioners of medicine" would be created for them. Despite all the sexist grumbling at the meetings, this ruling was an incredible victory.

That same month, Sophia, Isabel, and Edith attempted another path to the medical register. They applied to the Royal College of Surgeons of England to take the exam for a license in midwifery. Surely women wouldn't be barred from a *midwifery* exam. While none of the women were specifically interested in practicing midwifery, a license was a license and would get them on the medical register. The midwifery licensing requirements had been crafted with men in mind, so no one could argue the credentials inferior. Sophia said any existing exam was better than a new, specially created one.

Shocked and confused, the Royal College of Surgeons's board consulted their lawyers, who explained that they had no legal grounds for refusing the ladies' applications. In fact, the class and clinical work the trio managed to complete in Edinburgh far exceeded the college's licensure requirements. The women devoted the first two months of the new year to excitedly studying for the exam.

After so many years, this one little opening felt like a massive victory. Sophia celebrated her thirty-sixth birthday while studying for this exam. Feeling hopeful, she said, "It seems as if this year was really to gain what I have been fighting for in England for 7 years: Registration."

Their examiners, meanwhile, were busy seeking counsel from

their colleagues at the Obstetrical Society. Resist any and all attempts by women to take over your profession, the society men urged. A few days before the exam, the college made a public announcement. They had accepted the women's applications, but the entire board of examiners would be resigning. They would all rather quit than administer an exam to women. And in midwifery no less!

"The council calls upon the board to aid in placing on the medical register 'persons' possessing only fragmentary medical skill," declared Robert Barnes, the third and final examiner to quit. "Feeling deeply the danger of making women and children the subjects of inferior medical skill, I cannot reconcile it to my sense of right to assist [this]. With extreme regret, but without hesitation, I resign the office of examiner."

This was yet another extreme, knee-jerk reaction from these medical men. Their tantrums knew no bounds. And this time, the tantrum would have long-reaching consequences. When no one stepped forward to take their spots on the board, a license in midwifery became unattainable in Britain—by anyone—for many years. Sophia and the others were crushed at yet another opportunity to prove themselves taken away so unexpectedly.

Poor Lizzie was privately dealing with her own heartbreak. Her second child, the beautiful Margaret, fell gravely ill in October at thirteen months old. Drowsy and listless, the infant's fever had not abated after a few days. "She is now very ill poor pet," Lizzie wrote in a panic to Jamie, who was in Glasgow minding his shipyard. "It is hard work physically carrying her about and pacing the room hour after hour."

Jamie's brother Ford floated the idea that she was suffering from meningitis, but Lizzie saw no evidence for this claim. Two eminent physicians could offer nothing but a grim prognosis. Ford snuck up to the nursery, crouched down over Margaret's cot, and brushed his finger along her forehead in the shape of a sickle. He waited and watched for the telltale white track that followed, a sure sign of meningitis. Lizzie quietly crept up the stairs behind him. At once recognizing what he was doing, she erupted in tears and unleashed a deluge of angry words upon him. Meningitis meant death, and she couldn't face that.

At dawn on December 15, Margaret died, her tiny head resting softly against her father's cheek. For months, little Louisa toddled all around the house in a fruitless search for "Babee? Babee?" The loss of a child casts a shadow across a parent's heart, creating an area where the light will never fully return. For a doctor not to be able to save their ill child was an especially crushing experience, riddled with guilt and shame.

Lizzie apologized to Ford on the day of the burial. "You were right and I was wrong." Lizzie busied herself with the work of keeping her hospital afloat and stepped back from being quite so involved in the school.

Despite all the obstacles they faced, Elizabeth never lost hope in the school. She began conferring with her old friend Russell Gurney, whose wife Emelia had been head of her London committee back in 1859. Help was needed if she was going to form a group that could introduce an act to parliament decreeing that there was "nothing in any charter of University or Examining Board, shall prevent the examination of women simply on the ground of sex."

Gurney reintroduced his Enabling Bill in May 1876, which would give examining bodies permission to admit women to their exams. This resulted in a few months of debates in parliament. It was reported that during discussions in the House of Commons, Dr. Ward drew such a ghastly picture of the practice of medicine that "it would really seem better we all died, 'like gentlemen,' without any leech to look after us, than that we should subject any unhappy class of beings to a course of education so dangerous."

Incredibly, by August, the bill was signed into law. Now, all nineteen British examination boards could admit any qualified applicant to their exams, regardless of gender, if they chose to do so. It was an unequivocal triumph for the women.

Sophia knew they'd have no luck with the board at the University of London, at least, not yet, and that they'd exhausted all traces of goodwill in Scotland. They would head to Ireland. The two star students, Edith Pechey and Edith Shove, went straightaway with hopes of convincing the Royal College of Physicians of Ireland to allow students from their London school to take advantage of this new law. They agreed—they would be allowed to sit for the MD exam. Another triumph!

Finally, Sophia's little London school achieved one of the two key ingredients it needed to survive. Most exciting of all was that Sophia could finally take the MD exam herself.

"Miss Pechey has done wonders. I cannot realize that an examining body is absolutely open to us," Isabel bubbled to Sophia. "You have been the main-spring of the seven years' struggle, and to you we are all deeply indebted for the result."

Three women had enough training and classes under their belt to attempt the Dublin exam right away: Sophia, Edith, and Annie. Isabel was also qualified, but she had to stay home with her children. To brush up before the exam, they spent two months visiting hospitals and attending lectures in Bern, Switzerland. The trio even took the Bern MD exam. Sophia's thesis tackled childbed fever because she'd encountered an outbreak during her time in Boston. But the stress of it all activated Sophia's neuralgia and she had terrible trouble sleeping.

That winter, their London school held classes in pathology, demonstrations in anatomy, and practice of medicine. Stansfeld interrupted Sophia's revisions with updates from London. He kept her apprised of his attempts to secure a hospital affiliation in London for their school in his capacity as honorary treasurer.

"I met Mrs Garrett Anderson at dinner the other day; she did not seem to have much hope or plan about the School in any way," Stansfeld wrote to Sophia dejectedly. "I very much wish you were here." Another letter from a friend urged her not to hurry taking the MD exam, because if she failed, her enemies would never let her hear the end of it.

Not the words of encouragement she'd hoped for: "Are they all in league to shake my nerves?" Sophia demanded. This was essentially a test run. If she failed the Bern exam, she could still take the Dublin one. But she might have lost her courage to try again if she failed the first time. "How very happy or very wretched I shall be this time tomorrow!" she wrote in her diary on January 9, 1877, the day before the exam.

Soon it was all over: she had passed! "Now to see how much better an M.D. sleeps than other people!" Sophia cried. Edith and Annie passed it a few weeks later. They were doctors at long last. But to get on the British medical register, they would need to pass *another* MD exam in Dublin.

It was around this time that Stansfeld had a chance meeting with the chairman of the Royal Free Hospital's board while they were both on vacation. He promised to consider an association with the London school, though he did not appear to be in awe of the staff. Stansfeld set to work talking up the school.

Stansfeld wrote to Sophia once again, who was now home with her ailing mother in Brighton, to tell her the good news: London's Royal Free Hospital had unanimously accepted his proposal for clinical instruction. The college would have to pay them 300 guineas a year to compensate for the potential losses brought about by the relationship to a women's institute, and give them all student fees paid for clinical instruction, promising it would amount to no less than £700 per year. The hospital chairman's wife felt such a deep interest in the success of the movement that she donated £100.

At long last, the London school could provide a fully realized degree program offering clinical training at a local hospital. British women could achieve an MD in their own country.

Lizzie was convalescing after the birth of her third child—a boy they named Alan, who had "his father's nose exactly"—when she heard Stansfeld's good news. "As I was not able to join in the cheer which I am glad to hear was given for you at the School on Saturday, will you please accept my very heartiest thanks for your grand success," Lizzie wrote to Stansfeld. "We all owe more to you than to anyone. I shall hope to be able to contribute £50 a year as my share."

She must've been feeling flush since a week before giving birth, she'd arranged a charity concert by renowned German pianist and composer Clara Schumann. The event raised £600 for Lizzie's hospital, which had recently moved into a former army barracks on Gray's Inn Road. She'd personally sold £400 worth of tickets.

In May, Edith and Sophia went to Dublin to take the MD exam after a brief stint studying at the Brompton Hospital in London. Louisa Atkins soon joined them. "The various tests loom vague and large," Sophia mused in her diary. "Diagnosis at bedside, horrible, though enormously helped by Brompton experience. Recognition of drugs and things under microscope. Four written exams. Two hours oral [recitation]."

Frances Morgan and Eliza Walker Dunbar had passed the Dublin exam three months before, yet they were still defending their abilities. After news of their exam results spread, a letter in the *Standard* newspaper declared the Irish college had used a modified exam for women. Frances wrote a letter to the editor refuting the assertion.

"As one of the only two women who have as yet taken advantage of the liberality of the Irish College of Physicians and obtained their license, I beg to say that in my experience, not only was the examination not less stringent than that undergone by men, but that I had to undergo two examinations—one clinical, the other by written papers—from which, had I been a man, my six years' practice in the profession would have exempted me," Frances railed. "It is exactly the opposite of what has been stated. I had the same written papers, and the clinical and *viva voce* examinations were conducted at the same time and in the same room with the male candidates."

As for Sophia, Edith, and Louisa, all three of them passed the Dublin exam. A triumph! They could now practice medicine in the UK. In 1877, for the first time in twelve years, women's names were added to the British medical register. The number of legally practicing women doctors in Britain had more than tripled: Lizzie and Elizabeth were now joined by five other women.

Now that she held an MD, Sophia could be publicly associated with her school. She likely expected to be allowed to play a much bigger role in its administration. Maybe she could even hold one of the professorships! Surely she could now officially, publicly hold the position of honorary secretary. As far as most people knew, her name had only ever been associated with the school as a trustee.

Sophia returned from Dublin on cloud nine, only to be brought back down to earth with a thud. While she was in Ireland, her school's governing body had taken steps to wrest all control out of her hands. They'd taken it upon themselves to appoint an official honorary secretary, the role Sophia had been performing in an unofficial capacity. (They also decided that a clerical secretary would be hired to allow the honorary secretary to focus on larger administrative concerns.) Isabel nominated Sophia. Someone else put forth Lizzie. Both nominations were seconded.

Stansfeld admired Sophia—why, she "made the greatest of all contributions to the end attained," he asserted—but he backed Lizzie because he recognized the school's transition to relative stability meant they now needed a diplomatic representative, not a fearless fighter. The organizing secretary would need "the tact and judgement," Stansfeld reasoned, "to enable the working of the school and its students to go on smoothly with the hospital." Their agreement with the hospital was still in a provisional stage and he didn't want to jeopardize it in any way.

Lizzie wondered aloud why they needed anyone in this post, and whether they should at least wait until Sophia was present before voting. She told them this put her in an incredibly difficult position—slated to replace the founder and organizer of this school. Lizzie knew her character was more suited for the post but also knew how badly Sophia wanted it and how angry she would be to come home and find Lizzie had stolen her place at the table.

Honestly, Lizzie didn't even really want the job. She was too busy with her hospital work and young family. The vote was postponed until the following meeting. Sophia had returned. She and King Chambers urged Isabel as the best candidate for the post. Isabel was happy to take up the challenge, especially if it meant keeping the peace, but it meant the end of her studies toward an MD. Lucy Sewall once declared that of all the Edinburgh students, Isabel would make the best doctor. Now that her children were older, she had hoped to restart her medical school training, but the job of honorary secretary would not leave enough time for her to do both.

"About the best possible [choice], with her excellent sense and perfect temper," Sophia wrote in her diary of Isabel taking up her post officially. "So much better than I."

Now they faced a new problem—the school had run out of money. The £1,219 in students' fees and £1,903 in donations had all been spent on teaching and maintenance, so no classes could be held that summer. That didn't bode well for the school's longevity.

Lizzie must have had more hope in the school's success than she let on, because she spent part of her summer holiday crafting an index of named diseases that would be printed as a pocket book for the students to carry with them. Like a morbid game of bingo, students could make their way through the list by marking off diseases in the Seen column. At the time, the College of Physicians defined 1,146 known diseases.

"It is no exaggeration to say that a well-educated student ought to know the nature and bearing of every one of these," Lizzie told the students. "The list I have drawn up does not profess to include these 1,146 conditions. If it had, it would have been too bulky for a real pocket book. It includes almost everything you will find on the medical wards, and a small but important part of what you will see in the surgical wards."

The school's executive council set out to raise £5,000. Their fundraising kicked off at a lavish event at St. George's Hall featuring Sophia, Lizzie, King Chambers, Lady Anna Gore Langton, and MP W. Cowper Temple as speakers. Sophia donated another £52, her mother gave £105. Lizzie and Jamie threw in £250. Enough money was amassed within a few months to keep the school afloat.

Even more exciting was the University of London agreeing to admit women to its MD examination. This meant the students of the women's school would no longer have to travel to Ireland. This was just in time for the inaugural class of thirty-four students to finish their three years of theoretical study.

It was with a newfound sense of security and hope that the school reopened for the fall term in October. Lizzie was teaching practice of medicine, and Edith and Sophia were named honorary professors of hygiene. Joining the faculty were Ford Anderson and Louisa Atkins teaching midwifery and diseases of women. Now that the school's path to success was no longer murky, Lizzie began to take a renewed interest in the institution.

In notes written in preparation for a speech to deliver to students, Lizzie explains how her own experience uniquely situated her to help other young women find their vocation. Her handwriting on these notes is wider, looser, larger than the letters she penned as a younger woman.

"I was then a young woman living at home with nothing to do, in what authors call 'comfortable circumstances.' I was full of energy, vigor, and of the discontent that goes with unemployed activities. The memory of those days has often helped me [in] my dealings with other discontented young women. I have been able to say to them with sincerity 'my dear, take heart. The world is not such a bad place after all once you find work. When I was your age everything seemed wrong to me. But from the moment I got into steady work, the sky cleared, and it has been clear ever since.'"

These major wins Lizzie, Elizabeth, and Sophia accomplished together had created a clear path forward for women wanting to pursue medicine. There were blue skies indeed.

NINETEEN

On to Separate Paths

Sophia never fully recovered from the pain she felt at being ousted from her own school. That the administrators of her own school—the culmination of her life's work, her long-cherished dream realized—tried to push her out so coolly was almost beyond belief. It hurt more than she allowed herself to admit. Her dear ally Edith was not there to comfort her; she'd left to establish a private practice in Leeds.

So in 1878, for the second time in her life, Sophia left her life in London and moved to Edinburgh in hopes of leaving her heartbreak behind. Before departing, she went out of her way to avoid seeing Lizzie. Sophia remained on the school's governing body, but was no longer an active participant. Isabel was upset that she would choose the easy way out by leaving, instead of staying to fight for her school.

Instead, Sophia decided to open her own private practice in Edinburgh. When she hung the brass plate on her house announcing her services, she became Scotland's first and only woman doctor. Welcoming her back to Scotland were her old friends Agnes and Helen. Agnes's MD was nearly complete, but poor Helen was busy raising three young children alone because her *Scotsman* editor husband Alexander had died suddenly of a heart attack two years prior. Their former mentors Watson and Balfour were excited to help Sophia build professional relationships and develop her practice.

Notoriety both helped and hindered Sophia's success. Her practice grew slowly but steadily. As a lady, driving her own small carriage and eschewing most social invitations to concentrate on work made her appear odd, eccentric. Friends urged her to attend regular religious services as a way to become more accepted by the community. Unlike Lizzie, she had no interest in buttering up the city's wealthy ladies. Sophia was known to pointedly look at her watch and walk over to the door whenever she realized one of the upper-class women who'd come to consult her was not actually ill but bored.

Those who did become her patients, mostly working-class women, were enthralled with her. "What a comfort it is to see your dear supporting face," one patient exclaimed to her.

After Sophia responded to an emergency call in March 1878, her patient proclaimed, "It was like being lifted on a comet's tail when you came in, strong and swift, with your eagle wings, getting over distances in a third of the time other people take to do it."

Sophia sounds like a veritable superhero. To hear the way women patients spoke about their women doctors is an incredible contrast to the way stodgy medical men depicted them.

Soon, business was booming enough for Sophia to open a dispensary for the very poor, just as Elizabeth and Lizzie had done. "I know you will be pleased to hear that I yesterday received fees which just completed my first £50—earned in less than three months," she wrote to her mother. "I don't think there is much doubt about the 'demand' or my prospects."

Twenty-three patients had made nearly one hundred visits at her private practice. In its first two weeks, her dispensary treated many more. She may not have been the head of a school, but she was a successful, practicing physician. "What pleases me still better is that every one of my patients has done well," Sophia boasted. "Several have left my hands practically recovered. And as among them were two cases to which I was called when the patient was described as 'dying' (and both got well) I think I may very well be content."

The one secular pleasure she allowed herself was occasional theatergoing. When actor Henry Irving came to town, she attended three shows a week with her friends. To Sophia, Irving's portrayal of despotic French king Louis XI was masterful. Irving would soon become the inspiration for the character Count Dracula.

Her maid, Alice, had retired, but Sophia now employed a bevy of other servants: a cook, a housemaid, and a coachman, who was often left to garden while Sophia drove herself. After thirteen years together, her most loyal companion passed away: her precious dog, Turk, died in her arms. But the worst was still to come. Her mother died in 1881 of complications related to a kidney stone. Next, a young woman who'd been working as Sophia's assistant at the dispensary died suddenly. Rumors swirled that it was regular exposure to ether at work that was to blame. Sophia worried she'd worked the poor girl too hard.

All those losses and all so close together; it was all too much. Sophia's friends swooped in to help her close up her practice and find workers to replace her at the dispensary. Her old friend Ursula du Pre whisked her to the country to grieve and recuperate. It would be almost two years of near seclusion and depressive episodes before she fully returned to a normal professional routine.

Sophia eventually resumed private practice in Edinburgh at a lodge she rented from friends. Patients were less and less squeamish about consulting her. Soon, she expanded her dispensary to include inpatient beds: the Edinburgh Hospital and Dispensary for Women was born. An alumna of the London school, Dr. Catherine Urquhart, became the hospital's first resident medical officer.

Sophia delivered a series of health lectures to a women-only audience. The organizers wanted to charge a shilling, but Sophia insisted the lectures be free. "My lecture went off very well, the hall (which holds nearly two thousand) was crammed to the doors and stairways, and I lectured from slight notes, much better, Ursula says, than if I had read a lecture," she told a friend. "I have already had four new patients in consequence."

After the Royal College of Physicians and Surgeons of Edinburgh and of Glasgow announced they would permit women to take exams in medicine and surgery, it inspired a new generation of women to apply to the University of Edinburgh. But when they encountered the same old problems the Edinburgh Seven had, they went to Sophia for help. Here she was again, negotiating with professors to allow women students in their class, assuring them the fees would be covered. Eight women would join the school as students this time.

One of them was Margaret Todd, a shy, book-smart lady of twenty-seven with curly hair and thin lips. She'd left her job as a teacher in Glasgow to pursue medical studies. She didn't have any family in Edinburgh, so Sophia invited Margaret to live with her. The pair soon struck up a close friendship that would eventually grow into romance, in spite of their nineteen-year age difference.

In the winter term of 1886-87, the new women students at Edinburgh attended separate lectures at one of the men's schools, but according to Margaret, "it soon became obvious that separate premises, in which students could study and dissect, and change their dress, and generally make themselves at home, were, if not absolutely necessary, at least highly desirable."

Sophia thought of the nearby property she and a few of her

friends had purchased back in 1876, that still sat vacant. It would make a perfect study space. Now in disrepair, this Surgeon Square building was the former site of an infamous medical school where Professor Robert Knox had lectured students using frighteningly fresh cadavers "sourced" by killers Burke and Hare.

But why give Edinburgh's students access to their property? Why not build her own school? With the help of a newly formed executive committee, which included Agnes, Helen, Ursula, and doctors Balfour and Watson, Sophia established the Edinburgh School of Medicine for Women. She named herself dean.

Edith was working in India by now, so she couldn't be involved in this new venture. Isabel heartily disapproved of Sophia opening yet another school instead of toughing it out and claiming what she'd started in London. She surely felt abandoned.

Sophia guided tradesmen in the careful restoration of the building's lecture rooms and laboratories. Now, sunlight cascaded into the school's spacious dissecting room from the long rows of roof windows. The many vast zinc tables would soon hold lifeless bodies sheathed in fabric. The walls were lined in anatomical drawings, a skeleton hung from a bracket. The students' sitting room was cramped, but cozy: a warm fireplace, walls filled with bookshelves and pictures, a pretty lamp. In the evenings, deep red curtains were pulled across the windows, shutting out the view of the city's chimneys and roofs.

Arranging clinical training was a breeze. Leith Hospital was now large enough to host medical students, was fully recognized by the Royal Colleges, and felt such a school association would be to its benefit. The Edinburgh school's first class consisted of eight students; over the course of its twelve years in operation, thirty-three women achieved their degrees at Sophia's school and a total of eighty students received at least part of their education there.

Trouble soon found Sophia, when a few of her students grew angry about her treatment of another student. That student had failed an exam, but gone back to the examiners and appealed, saying she'd been unwell at the time of the test. She was granted a pass. Sophia did not like women seeking such special treatment, and she made these feelings known to this student. The other students thought she was being too harsh, and they mounted a rebellion. After the two main antagonizers—the Cadell sisters, Ina and Grace—were expelled, they promptly sued the school.

Outraged by the expulsions, Elsie Inglis, one of Sophia's brightest students, decided to establish a rival institution, the Medical College for Women. Other students were convinced to defect, and the Cadells also joined them. Sophia's school couldn't compete and soon folded.

Now, it's Elsie who's remembered in Edinburgh: a display celebrating her in the Surgeons' Hall Museum, a building and a quadrangle named after her at the University of Edinburgh, a plaque at the city's central library, a maternity hospital bearing her name. Yes, her legacy as suffragist surgeon, war doctor in Serbia, and founder of the Scottish Women's Hospitals for Foreign Service is deservingly laudable, but to walk the city and find so many traces of her and virtually none of Sophia is disheartening. The newspapers of her day may have loved Sophia for the copy she prompted, but once her newsworthy exploits faded, so did their interest in her.

Well-behaved women rarely make history, so the platitude goes. The truth is that history favors noteworthy ladies who most closely adhere to societal ideals of womanhood. A more accurate, if less bumper-stickerable, sentiment comes from prolific eighteenth-century translator and Biblical scholar Elizabeth Smith: "A woman must have uncommon sweetness of disposition and manners to be forgiven for possessing superior talents."

Lizzie, for instance, offers a tidy little tale: a dainty, demure, dutiful wife and mother who didn't overly ripple the status quo when she waded through sexist antagonism to become a "first." She is easier to laud than Sophia, an outspoken, heavy-set lesbian who struggled with a short temper, coveted the driver's seat, and ruffled every feather she encountered. But flouting social norms doesn't negate your contributions. It just makes you human. Sophia did so much to further the cause that it's difficult to see her faults muddy her legacy, especially since so many men's legacies have never been besmirched by their terrible opinions or bad behavior.

"They might like her or dislike her, but she went on her way, doing her work absolutely without ostentation," Margaret later wrote of Sophia. "She was impulsive, she made mistakes. She held out at times about trifles—failed to see that they *were* trifles—and at times she terrified people more than she knew. Of her indeed it might be said that she heard the beat of a different drummer. But there was another side to the picture. Many of those who criticised details were yet forced to bow before the big transparent honesty, the fine unflinching consistency, of her life."

It took Margaret eight years to complete her degree, because she was also writing while studying. She published the novel *Mona Maclean, Medical Student* under the male pseudonym Graham Travers. The book illustrated the indispensability of women doctors. It sat among the broader trend of women authors beginning to use novels to convince the wider public that female physicians could be competent, professional healers (not just greedy, nefarious abortionists). Margaret would go on to write a total of six novels, a biography of Sophia, and several short stories. She also coined the term *isotope*.

After passing her MD exams in Brussels, she became Sophia's assistant physician at Edinburgh Hospital and Dispensary for Women and Children. The pair fell deeply in love while working so closely together. Sophia's school may have been failing, but her women's hospital was thriving.

"My life is full and complete again, if somewhat greyer for all the past pain," Sophia wrote in her diary.

Even though she'd found a fulfilling, devoted relationship, Sophia never forgot about Octavia, even following her career from afar with great interest. Some twenty years after their breakup, she wrote in her diary that she always maintained a "fanciful faithfulness" that even in this life their friendship might be rekindled.

In 1883, Norton announced his resignation from the London school, so Sophia and many other typically absent council members returned for the meeting where the next dean would be decided. Six members were normally present for meetings; this one included fifteen. Knowing that she would likely be put forth as a candidate for dean, Lizzie did not attend. Sophia and King Chambers suggested Edith also be put forward for consideration, but they couldn't gain enough support. Lizzie's nomination was approved fourteen to one.

Lizzie's first act as dean was to present the first two ladies who passed the London University MD exams to Lord Granville for their graduation. She invited her father as thanks for all of his help in getting her where she was today.

In 1896, Sophia finally quit the London school's governing board after disagreements over their plans to use funds to expand to larger premises. Three years later, she retired from her Edinburgh hospital. The institute moved into her lodge home, becoming the Bruntsfield Hospital, where it continued to serve the city's women patients for eighty years. After Sophia died in 1912, Margaret used Sophia's personal journals and papers to write her biography and then destroyed them, just as Sophia requested. Once the book was published, Margaret died by suicide.

Back in New York, Emily served as dean and professor of obstetrics and gynecology at the Woman's Medical College of the New York Infirmary for thirty years. She even eventually asked Elizabeth Cushier to move in with her. While women didn't need to be accepted at regular universities to legally practice medicine in America, they still wanted to be free to do so. Emily, Marie, Lucy, and Mary raised a $50,000 donation to Harvard University to establish a medical degree program for women there. (Harvard rejected the funds.) They also rallied women across the country to lobby each state's top medical schools to admit women. By the time the Woman's Medical College of the New York Infirmary closed in 1899, 364 women had earned their degrees there.

Elizabeth resigned from her position as professor of diseases of women at the London School of Medicine for Women at the end of the fall 1877 term, but remained on the school's governing body until 1899. Elizabeth and Kitty moved one final time, to a house overlooking the sea on the southeast coast of England in the tiny town of Hastings (where Sophia was born). Before long, her sisters Marian and Anna moved into town as well, so the three sisters could spend their final years together. When Elizabeth died on May 31, 1910, nearly 7,400 women had become licensed physicians and surgeons in the United States. Emily died a few months later.

"The work of Dr. Garrett Anderson and Dr. Sophia Jex Blake will always be remembered," Elizabeth fondly remarked. "It was my privilege and pleasure, in some small degree, to encourage these brave workers in their pioneer enterprise in England."

The London School of Medicine for Women enjoyed extended longevity. It was the only school in Great Britain offering a medical education to women until 1886. Lizzie was a lecturer for twenty-three years and served as dean until 1903. Attendance grew exponentially. In 1887, there were seventy-seven students. The institution expanded its premises again in 1914, when it could barely contain all three hundred of its students. By 1917, it boasted 441 students. In 1998, the school merged with University College Hospital Medical School to become the Royal Free and University College Medical School, which is still in operation.

Lizzie enjoyed a long, steady career working as a highly respected senior physician at her hospital for twenty-four years.

She also served as president of the East Anglian branch of the British Medical Association. Even after retiring, she still wasn't finished making firsts. She returned to her hometown of Aldeburgh, and in 1908, at age seventy-one, Lizzie became the first woman mayor in Britain. In 1918, the year after Lizzie died, the New Hospital for Women was renamed the Elizabeth Garrett Anderson Hospital.

Lizzie's daughter Louisa grew up to become an accomplished surgeon after attending the London School of Medicine for Women. She and fellow alum Flora Murray founded a hospital for women and children in a working-class London neighborhood. The pair also created a military hospital during World War I that paved the way for women to treat adult male patients.

Thanks to the London school, the UK eventually made strides toward catching up to the US in terms of its number of practicing women physicians. In 1881, there were only twenty-five women doctors registered in England and Wales; by 1911, there were 495.

Around the 1880s, physicians began to wear white lab coats. They were a sign of doctors' newfound "scientificness" and symbolized the cleanliness and purity that germ theory and asepsis had brought about. Medicine was now rooted in the laboratory and so its practitioners had to create a recognizable way to differentiate themselves from the old days of quacks, leeches, and stabs in the dark.

While it isn't clear whether or not these three women donned white coats during their careers, the younger two of them were still practicing when the switch came about, so it's very likely. One thing's for sure, they opened the door and ushered in a group of medical students who would be the first women in white coats.

EPILOGUE

A Lasting Legacy

The hard work of these trailblazing women was not in vain. How many lifesaving breakthroughs would never have been made had these Victorian ladies not stood up and said, *Women are just as capable as men*? How many pharmaceutical discoveries, treatment innovations, instrument inventions, medical tech, wouldn't exist had women not demanded their voices were just as valid, their brains just as bright?

The more women doctors there were, the more accepted they became by society, and the more society benefited from them. The women who trained at these first women's medical schools and hospitals fanned out and established their own clinics and hospitals across the globe, raising the bar for the healthcare received by women, especially poor women. Many also made significant contributions to medicine.

Janet Lane-Claypon, who entered the London School of Medicine for Women in 1898, helped found the discipline of epide-

OLIVIA CAMPBELL

miology, spearheading the use of cohort and case-control studies. After graduating from the LSMW, Eleanor Davies-Colley co-founded the South London Hospital for Women and Children and became the first woman member of the Fellowship of the Royal Colleges of Surgeons. Alum Lucy Wills discovered the protective effects of folic acid in pregnancy in the 1920s. Thanks to her, all pregnant women are still encouraged to take the supplement to prevent anemia and neural tube defects.

Lizzie's protégé Eliza Walker Dunbar established a hospital for women and children in Bristol, England, staffed entirely by women doctors. One of the original Edinburgh Seven, Matilda Chaplin, created a midwifery school in Tokyo. Gertrude Herzfeld, the first practicing woman surgeon in Scotland, worked at Sophia's Edinburgh hospital from 1920-1955. She became a leading authority on pediatric surgery, particularly neonatal procedures.

Mary Putnam Jacobi published nine books and over 120 scientific papers. Her research-filled essay proving women's vigor was unaffected by menstrual cycles helped women fight for better education. After serving as the New York Infirmary's sanitary visitor, Rebecca Cole returned to Philadelphia and opened a center where poor women and children could obtain medical and legal services. Mary Harris Thompson, who interned at the Blackwells' infirmary, founded the Chicago Hospital for Women and Children in 1865.

Three years after graduating from the Blackwells' college, Anna Wessels Williams isolated a strain of diphtheria bacillus to develop an antitoxin for the deadly malady. Alum Sara Josephine Baker became the first director of New York's Bureau of Child Hygiene in 1908. An innovator in public health, her work in improving child and maternal health in the city became a national model. Baker collected the specimens implicating "Typhoid Mary," the super-spreader cook who infected at least forty-eight people. She also designed a foolproof applicator for the medication given to newborns to prevent blindness.

Throughout the decades, women have continued to be the driving force behind medical advances of all kinds. If you've ever had chemotherapy, radiation treatment, open-heart surgery, fertility treatment, an X-ray, Pap smear, blood transfusion, Tdap vaccination, organ transplant, or been treated for diabetes, leukemia, malaria, herpes, gout, Alzheimer's disease, cerebral palsy, Parkinson's disease, or schizophrenia, then you've benefited from women in medical sciences.

Recent research shows women may actually be better doctors. They are more likely to follow clinical guidelines and provide preventive care than their male counterparts. Data from 1.5 million hospitalizations concluded that patients treated by women are significantly less likely to die or be readmitted. Patients operated on by female surgeons are also less likely to die. In 2017, for the first time ever in the US, there were more women medical students than men. What a glorious rebuke to all of those nasty Victorian naysayers who claimed women were entirely unfit to practice medicine.

In 1892, the University of Edinburgh finally began accepting women students. In 2019—the 150th anniversary of the Edinburgh Seven's matriculation at the University of Edinburgh—Sophia Jex-Blake, Isabel Thorne, Edith Pechey, Matilda Chaplin, Helen Evans, Mary Anderson Marshall, and Emily Bovell were finally, posthumously, awarded honorary degrees.

"I do not consider the time wasted," Isabel reflected on their Edinburgh attempt. "It seems to me that it is greatly due to the struggle in Edinburgh that it is now possible for women to obtain a fully qualifying medical education."

A world where only men are physicians seems almost unimaginable today. Were it not for these ambitious, tenacious, and incredibly persistent women, we might still be living in such a world. They could have easily given up their quest at any point and no one could've blamed them, but they never once wavered. We have these women to thank for the fact that today, when a little girl dreams of becoming a doctor, that dream can become a reality.

★ ★ ★ ★ ★

ACKNOWLEDGMENTS

It seems odd to claim that I alone created this book since so many people played a part in shaping it. First, I want to thank my amazing editor, Laura Brown at Park Row Books/Harper-Collins. Her thoughtful, comprehensive feedback helped ensure the story of these intrepid women became a compelling tale accessible to all readers. The entire team at Park Row, from the designers and copy editors to the legal, marketing, and publicity teams, have been instrumental in making this book something I'm incredibly proud to share with the world. I owe so much to my agent, Zoe Sandler at ICM Partners. I truly would not be where I am today without her. She's an amazing advocate and great friend. It's thanks to her comments and ideas on my book proposal that a marketable book idea was born. I'd also like to thank the editors who rejected early versions of my book proposal. Their considerate critique helped me hone the focus of the book into a tighter, more cohesive narrative, which subsequently interested several publishers.

To all of the staff at the archives I utilized in person—the

Women's Library Archives at the London School of Economics, the London Metropolitan Archives, the Centre for Research Collections at the Edinburgh University Library, and the Rare Book & Manuscript Library at Columbia University—and those I accessed online—the Schlesinger Library at Harvard University, the National Library of Medicine, and the Library of Congress—thank you for your tireless work of both keeping history alive and helping researchers quickly and easily access it.

I'm forever thankful to my husband and three sons for their constant, loving support of me and my work. To my grandfather, for dedicating his life to being an incredible doctor. To my parents, for always believing in me. To my siblings, for always keeping it real. To Louisa, for always championing my work. To Cindy, for always helping with the business side of this profession. To my friends, for always asking how the book is going. To my writing professors, for their passion and insight. To my antidepressant medication, for reigniting my interest and ability to write. And lastly, to my dearest lap cat, Rosie. I hope I managed to delete all of the random letters you added to the text when you walked all over my keyboard.

AUTHOR NOTE

This book is the product of many years of research. While digitization has made many important archival collections available remotely, not everything is online. I was lucky enough to be able to travel to the relevant archives across the US and UK in order to piece together a clear picture of these women. (Sophia was the most difficult to write about since she requested all of her private papers be destroyed upon her death.) Holding letters and notes handwritten by these women was truly electrifying and helped me feel connected to them and their lives. I hope I have done them justice.

There are many instances in this book where words or short sections of quotes have been removed. In every case, the condensations only aim to make the quotes more easily understood by a modern audience, and never to change the meaning or intent. I have largely forgone the use of ellipses so as not to distract the reader. There are only a small handful of instances when I quote handwritten text that included difficult-to-decipher words. No quoted words have been knowingly changed.

SELECT BIBLIOGRAPHY

Books:

Abram, Ruth J., ed. *Send Us a Lady Physician: Women Doctors in America, 1835-1920.* New York: W.W. Norton & Company, Inc., 1985.

Blackwell, Elizabeth. *Pioneer Work in Opening the Medical Profession to Women.* London, 1895.

Boyd, Julia. *The Excellent Doctor Blackwell: The Life of the First Woman Physician.* London: Thistle Publishing, 2013.

Brock, Claire. *British Women Surgeons and their Patients, 1860–1918.* New York: Cambridge University Press, 2017.

Ehrenreich, Barbara, and Deirdre English. *Witches, Midwives, & Nurses: A History of Women Healers.* 2nd ed. New York: The Feminist Press at CUNY, 2010.

Fitzharris, Lindsey. *The Butchering Art: Joseph Lister's Quest to Transform the Grisly World of Victorian Medicine.* New York: Scientific American / Farrar, Straus and Giroux, 2017.

Garrett Anderson, Louisa. *Elizabeth Garrett Anderson, 1836–1917*. London: Faber and Faber, 1939.

Hays, Elinor Rice. *Those Extraordinary Blackwells: The Story of a Journey to a Better World*. New York: Harcourt, Brace & Ward, Inc., 1967.

James, Edward T., Janet Wilson James, and Paul S. Boyer, eds. *Notable American Women, 1607-1950: A Biographical Dictionary, Volume 2*. Cambridge, MA: Harvard University Press, Radcliffe College, 1971.

Jex-Blake, Sophia. *Medical Women: Two Essays*. Edinburgh, 1872. (And Second Edition: *Medical Women: A Thesis and a History*, Edinburgh, 1886.)

Kang, Lydia, and Nate Pedersen. *Quackery: A Brief History of the Worst Ways to Cure Everything*. New York: Workman Publishing, 2017.

Manton, Jo. *Elizabeth Garrett Anderson*. New York: E. P. Dutton & Co., Inc., 1965.

Morantz-Sanchez, Regina. *Sympathy and Science: Women Physicians in American Medicine*. Chapel Hill, NC: University of North Carolina Press, 2000.

Roberts, Shirley. *Sophia Jex-Blake: A Woman Pioneer in Nineteenth-Century Medical Reform*. New York: Routledge, 1993.

Thorne, Isabel. *Sketch of the Foundation and Development of the London School of Medicine for Women*. London: G. Sharrow, 1905.

Todd, Margaret G. (Graham Travers, pseud.). *The Life of Sophia Jex-Blake*. London: Macmillan and Co., Limited, 1918.

Tuchman, Arleen. *Science Has No Sex: The Life of Marie Zakrzewska, M.D.* Chapel Hill, NC: University of North Carolina Press, 2006.

Zakrzewska, Marie Elizabeth. *A Woman's Quest: The Life of Marie E. Zakrzewska, M.D.* New York: D. Appleton and Company, 1924.

Manuscript Sources:

Bethesda, MD. National Library of Medicine (NLM).
   Elizabeth Blackwell Papers; New York Infirmary for Women and
   Children Records; Woman's Medical College of the New York
   Infirmary Records.

Cambridge, MA. Schlesinger Library, Harvard University Radcliffe
Institute for Advanced Study (HU).
   Blackwell Family Papers.
   http://schlesinger.radcliffe.harvard.edu/onlinecollections/blackwell.

Edinburgh. University of Edinburgh Library Centre for Research
Collections, Special Collections (UE).
   Edinburgh School of Medicine for Women Records; Isabel J. Thorne
   Diary; Sir Henry Littlejohn Lecture Notes; Sophia Jex-Blake Papers.

London. Women's Library Archives, London School of Economics (LSE).
   Autograph Letter Collection: Women in Medicine; Elizabeth Garrett
   Anderson Papers.

London. London Metropolitan Archives (LMA).
   Elizabeth Garrett Anderson Papers; London School of Medicine for
   Women: 1874-1998 Records; New Hospital for Women Records;
   Sophia Jex-Blake Papers; St. Mary's Dispensary for Women and
   Children Records.

New York. Rare Book & Manuscript Library, Columbia University (CU).
   Elinor Rice Hays papers; Elizabeth Blackwell Papers; Emily Blackwell
   Diary.

Washington, D.C. Library of Congress (LOC).
   Blackwell Family Papers.

NOTES ON SOURCES

Prologue: The Forgotten History of Healing

Women have delivered…: Elisabeth Brooke, *Women Healers: Portraits of Herb-alists, Physicians, and Midwives.* Rochester, VT: Healing Arts Press, 1995, pp. 6-9.

Agnodice…: Brooke, *Women Healers*, 11-12; Helen King, "Agnodike and The Profession of Medicine," *Proceedings of the Cambridge Philological Society*, New Series, No. 32 (212) (1986), pp. 53-77. JSTOR, www.jstor.org/stable/44696917.

A relative scarcity…: Mary E. Fissell, "Introduction: Women, Health, and Healing in Early Modern Europe," *Bulletin of the History of Medicine*, Vol. 82, No. 1, Special Issue: Women, Health, and Healing in Early Modern Europe, Spring 2008, pp. 1-17, www.jstor.org/stable/44448504.

As late as…: "A Pioneer of Modern Medical Women and Her Predecessors of the Middle Ages," *The Lancet*, January 18, 1908, pp. 173-174, https://doi.org/10.1016/S0140-6736(01)61655-6.

In medieval France…: Monica Green, "Women's Medical Practice and Health Care in Medieval Europe," *Signs*, Vol. 14, No. 2, Working Together in the Middle Ages: Perspectives on Women's Communities, Winter 1989, pp. 434-473, www.jstor.org/stable/3174557.

Nuns soon became…: John Augustine Zahm, *Woman in Science*, New York: D. Appleton and Company, 1913, pp. 274-281.

When medicine began…: Barbara Ehrenreich et al., *Witches, Midwives, & Nurses*, 53-54.

In 1390…: Leigh Whaley, *Women and the Practice of Medical Care in Early Modern Europe, 1400–1800*, London: Palgrave Macmillan, 2011.

In 1421…: Ehrenreich et al., *Witches, Midwives, & Nurses*, 55.

Between 1400 and…: Ehrenreich et al., *Witches, Midwives, & Nurses*, 14, 31-49.

Chapter 1: A Lady Doctor

Mary Donaldson…: Leo Trachtenberg, "New York's First 'Lady Doctor'," *City Journal*, Winter 2000, www.city-journal.org/html/new-york's-first—"lady-doctor"-11937.html.

Elizabeth was a…: Anna Blackwell, "Elizabeth Blackwell, M.D.," *The English Woman's Journal*, April 1, 1858, pp. 80-100, https://ncse.ac.uk/periodicals/ewj/issues/ewj_01041858.

He lovingly referred…: Anna Blackwell, "Elizabeth Blackwell, M.D.," *The English Woman's Journal*, April 1, 1858, p. 81, https://ncse.ac.uk/periodicals/ewj/issues/ewj_01041858.

The worst part…: Elizabeth Blackwell, *Pioneer Work*, chap. 2.

Heroic measures…: Robert B. Sullivan, "Sanguine Practices: A Historical and Historiographic Reconsideration of Heroic Therapy in the Age of Rush," *Bulletin of the History of Medicine*, Vol. 68, No. 2, Summer 1994, pp. 211-234, www.jstor.org/stable/44444366.

Hippocrates' theory…: "'And there's the humor of it,' Shakespeare and the Four Humors," National Library of Medicine exhibition, www.nlm.nih.gov/exhibition/shakespeare/fourhumors.html.

Infections were thought…: Cristie Columbus, "In a world with no antibiotics, how did doctors treat infections?" *The Conversation*, January 29, 2016, https://theconversation.com/in-a-world-with-no-antibiotics-how-did-doctors-treat-infections-53376.

Toxic metals...: Kang et al., *Quackery*, 3-14.

Around the 1840s...: Guenter B. Risse, "Calomel and the American Medical Sects during the Nineteenth Century," *Mayo Clinic Proceedings*, Vol. 48, January 1973, pp. 57–64.

Arsenic tinctures...: J. C. Saha, "A Review of Arsenic Poisoning and its Effects on Human Health," Environmental Protection Agency, March 2014, www.epa.gov/sites/production/files/2014-03/documents/a_review_of_arsenic_poisoning_and_its_effects_on_human_health_3v.pdf.

Another popular remedy...: Kang et al., *Quackery*, 20-21.

Diseases of the reproductive...: Ornella Moscucci, "Gender and Cancer in Britain, 1860–1910: The Emergence of Cancer as a Public Health Concern," *American Journal of Public Health*, August 2005, 95(8): 1312–1321, https://doi.org/10.2105/AJPH.2004.046458.

Among the many...: Shannon Selin, "Cancer Treatment in the 19th Century," https://shannonselin.com/2017/08/cancer-treatment-19th-century.

My friend died...: Blackwell, *Pioneer Work*, chap. 2.

Elizabeth dreamed of discovering...: Blackwell, *Pioneer Work*, chap. 2.

Once, as a young...: Anna Blackwell, "Elizabeth Blackwell, M.D."

Elizabeth's desire...: Boyd, *Excellent Doctor Blackwell*, 50.

Women were narrow-minded...: Elizabeth Blackwell to Emily Collins, August 12, 1848 in *History Of Woman Suffrage—Part 1, 1848-1861*, 2nd ed., eds. Elizabeth Cady Stanton, Susan B. Anthony, and Matilda Joslyn Gage, Rochester, 1899, pp. 90–91.

Her other neighbor...: Blackwell, *Pioneer Work*, chap. 2.

I was severing...: Blackwell, *Pioneer Work*, chap. 2.

Her religious upbringing...: Blackwell, *Pioneer Work*, chap. 2.

Having something...: Blackwell, *Pioneer Work*, chap. 2.

Chapter 2: Surely, She Is a Joke

A woman who dissects...: "Medical Women," *The Australian Medical Journal*, July 1865, pp. 233-235, https://digitised-collections.unimelb.edu.au/bitstream/handle/11343/23129/267469_UDS2010779-115.pdf.

The struggle with...: Blackwell, *Pioneer Work*, chap. 2.

I really now feel...: Elizabeth Blackwell to Marian Blackwell, March 22, 1846, HU.

My mind is...: Elizabeth Blackwell to Marian Blackwell, November 7, 1846, HU.

Medical schools had...: J. Collins Warren, "Medical Education in the United States," *Journal of the American Medical Association*, Volume 21, September 9, 1893, pp. 375–382.

In 1765...: Penn University Archives & Records Center, "Brief Histories of the Schools of the University of Pennsylvania, School of Medicine: A Brief History," https://archives.upenn.edu/exhibits/penn-history/school-histories/medicine.

Warrington was dedicated...: Penn Medicine, History of Pennsylvania Hospital, "Obstetrics: A Brief History of Obstetrical Care at Pennsylvania Hospital," www.uphs.upenn.edu/paharc/timeline/1801/tline10.html.

I confess, my dear...: Blackwell, *Pioneer Work*, chap. 2.

So revolutionary seemed...: Blackwell, *Pioneer Work*, chap. 3.

Well, what is it...: Blackwell, *Pioneer Work*, chap. 3.

The beauty of...: Blackwell, *Pioneer Work*, chap. 3.

I begin to think...: Elizabeth Blackwell to Marian Blackwell, June 27, 1847, Blackwell Family Papers, Library of Congress.

Such sects included...: Ronald L. Numbers, "Do-It-Yourself the Sectarian Way," in *Send Us a Lady Physician*, ed. Ruth J. Abram.

Harriot Hunt...: Boyd, *Excellent Doctor Blackwell*, 54.

You, a young unmarried...: Blackwell, *Pioneer Work*, chap. 3.

I have tried...: Blackwell, *Pioneer Work*, chap. 3.

You cannot expect...: Blackwell, *Pioneer Work*, chap. 3.

Elizabeth it is...: Blackwell, *Pioneer Work*, chap. 3.

But when it...: Stephen Smith, "The Co-education of the Sexes," *Physician and Surgeon, a Journal of the Medical Sciences*, Vol. 13, 1891, pp. 45–48.

Elizabeth left for...: Boyd, *Excellent Doctor Blackwell*, 78.

Between 1790 and...: Meryl S. Justin, "The Entry of Women into Medicine in America: Education and Obstacles 1847-1910," Hobart and William Smith Colleges, History of the Colleges, www.hws.edu/about/blackwell/articles/womenmedicine.aspx.

In 1847...: Nathan Smith Davis, *History of the American Medical Association from Its Organization Up to January 1855*, Philadelphia: Lippincott, Grambo & Company, 1855.

The female student...: Stephen Smith, "The Co-education of the Sexes," *Physician and Surgeon, a Journal of the Medical Sciences*, Vol. 13, 1891, pp. 45-48.

After her first...: Blackwell, *Pioneer Work*, chap. 3.

Your plan is...: Blackwell, *Pioneer Work*, chap. 3.

A very notable...: Blackwell, *Pioneer Work*, chap. 3.

I sit quietly...: Blackwell, *Pioneer Work*, chap. 3.

Here she comes...: Anna Blackwell, "Elizabeth Blackwell, M.D."

I had not the...: Blackwell, *Pioneer Work*, chap. 3.

She felt, instinctively...: Anna Blackwell, "Elizabeth Blackwell, M.D."

The study of anatomy...: Blackwell, *Pioneer Work*, chap. 3.

My delicacy was...: Blackwell, *Pioneer Work*, chap. 3.

The wonderful arrangements...: Blackwell, *Pioneer Work*, chap. 3.

Blockley was a...: Boyd, *Excellent Doctor Blackwell*, 84.

This unanimity...: Blackwell, *Pioneer Work*, chap. 3.

She was quite...: Blackwell, *Pioneer Work*, chap. 3.

I see frequently...: Elizabeth Blackwell to George Washington Blackwell, undated, HU.

Her notes from...: Elizabeth Blackwell, notes from materia medica lecture given by Charles Lee, undated, Blackwell Family Papers, Library of Congress.

My face burned...: Blackwell, *Pioneer Work*, chap. 3.

I found E....: Blackwell, *Pioneer Work*, chap. 3.

It wouldn't be…: Blackwell, *Pioneer Work*, chap. 3.

I can neither…: Anna Blackwell, "Elizabeth Blackwell, M.D."

Sir, I thank you…: Blackwell, *Pioneer Work*, chap. 3.

Chapter 3: Another Elizabeth Blazes the Trail

Nine years later…: Jo Manton, *Elizabeth Garrett Anderson*, 44–45.

Later dubbed the…: Beverley Cook et al., "Breathing in London's History: From the Great Stink to the Great Smog," Museum of London, August 24, 2017, www.museumoflondon.org.uk/discover/londons-past-air.

In an effort to…: Michael J. D. Roberts, "The Politics of Professionalization: MPs, Medical Men, and the 1858 Medical Act," Medical History, January 2009, 53(1), pp. 37–56, https://doi.org/10.1017/s0025727300003306.

At its height…: Jim Mussell, "*The English Woman's Journal*," Nineteenth-Century Serials Edition, https://ncse.ac.uk/headnotes/ewj.html.

The first article…: *The English Woman's Journal*, Vol. 1, No. 2, April 1, 1858, https://ncse.ac.uk/periodicals/ewj.

Endowed by nature…: Anna Blackwell, "Elizabeth Blackwell, M.D."

The Cult of True…: Barbara Welter, "The Cult of True Womanhood: 1820-1860," *American Quarterly*, Vol. 18, No. 2, Part 1, Summer 1966, pp. 151-174, https://doi.org/10.2307/2711179, www.jstor.org/stable/2711179.

The 1829 publication…: *The young lady's book: a manual of elegant recreations, exercises, and pursuits*, London, 1829, https://books.google.com/books?id=-8p-9OoTSLIC.

Recognizing a growing…: Manton, *Elizabeth Garrett Anderson*, 27.

In the mid-1800s…: Max Roser and Esteban Ortiz-Ospina, "Literacy," Our World In Data, https://ourworldindata.org/literacy.

In fact, recalling…: Louisa Garrett Anderson, *Elizabeth Garrett Anderson*, 33.

The sisters became…: Manton, *Elizabeth Garrett Anderson*, 36.

In January 1859…: Manton, *Elizabeth Garrett Anderson*, 46.

Toying with the…: Boyd, *Excellent Doctor Blackwell*, 198.

Those who'd earned...: Boyd, *Excellent Doctor Blackwell*, 219.

Not everyone in England...: C. Willett Cunnington, *Feminine Attitudes in the Nineteenth Century*, New York: Macmillan, 1936, p. 144.

It is impossible...: C. Willett Cunnington, *Feminine Attitudes in the Nineteenth Century*, 144.

How can you...: Manton, *Elizabeth Garrett Anderson*, 47.

Upon hearing about...: Manton, *Elizabeth Garrett Anderson*, 48.

For the purpose...: Hester Burton, *Barbara Bodichon: 1827-1891*, London: J. Murray, 1949.

It is work...: Bessie Rayner Parkes, "Association for Promoting the Employment of Women," *The English Woman's Journal*, Vol. 4, No. 19, September 1, 1859, p. 54, https://ncse.ac.uk/periodicals/ewj/.

Barbara had decorated...: Blackwell, *Pioneer Work*, chap. 6.

Lizzie was among...: Blackwell, *Pioneer Work*, chap. 6.

Her sisters had...: Boyd, *Excellent Doctor Blackwell*, 197.

In her speech...: Elizabeth and Emily Blackwell, *Medicine as a Profession for Women*, New York, 1860.

She assumed that...: Garrett Anderson, *Elizabeth Garrett Anderson*, 42.

In fact, Lizzie...: Manton, *Elizabeth Garrett Anderson*, 52.

It seemed to...: Manton, *Elizabeth Garrett Anderson*, 53-54.

I'm going to...: Manton, *Elizabeth Garrett Anderson*, 54.

Women can get...: Garrett Anderson, *Elizabeth Garrett Anderson*, 48.

The London lectures...: Blackwell, *Pioneer Work*, chap. 6.

Students should be...: Elizabeth Blackwell, "Letter to Ladies Desirous of Studying Medicine," *The English Woman's Journal*, January 23, 1860, pp. 329-332.

I wish to study...: Elizabeth Garrett to Emily Davies, June 15, 1860, LSE; Manton, *Elizabeth Garrett Anderson*, 73-74.

The disgrace...: Garrett Anderson, *Elizabeth Garrett Anderson*, 47.

But Lizzie...: Manton, *Elizabeth Garrett Anderson*, 75.

They naturally feel...: Garrett Anderson, *Elizabeth Garrett Anderson*, 46–47.

When Lizzie's cousin...: Manton, *Elizabeth Garrett Anderson*, 75.

The street was...: "History of Harley Street," www.harleystreet.com/why-harley-street/history.

Why not be...: Garrett Anderson, *Elizabeth Garrett Anderson*, 50.

During the last...: Elizabeth Garrett to her aunt, Mrs. Richard Garrett, July 13, 1860, LSE.

Emelia's charm...: Garrett Anderson, *Elizabeth Garrett Anderson*, 51–52.

It is because...: Garrett Anderson, *Elizabeth Garrett Anderson*, 55.

Chapter 4: More Than a Nurse

Surgery in the...: Fitzharris, *The Butchering Art*.

At last patients...: Edward H. Clarke, "Practical Medicine," in *A Century of American Medicine, 1776-1876*, Philadelphia, 1876, p. 67.

Between 1795...: Fitzharris, *The Butchering Art*; Tom Koch, "Mapping the Miasma: Air, Health, and Place in Early Medical Mapping," *Cartographic Perspectives*, No. 52, Fall 2005, https://doi.org/10.14714/CP52.376.

Semmelweis noticed...: William Charney, ed., *Epidemic of Medical Errors and Hospital-Acquired Infections: Systemic and Social Causes*, Boca Raton, FL: CRC Press, 2012, p. 81.

In this pre-antiseptic...: Fitzharris, *The Butchering Art*, 139.

I begin at once...: Elizabeth Garrett to Emily Davies, August 7, 1860, LSE.

A bald man...: Garrett Anderson, *Elizabeth Garrett Anderson*, 59.

There was a small...: Elizabeth Garrett to Emily Davies, August 7, 1860, LSE.

The museum reading...: Elizabeth Garrett to Emily Davies, March 6, 1861, LSE.

Lizzie had been...: Elizabeth Garrett to Emily Davies, August 17, 1860, LSE.

I think this is...: Elizabeth Garrett to Emily Davies, August 17, 1860, LSE.

As for her fellow...: Elizabeth Garrett to Emily Davies, August 17, 1860, LSE.

Willis would later...: Yasuko Shidara, "'The Shadow-Line's' 'Sympathetic

Doctor': Dr William Willis in Bangkok, 1888," *The Conradian*, Vol. 30, No. 1, Spring 2005, pp. 97-110, www.jstor.org/stable/20873541.

I did not feel...: Elizabeth Garrett to Emily Davies, September 5, 1860, LSE.

Sometimes I fear...: Elizabeth Garrett to Emily Davies, September 9, 1860, LSE.

It was very...: Blackwell, *Pioneer Work*, chap. 6.

She has short...: Garrett Anderson, *Elizabeth Garrett Anderson*, 68.

Impossible...: Garrett Anderson, *Elizabeth Garrett Anderson*, 67.

Lizzie wrote to Emily...: Garrett Anderson, *Elizabeth Garrett Anderson*, 70.

Plaskitt believed...: Elizabeth Garrett to Emily Davies, November 18, 1860, LSE.

The general feeling...: Blackwell, *Pioneer Work*, chap. 6.

While she expected...: Elizabeth Garrett to Emily Davies, March 19, 1861, LSE.

Last Saturday I...: Elizabeth Garrett to Emily Davies, March 23, 1861, LSE.

The male students...: Elizabeth Garrett to Emily Davies, March 23, 1861, LSE.

I am very much...: Elizabeth Garrett to Emily Davies, March 23, 1861, LSE.

Much surprise has...: Letter to the Editors, Elizabeth Garrett, *The English Woman's Journal*, Vol. 7, No. 40, June 1, 1861, pp. 282-283, https://ncse. ac.uk/periodicals/ewj/.

Celebrated feminist author...: Carolyn Heilbrun, *Writing a Woman's Life*, New York: Ballantine Books, 1988, p. 81.

Happily, she found...: Elizabeth Garrett to Emily Davies, March 23, 1861, LSE.

I have been talking...: Elizabeth Garrett to Emily Davies, March 19, 1861, LSE.

It is hard to...: Garrett Anderson, *Elizabeth Garrett Anderson*, 68.

I feel so mean...: Garrett Anderson, *Elizabeth Garrett Anderson*, 77.

Lizzie signed the...: Garrett Anderson, *Elizabeth Garrett Anderson*, 77.

Many of the doctors...: Elizabeth Garrett to Emily Davies, March 19, 1861, LSE.

Lizzie worried about...: Elizabeth Garrett to Emily Davies, November 18, 1860, LSE.

Dr. Thompson was…: Elizabeth Garrett to Newson Garrett, date unknown, 1861, LMA.

The students dare not…: Elizabeth Garrett to Emily Davies, June 11, 1861, LSE.

The response…: Manton, *Elizabeth Garrett Anderson*, 106.

I believe my…: Elizabeth Garrett to Emily Davies, June 11, 1861, LSE.

When Nunn heard…: Elizabeth Garrett to Emily Davies, June 14, 1861, LSE.

They did regret…: Manton, *Elizabeth Garrett Anderson*, 110.

I felt horribly…: Garrett Anderson, *Elizabeth Garrett Anderson*, 81.

You will be sorry…: Elizabeth Garrett to Newson Garrett, date unknown, 1861, LMA.

A lady has…: "A Lady Amongst the Students," *The Lancet*, July 6, 1861, p. 16, https://books.google.com/books?id=44hMAQAAMAAJ.

It was a most…: Elizabeth Garrett to Emily Davies, August 21, 1861, LSE.

A few weeks…: "Female Medical Students," *The Lancet*, August 3, 1861, p. 116, https://books.google.com/books?id=44hMAQAAMAAJ.

Small talk had…: Elizabeth Garrett to Emily Davies, August 21, 1861, LSE.

It is a very large…: Elizabeth Garrett to Emily Davies, October 8, 1861, LSE.

Let us have…: Thomas Henry Huxley, "Emancipation—Black and White," (1865), *Science & Education: Essays*, New York: 1904, https://books.google.com/books?id=XOhKAAAAYAAJ.

She has some…: Manton, *Elizabeth Garrett Anderson*, 128.

I shall be very…: Elizabeth Garrett to Emily Davies, October 19, 1861, LSE.

Chapter 5: Young Sophia

To gain her…: Margaret G. Todd, *The Life of Sophia Jex-Blake*, 63.

Being strict Evangelical…: Todd, *The Life of Sophia Jex-Blake*, 4.

Left to create…: Shirley Roberts, *Sophia Jex-Blake: A Woman Pioneer in Nineteenth-Century Medical Reform*, 9.

More sad and…: Todd, *The Life of Sophia Jex-Blake*, 25.

My little child…: Todd, *The Life of Sophia Jex-Blake*, 17.

One schoolmate…: Todd, *The Life of Sophia Jex-Blake*, 33.

Although Sophia had…: Todd, *The Life of Sophia Jex-Blake*, 65.

Sophia describes one…: Todd, *The Life of Sophia Jex-Blake*, 86.

I wonder if it…: Todd, *The Life of Sophia Jex-Blake*, Footnote 26.

Sophia lamented…: Todd, *The Life of Sophia Jex-Blake*, 116.

I want you to…: Todd, *The Life of Sophia Jex-Blake*, 118.

Miss Garrett and her…: Todd, *The Life of Sophia Jex-Blake*, 117.

Actress Tilda Swinton…: Tilda Swinton biography, IMDB, www.imdb.com/
name/nm0842770/bio.

Founded in 1726…: "Medicine at the University of Edinburgh," www.ed.ac.
uk/medicine-vet-medicine/about/history/medicine.

While talking about…: Todd, *The Life of Sophia Jex-Blake*, 119.

To celebrate…: Manton, *Elizabeth Garrett Anderson*, 129.

Oh, I've annihilated…: Todd, *The Life of Sophia Jex-Blake*, 120.

I do not know…: Todd, *The Life of Sophia Jex-Blake*, 119.

Miss Garrett was…: Todd, *The Life of Sophia Jex-Blake*, 130.

And now I have…: Todd, *The Life of Sophia Jex-Blake*, 128.

It brought a smile…: Todd, *The Life of Sophia Jex-Blake*, 128.

I seem so oppressed…: Todd, *The Life of Sophia Jex-Blake*, 135.

You cannot sing…: Todd, *The Life of Sophia Jex-Blake*, 136.

Cold. Therefore rather…: Todd, *The Life of Sophia Jex-Blake*, 135.

Chapter 6: Sophia in America

We were summoned…: Todd, *The Life of Sophia Jex-Blake*, 160.

Ralph Waldo Emerson…: Ralph Waldo Emerson, Academy of American
Poets, https://poets.org/poet/ralph-waldo-emerson.

Though officially neutral…: Roberts, *Sophia Jex-Blake*, 47; "Anglo-American relations during the Civil War," British Library, www.bl.uk/onlinegallery/onlineex/uscivilwar/britain/britainamericancivilwar.html.

Elizabeth Peabody…: Chloe Morse-Harding, "Elizabeth Palmer Peabody," *Boston Athenaeum*, July 2013, www.bostonathenaeum.org/library/book-recommendations/athenaeum-authors/elizabeth-palmer-peabody.

She was already…: Edward T. James, et al., eds. *Notable American Women*, p. 268.

First came the…: Morantz-Sanchez, *Sympathy and Science*, 81.

The Female Medical…: Morantz-Sanchez, *Sympathy and Science*, 76.

However, a degree…: Kate Campbell Hurd-Mead, *Medical women of America: A short history of the pioneer medical women of America and a few of their colleagues in England*, New York: Froben Press, 1933, p. 33.

Some appeared…: Todd, *The Life of Sophia Jex-Blake*, 163.

I can't tell you…: Todd, *The Life of Sophia Jex-Blake*, 173.

You don't know what…: Todd, *The Life of Sophia Jex-Blake*, 165.

These machines used…: Anna Wexler, "The Medical Battery in The United States (1870–1920): Electrotherapy at Home and in the Clinic," *Journal of the History of Medicine and Allied Sciences*, Volume 72, Issue 2, April 2017, pp. 166–192, https://doi.org/10.1093/jhmas/jrx001.

After watching her…: Todd, *The Life of Sophia Jex-Blake*, 164.

I am so exceedingly…: Todd, *The Life of Sophia Jex-Blake*, 173.

It is such a joy…: Todd, *The Life of Sophia Jex-Blake*, 185.

Before long…: Todd, *The Life of Sophia Jex-Blake*, 172.

Sophia accompanied…: Todd, *The Life of Sophia Jex-Blake*, 174.

This hospital life…: Todd, *The Life of Sophia Jex-Blake*, 173.

Oh, I could not…: Sophia Jex-Blake, *Medical Women*, 41.

I think anyone…: Todd, *The Life of Sophia Jex-Blake*, 174.

I believe that…: Jex-Blake, *Medical Women*, 42.

Such theories grew…: Helen King, "Once Upon a Text: Hysteria From Hippocrates," in *Hysteria Beyond Freud*, Sander L. Gilman, et al., Berkeley: University of California Press, pp. 3-90, https://books.google.com/books?id=LdxmV5J0pPkC.

Before long, the…: Edward Shorter, "Paralysis: The Rise and Fall of a 'Hysterical' Symptom," *Journal of Social History*, Volume 19, Issue 4, Summer 1986, pp. 549–582, https://doi.org/10.1353/jsh/19.4.549.

By the Victorian…: Kathleen E. McCrone, *Playing the Game: Sport and the Physical Emancipation of English Women, 1870-1914*, Lexington, KY: University Press of Kentucky, 1988.

Why, if a woman…: Ben Rooney, "Women And Children First: Technology And Moral Panic," *The Wall Street Journal*, July 11, 2011, https://blogs.wsj.com/tech-europe/2011/07/11/women-and-children-first-technology-and-moral-panic.

In actuality…: Anita M. Harris, *Broken Patterns: Professional Women and the Quest for a New Feminine Identity*. Detroit, MI: Wayne State University Press, 1995, p. 46.

The principal reason…: Edward John Tilt, *Handbook of Uterine Therapeutics*, New York, 1869.

Well, I guess the…: Todd, *The Life of Sophia Jex-Blake*, 176.

Infanticide and infant…: Paul A. Gilje, "Infant Abandonment in Early Nineteenth-Century New York City: Three Cases." *Signs*, Vol. 8, No. 3, 1983: 580-90, www.jstor.org/stable/3173958.

When humoural…: Sarah Handley-Cousins, "Abortion in the 19th Century," National Museum of Civil War Medicine, February 9, 2016, www.civilwarmed.org/abortion1.

I find myself…: Todd, *The Life of Sophia Jex-Blake*, 173.

But won't Elizabeth…: Todd, *The Life of Sophia Jex-Blake*, 184.

If you feel you…: Todd, *The Life of Sophia Jex-Blake*, 183.

Most people are…: Todd, *The Life of Sophia Jex-Blake*, 186.

I really feel quite…: Todd, *The Life of Sophia Jex-Blake*, 186.

At least one…: Arleen Tuchman, *Science Has No Sex*, 115.

Boston Marriages…: Tuchman, *Science Has No Sex*, 114-118.

I don't mean…: Todd, *The Life of Sophia Jex-Blake*, endnote 43.

When Harriot Hunt…: Abram, "Will There Be a Monument? Six Pioneer Women Doctors Tell Their Own Stories," in *Send Us a Lady Physician*, ed. Abram, 71-74.

The university's terse…: Todd, *The Life of Sophia Jex-Blake*, 191.

Chapter 7: Facing Down Hurdles as America's First Woman Doctor

A letter to the…: Letter to the Editor from "D.K." "The Late Medical Degree to a Female," *Boston Medical and Surgical Journal*, Vol. 40, No. 3, February 21, 1849, pp. 58-59, https://books.google.com/books?id=U7YEAAAAYAAJ.

A Massachusetts Medical College…: John Ware, "Success in the medical profession," an introductory lecture delivered at the Massachusetts Medical College, November 6, 1850, https://books.google.com/books?id=_wYJAAAAIAAJ.

The satirical British…: Blackwell, *Pioneer Work*, chap. 3; appendix 2.

The invention of…: Ariel Roguin, "Rene Theophile Hyacinthe Laënnec (1781–1826): The Man Behind the Stethoscope," *Clinical Medicine and Research*, September 2006, 4(3): 230–235, https://doi.org/10.3121/cmr.4.3.230.

To train in Paris…: John Duffy, *From Humors to Medical Science: A History of American Medicine*, Urbana: University of Illinois Press, 2nd ed., 1993 (McGraw-Hill 1976), pp. 72-73.

Within a few…: Blackwell, *Pioneer Work*, chap. 4.

Baby after baby…: Blackwell, *Pioneer Work*, chap. 4.

I think he must…: Blackwell, *Pioneer Work*, chap. 4.

On Sunday, November…: Blackwell, *Pioneer Work*, chap. 4.

It wouldn't be…: Adela Matejcek, "Treatment and prevention of ophthalmia neonatorum," *Canadian Family Physician*, November 2013, 59(11), 1187-1190, https://www.ncbi.nlm.nih.gov/pmc/articles/PMC3828094.

When Elizabeth finally…: Boyd, *Excellent Doctor Blackwell*, 138.

In a tiny room…: Boyd, *Excellent Doctor Blackwell*, 135-137.

Do you know…: Blackwell, *Pioneer Work*, chap. 4.

Within a few years…: Florence Nightingale, *Notes on Hospitals*, London, 1863.

They were within…: Louisa Martindale, *The Woman Doctor And Her Future*, Plymouth, UK: The Mayflower Press, 1922, p. 39.

The notorious…: Karen Abbott, "Madame Restell: The Abortionist of Fifth Avenue," *Smithsonian Magazine*, November 27, 2012, www.smithsonianmag.com/history/madame-restell-the-abortionist-of-fifth-avenue-145109198.

Dime novelists…: Karen Weingarten, *Abortion in the American Imagination: Before Life and Choice*, 1880-1940, New Brunswick, NJ: Rutgers University Press, 2014.

I like the room…: Boyd, *Excellent Doctor Blackwell*, 154.

Progressive New York…: Boyd, *Excellent Doctor Blackwell*, 155.

The first seven…: Blackwell, *Pioneer Work*, chap. 5.

She was plagued…: Blackwell, *Pioneer Work*, chap. 5.

I had no medical…: Blackwell, *Pioneer Work*, chap. 5.

She confided to…: Blackwell, *Pioneer Work*, chap. 5.

Oh for life…: Edward T. James, et al., eds. *Notable American Women*, 165.

Take an extra…: Anna Blackwell, "Elizabeth Blackwell, M.D."

That fragile lady…: Abram, *Send Us a Lady Physician*, 81.

Chapter 8: Changing the Culture,
One Patient at a Time

Hoping to drum…: Elizabeth Blackwell, *The Laws of Life, With Special Reference to the Physical Education of Girls*, New York, 1852.

Elizabeth said she…: Anna Blackwell, "Elizabeth Blackwell, M.D.," 95.

A most extraordinary…: Blackwell, *Pioneer Work*, chap. 5.

Typical remedies…: Jane McHugh, et al., "Death in the White House: President William Henry Harrison's Atypical Pneumonia," *Clinical Infectious Diseases*, Vol. 59, Issue 7, October 1, 2014, pp. 990–995, https://doi.org/10.1093/cid/ciu470.

When Emily…: Boyd, *Excellent Doctor Blackwell*, 160.

A blank wall of…: James, et al., eds., *Notable American Women*, 165.

Emily was a handsome…: S. Josephine Baker, *Fighting for Life*, New York Review of Books, 1939, pp. 33–35.

On January 20…: Blackwell, *Pioneer Work*, appendix 3.

I have at last…: Blackwell, *Pioneer Work*, chap. 5.

Born in Germany…: "Dr. Marie E. Zakrzewska," Changing the Face of Medicine series, National Library of Medicine, https://cfmedicine.nlm.nih.gov/physicians/biography_338.html.

These malicious stories…: Blackwell, *Pioneer Work*, chap. 5.

I was very…: Boyd, *Excellent Doctor Blackwell*, 174.

So she did…: Boyd, *Excellent Doctor Blackwell*, 174.

Who will ever…: Blackwell, *Pioneer Work*, chap. 5.

It would ensure…: Blackwell, *Pioneer Work*, chap. 5.

After graduating…: James, et al., eds., *Notable American Women*, 165–166.

In Edinburgh…: Blackwell, *Pioneer Work*, chap. 5.

Appointed professor…: "James Young Simpson," Wikipedia, https://en.wikipedia.org/wiki/James_Young_Simpson.

He derived great…: Blackwell, *Pioneer Work*, chap. 5.

As this movement…: Sarah J. McNutt, "Response to the Toast 'Pioneers of Yesterday in Medicine,'" *The Woman's Medical Journal*, Vol. 29, Issue 9, September 1919, pp. 191–192.

Approximately 15,000…: Kenneth M. Ludmerer, *Let Me Heal: The Opportunity to Preserve Excellence in American Medicine*, New York: Oxford University Press, 2015, p. 10.

For the first…: Kenneth M. Ludmerer, *Learning to Heal: The Development of American Medical Education*, New York: Basic Books, 1985.

Marie's father…: Susan Wells, *Out of the Dead House: Nineteenth-Century Women Physicians and the Writing of Medicine*, Madison, WI: The University of Wisconsin Press, 2001, p. 4.

After ordering…: Boyd, *Excellent Doctor Blackwell*, 188.

They do wrong...: Boyd, *Excellent Doctor Blackwell*, 190.

Ann Preston...: Abram, *Send Us a Lady Physician*, 87.

The front...: Boyd, *Excellent Doctor Blackwell*, 188.

Irish Catholic...: Five Points, Wikipedia, https://en.wikipedia.org/wiki/Five_Points,_Manhattan.

During the Infirmary's...: Boyd, *Excellent Doctor Blackwell*, 190-191.

Through a cloud...: Blackwell, *Pioneer Work*, chap. 5.

We established a...: Blackwell, *Pioneer Work*, chap. 6.

She once recorded...: Marie Zakrzewska, *A Woman's Quest*, pp. 213-214.

How good work...: Elizabeth Blackwell to Barbara Bodichon, May 25, 1860, CU.

Marie referred...: Zakrzewska, *A Woman's Quest*, 211.

Newly minted MDs...: Richard W. Wertz and Dorothy C. Wertz, *Lying-in: A History of Childbirth in America*, expanded edition, New Haven, CT: Yale University Press, 1989, p. 63.

Leeches applied...: Deborah Kuhn McGregor, *From Midwives to Medicine: The Birth of American Gynecology*, New Brunswick, NJ: Rutgers University Press, 1998, pp. 139-140; Vaginal speculum for applying leeches, Science Museum Group, https://collection.sciencemuseumgroup.org.uk/objects/co91167/vaginal-speculum-for-applying-leeches-vaginal-speculum.

We have only...: *Medicine as a Profession for Women*, address delivered by Elizabeth Blackwell at Clinton Hall, December 2, 1859, prepared by Elizabeth and Emily Blackwell, published New York, 1860.

Upon hearing this...: Blackwell, *Pioneer Work*, chap. 5.

Women physicians are...: Zakrzewska, *A Woman's Quest*, 218-219.

Dr. J. Marion Sims...: Brynn Holland, "The 'Father of Modern Gynecology' Performed Shocking Experiments On Slaves," History.com, August 29, 2017, updated December 4, 2018, www.history.com/news/the-father-of-modern-gynecology-performed-shocking-experiments-on-slaves.

Elizabeth, by contrast...: Boyd, *Excellent Doctor Blackwell*, 230-231.

In all, 120 people...: New York City draft riots, Wikipedia, https://en.wikipedia.org/wiki/New_York_City_draft_riots.

Marie's initial...: Zakrzewska, *A Woman's Quest*, 250-51.

She secured...: James, et al., eds. *Notable American Women*, 166.

It was a three-story...: Damien Farley, "Orpheum Theatre," Cinema Treasures, http://cinematreasures.org/theaters/13829.

The master carpenters...: Elizabeth Blackwell to Barbara Bodichon, April 25, 1860, CU.

The first annual...: James, et al., eds. *Notable American Women*, 166.

In 1862...: Boyd, *Excellent Doctor Blackwell*, 235-236.

I have yet...: Boyd, *Excellent Doctor Blackwell*, 235-236.

I watched lately...: Elizabeth Blackwell to Barbara Bodichon, January 18, 1865, CU.

Some three hundred...: Elizabeth and Emily Blackwell, *Medicine as a Profession for Women*.

Chapter 9: Lizzie Is Pushed into Private Study

I had been thinking...: Elizabeth Garrett to Louisa Garrett, June 18, 1862, LMA.

This slow romancing...: Manton, *Elizabeth Garrett Anderson*, 130.

Believing as I...: Elizabeth Garrett to Louisa Garrett, June 18, 1862, LMA.

I suppose I...: Manton, *Elizabeth Garrett Anderson*, 123.

One of the...: W. M. Moorman, "The Medical Profession And Women's Rights," *The Lancet*, Vol. 80, Issue 2036, pp. 268-269, September 6, 1862.

But she simply...: Manton, *Elizabeth Garrett Anderson*, 132.

The students are...: Garrett Anderson, *Elizabeth Garrett Anderson*, 98.

The chance to...: Garrett Anderson, *Elizabeth Garrett Anderson*, 281.

Still, she says...: Manton, *Elizabeth Garrett Anderson*, 134.

It was for this...: Manton, *Elizabeth Garrett Anderson*, 135.

The Senate ruled...: Manton, *Elizabeth Garrett Anderson*, 136.

The female doctor...: Manton, *Elizabeth Garrett Anderson*, 138.

On a three-hour...: Manton, *Elizabeth Garrett Anderson*, 138-139.

My dear little...: Elizabeth Garrett to Louisa Smith, (undated) 1863, LSE.

Mothers also died...: Geoffrey Chamberlain, "British maternal mortality in the 19th and early 20th centuries," *Journal of the Royal Society of Medicine*, vol. 99, 11, 2006, pp. 559-563, https://doi.org/10.1258/jrsm.99.11.559.

The responsibility for...: Elizabeth Garrett Anderson, "Deaths in childbirth," *British Medical Journal*, October 15, 1898, 2, p. 1198, https://doi.org/10.1136/bmj.2.1972.1198.

I must decline...: Garrett Anderson, *Elizabeth Garrett Anderson*, 108.

Something 'just as good'...: Manton, *Elizabeth Garrett Anderson*, 146.

The large institution...: E. W. Morris, *A History of the London Hospital*, London: Edward Arnold, 1910.

In the mid-1700s...: E. W. Morris, *A History of the London Hospital*.

Lizzie told Emily...: Garrett Anderson, *Elizabeth Garrett Anderson*, 111.

An operative vaginal...: James A. Low, "Operative Delivery: Yesterday and Today," *Journal of Obstetrics and Gynecology Canada*, February 2009, Vol. 31, Issue 2, pp. 132–141, https://doi.org/10.1016/S1701-2163(16)34097-X.

It's estimated...: "Cesarean Section—A Brief History," Part 2, National Library of Medicine, History of Medicine series, www.nlm.nih.gov/exhibition/cesarean/part2.html.

I feel seedy...: Elizabeth Garrett to Emily Davies, February 3, 1864, LSE.

A storm is...: Garrett Anderson, *Elizabeth Garrett Anderson*, 112.

Snubbing is unpleasant...: Garrett Anderson, *Elizabeth Garrett Anderson*, 111.

I had heard...: Garrett Anderson, *Elizabeth Garrett Anderson*, 113.

My courage rose...: Garrett Anderson, *Elizabeth Garrett Anderson*, 113.

A political economy...: Manton, *Elizabeth Garrett Anderson*, 156.

Are you Miss...: Manton, *Elizabeth Garrett Anderson*, 159.

That summer...: Claudette Fillard, et al., ed. *Exchanges and Correspondence:*

The Construction of Feminism, Newcastle upon Tyne: Cambridge Scholars Publishing, 2010, p. 196.

At 5 o'clock…: Manton, *Elizabeth Garrett Anderson*, 162.

Above the door…: Apothecaries' Hall, London, Wikipedia, https://en. wikipedia.org/wiki/Apothecaries%27_Hall,_London.

Chapter 10: The Blackwells Welcome
Sophia in New York

Their movement…: Blackwell, *Pioneer Work*, chap. 5.

Consider how women…: Elizabeth and Emily Blackwell, *Address on the Medical Education of Women*, read at a meeting at The New York Infirmary for Women and Children on December 19, 1863, published New York, 1864, https:// en.wikisource.org/wiki/Address_on_the_Medical_Education_of_Women.

They fell short…: "New York Infirmary for Women and Children Annual Report," *The New York Times*, March 31, 1869, p. 4, https://timesmachine. nytimes.com/timesmachine/1869/03/31/issue.html; Boyd, *Excellent Doctor Blackwell*, 246.

In this way…: Elizabeth Blackwell, *Address delivered at the opening of the Woman's Medical College of the New York Infirmary*, November 2, 1868, published New York, 1869, https://guides.upstate.edu/ld.php?content_ id=28856148.

At St. Bartholomew's…: "Saint Bartholomew's Hospital and Medical College Brief History During The Snow Era (1813-58)," UCLA Fielding School of Public Health, Epidemiology, www.ph.ucla.edu/epi/snow/1859map/ stbartholomews_hosp.html.

And the shortest…: Elinor Rice Hays, *Those Extraordinary Blackwells*, 163-164.

As for the nurses…: Boyd, *Excellent Doctor Blackwell*, 227.

Florence complained…: Philip A. Mackowiak, "Florence Nightingale's Syphilis That Wasn't," Oxford University Press Blog, August 13, 2015, https:// blog.oup.com/2015/08/florence-nightingale-syphilis-death.

The Blackwells also…: Morantz-Sanchez, *Sympathy and Science*, 73-78.

Foremost in her…: Blackwell, *Address delivered at the opening of the Woman's Medical College of the New York Infirmary*.

The school's overall...: Boyd, *Excellent Doctor Blackwell*, 238-239.

I think hygiene...: Hays, *Those Extraordinary Blackwells*, 164.

Smallpox was the...: The History of Vaccines, An Educational Resource by the College of Physicians of Philadelphia, www.historyofvaccines.org/timeline/all.

Oh, dear...: Todd, *The Life of Sophia Jex-Blake*, 199.

Why don't you...: Todd, *The Life of Sophia Jex-Blake*, 199; Dorothy Clarke Wilson, *Lone Woman: The Story of Elizabeth Blackwell, the First Woman Doctor*, Boston: Little, Brown & Company, 1970, p. 404.

We sleep in...: Trachtenberg, "New York's First 'Lady Doctor'."

English ladies are...: Todd, *The Life of Sophia Jex-Blake*, 199.

This last week...: Todd, *The Life of Sophia Jex-Blake*, 205.

She worried...: Todd, *The Life of Sophia Jex-Blake*, 205.

We have been...: Blackwell, *Address delivered at the opening of the Woman's Medical College of the New York Infirmary*.

An Australian Medical...: "Medical Women," *The Australian Medical Journal*, July 1865.

As far as Sophia...: Sophia Jex-Blake, "The Medical Education of Women," *Transactions of the National Association for the Promotion of Social Science*, London, 1874, pp. 385-393, https://books.google.com/books?id=JHQzAQAAMAAJ.

A full course...: Joseph Shannon, "New York Infirmary and Women's Medical College," *Manual of the Corporation of the City of New York*, 1868, pp. 363-366, https://books.google.com/books?id=XwoAAAAAMAAJ.

The teaching is...: Todd, *The Life of Sophia Jex-Blake*, 207.

Elizabeth feared Sophia...: Elizabeth Blackwell to Barbara Bodichon, October 28, 1868, CU.

As many as...: Shannon, "New York Infirmary and Women's Medical College," *Manual of the Corporation of the City of New York*.

Elizabeth heard...: Elizabeth Blackwell to Barbara Bodichon, January 18, 1865, CU.

Students of today...: "Only Heroic Women Were Doctors Then," *The New*

York Times, April 9, 1916, p. 10, https://timesmachine.nytimes.com/timesmachine/1916/04/09/104022125.html.

I believe if…: Todd, *The Life of Sophia Jex-Blake*, 207.

We are so sorry…: Wilson, *Lone Woman*, 419.

I want to write…: Todd, *The Life of Sophia Jex-Blake*, 213.

If you don't…: Todd, *The Life of Sophia Jex-Blake*, 209.

But we will be…: Todd, *The Life of Sophia Jex-Blake*, 215.

Chapter 11: Lizzie Takes On London

However, it surmised…: "Frocks and Gowns," *The Lancet*, October 7, 1865, pp. 415-416, https://books.google.com/books?id=mLM1AQAAMAAJ.

I don't like…: Garrett Anderson, Elizabeth Garrett Anderson, 118.

Louie suggested…: Garrett Anderson, Elizabeth Garrett Anderson, 118.

When word got…: Elizabeth Crawford, *The Women's Suffrage Movement: A Reference Guide 1866-1928*, London: UCL Press, 1999, p. 10.

Everyone cared more…: Manton, *Elizabeth Garrett Anderson*, 170.

I was in the…: Manton, *Elizabeth Garrett Anderson*, 163.

Over the course…: Cook, "Breathing in London's history," Museum of London, August 24, 2017.

For those born…: Cook, "Breathing in London's history," Museum of London, August 24, 2017.

There are foul…: Charles Dickens, "Health by Act of Parliament," *Household Words*, Vol. 1, No. 20, August 10, 1850, pp. 460-463, https://books.google.com/books?id=mofice8Ca7cC.

In 1865…: Octavia Hill, "Organized Work Among the Poor," *Macmillan's Magazine*, Vol. 20, July 1869, pp. 219-226, https://books.google.com/books?id=V7YZAQAAIAAJ.

Rancid food…: Jan Marsh, "Health & Medicine in the 19th Century," Victoria and Albert Museum, www.vam.ac.uk/content/articles/h/health-and-medicine-in-the-19th-century.

Scottish physician...: Marsh, "Health & Medicine in the 19th Century," Victoria and Albert Museum.

It wasn't until...: Judith Summers, "Broad Street Pump Outbreak," UCLA Fielding School of Public Health, Epidemiology, www.ph.ucla.edu/epi/snow/broadstreetpump.html.

During each short...: Manton, *Elizabeth Garrett Anderson*, 174.

She cared for...: Manton, *Elizabeth Garrett Anderson*, 175.

Her patients were...: Manton, *Elizabeth Garrett Anderson*, 174–175.

Lizzie quickly made...: Manton, *Elizabeth Garrett Anderson*, 175.

From Lizzie, Butler...: Manton, *Elizabeth Garrett Anderson*, 172.

Oh if men...: Patricia A. Vertinsky, *The Eternally Wounded Woman: Women, Doctors, and Exercise in the Late Nineteenth Century*, Urbana: University of Illinois Press, 1994, p. 113.

By this law...: Josephine Butler ("An English Mother"), *An Appeal to the People of England on the Recognition and Superintendence of Prostitution by Governments*, Nottingham, 1869.

Elizabeth Blackwell also...: Blackwell, *Pioneer Work*, chap. 7.

Hospitals do not...: Manton, *Elizabeth Garrett Anderson*, 180.

After five years...: New Hospital for Women Annual Report: 1872, LMA.

Chapter 12: Sophia Storms Edinburgh

The well-ordered...: Todd, *The Life of Sophia Jex-Blake*, 214.

By January...: Todd, *The Life of Sophia Jex-Blake*, 219.

By special order...: Todd, *The Life of Sophia Jex-Blake*, 233.

That woman certainly...: Todd, *The Life of Sophia Jex-Blake*, 233.

Sophia had four...: Todd, *The Life of Sophia Jex-Blake*, 234–238.

A skilled toxicologist...: Adam Nightingale, *Masters of Crime: Fiction's Finest Villains and Their Real-life Inspirations*, Stroud, UK: The History Press, 2011, chap. 6, https://books.google.com/books?id=WFODDQAAQBAJ.

Muirhead was backed…: Roberts, *Sophia Jex-Blake*, 85.

All were concerned…: Todd, *The Life of Sophia Jex-Blake*, 248.

Elizabeth said she…: Elizabeth Blackwell to Barbara Bodichon, August 30, 1869, CU.

In fact, nothing…: Sophia Jex-Blake, "Medicine as a Profession for Women," *Medical Women: Two Essays*, Footnote 4.

In her essay…: Jex-Blake, *Medical Women*.

If it is indeed…: Jex-Blake, *Medical Women*.

Isabel had realized…: Diary of Isabel Jane Thorne, 1887, UE.

I was anxious…: Diary of Isabel Jane Thorne, 1887, UE.

They were all…: Diary of Isabel Jane Thorne, 1887, UE.

Helen was born…: Helen Evans, Wikipedia, https://en.wikipedia.org/wiki/Helen_Evans.

Do you think…: Todd, *The Life of Sophia Jex-Blake*, 255.

All five women…: Lauren Fuge, "The Wake of the Edinburgh Seven," *Lateral Magazine*, February 26, 2018, www.lateralmag.com/articles/issue-25/the-wake-of-the-edinburgh-seven.

I do indeed…: Todd, *The Life of Sophia Jex-Blake*, 264.

Ann Preston, dean…: Steve J. Peitzman, *A New and Untried Course: Women's Medical College and Medical College of Pennsylvania, 1850-1998*. New Brunswick, NJ: Rutgers University Press, 2000.

I wonder if…: *The Scotsman*, December 4, 1869, p. 2.

Dr. Thomas Charles Hope…: Dr. Thomas Charles Hope, Wikipedia, https://en.wikipedia.org/wiki/Thomas_Charles_Hope.

He was so…: Todd, *The Life of Sophia Jex-Blake*, 269.

A writer in…: Jex-Blake, *Medical Women*, Note I, p. 145.

While in The Spectator…: Jex-Blake, *Medical Women*, Note I, p. 145.

The Times took…: Jex-Blake, *Medical Women*, Note I, p. 145.

The results of…: Jex-Blake, *Medical Women*, 94.

Turner, Joseph Lister...: Todd, *The Life of Sophia Jex-Blake*, 273.

Lister argued...: Joseph Lister, Letter to the Editor, *British Medical Journal*, February 9, 1878, p. 213.

Having ladies attend...: Roberts, *Sophia Jex-Blake*, 133.

Eminent medical men...: Alison Moulds, "The Woman (Doctor) Question and Nineteenth-Century Medical Journals," January 30, 2015, and "Why Women Shouldn't be Doctors (According to Victorian medical men)," June 28, 2015, The Victorian Clinic, https://victorianclinic.wordpress.com/; Moulds, "Women: Perspectives from the Victorian medical profession," Royal College of Surgeons of England, The Bulletin, July 2017, Vol. 99, Issue 7, https://publishing.rcseng.ac.uk/doi/pdf/10.1308/rcsbull.2017.255, pp. 255-257; "The Medical Education of Women," *The Lancet*, May 7, 1870, p. 673; "The Female Physician," *The Medical Times and Register*, Vol. 24, March 5, 1892.

One concerned female...: Letter to the Editor from "Mater," "A Lady on Lady Doctors," *The Lancet*, May 7, 1870, p. 680, https://books.google.com/books?id=SHdMAQAAMAAJ.

In The BMJ...: "Lady Surgeons," *British Medical Journal*, April 2, 1870, pp. 338–339.

The Medical Mirror...: "Notes and Comments: Female Physicians," *Medical Mirror*, December 1, 1869, p. 173.

Ladies are all very...: Letter to the Editor from "A Country Gentleman, and MRCS," *Medical Press and Circular*, January 5, 1870.

The journal also made...: "Lady Doctors," *Medical Press and Circular*, February 23, 1870.

Dear Goddess of Health...: Garrett Anderson, *Elizabeth Garrett Anderson*, 136.

What right have women...: Henry Bennet, "Women as Practitioners of Midwifery," *The Lancet*, Vol. 95, Issue 2442, June 18, 1870, pp. 887–888, https://doi.org/10.1016/S0140-6736(02)68011-0.

After saying that...: Jex-Blake, *Medical Women*, Note B, p. 138.

That was how...: Jex-Blake, *Medical Women*, 97.

To help their...: Jex-Blake, *Medical Women*, 98-99.

Human remains for...: Sanjib Kumar Ghosh, "Human cadaveric dissection: a historical account from ancient Greece to the modern era," *Anatomy &*

Cell Biology, September 2015, 48(3), pp. 153–169, https://doi.org/10.5115/acb.2015.48.3.153.

Before the discovery…: Erich Brenner, "Human body preservation—old and new techniques," *Journal of Anatomy*, January 18, 2014, https://doi.org/10.1111/joa.12160.

The first person…: Elizabeth H. Oakes, *Encyclopedia of World Scientists*, Revised Edition, New York: Infobase Publishing, 2007, pp. 273-274, https://books.google.com/books?id=uPRB-OED1bcC.

The male students…: Jex-Blake, *Medical Women*, 100.

The conduct of…: Todd, *The Life of Sophia Jex-Blake*, 299.

They obtained…: Todd, *The Life of Sophia Jex-Blake*, 290.

Several male students…: Jex-Blake, *Medical Women*, 101-102.

Along the street…: Todd, *The Life of Sophia Jex-Blake*, 290-292; Roberts, *Sophia Jex-Blake*, 103.

The men were…: Todd, *The Life of Sophia Jex-Blake*, 291.

Most of them…: Jex-Blake, *Medical Women*, Footnote 90.

As for the…: Isabel Thorne, *London School of Medicine for Women*, 10.

The sheriff would…: *The Scotsman*, November 23, 1870.

I began the…: Todd, *The Life of Sophia Jex-Blake*, 318-319.

By coming in…: Jex-Blake, *Medical Women*, 160.

Chapter 13: Emily's Turn to Shine in New York

The more I see…: Blackwell, *Pioneer Work*, chap. 6.

In fact, she…: Boyd, *Excellent Doctor Blackwell*, 245.

I am more…: Boyd, *Excellent Doctor Blackwell*, 245.

Sara Josephine Baker…: Baker, *Fighting for Life*, 33.

I have seen…: Emily Blackwell to Elizabeth Blackwell, December 20, 1852, HU.

I went to the...: Emily Blackwell to Elizabeth Blackwell, December 1852, HU.

I know you...: Boyd, *Excellent Doctor Blackwell*, 166.

Operations, though the...: Emily Blackwell diary, January 9, 1853, HU.

Before long, they...: James, et al., eds., *Notable American Women*, 165-166.

Emily adopted a...: Lillian Faderman, *To Believe in Women: What Lesbians Have Done For America—A History*, New York: Houghton Mifflin Company, 1999, pp. 281-282.

She is a remarkable...: Mary Putnam Jacobi to Elizabeth Blackwell, December 25, 1888, LOC.

I have sufficient...: Carla Bittel, *Mary Putnam Jacobi and the Politics of Medicine in Nineteenth-Century America*, Chapel Hill, NC: University of North Carolina Press, 2009, p. 84.

It is perfectly...: Mary Putnam Jacobi, "Woman in Medicine," in *Woman's Work in America*, ed. Annie Nathan Meyer, Henry Holt & Co., 1891, pp. 139-205.

She said her...: Abram, "Will There Be a Monument?" in *Send Us a Lady Physician*, ed. Abram, 97.

In America...: *The Scotsman*, December 4, 1869.

While she always...: Emily Blackwell, "Women in Medicine," speech read at the fortieth anniversary of the first National Woman's Rights Convention, *The Woman's Journal*, February 14, 1891, Vol. 22, No. 7, https://iiif.lib.harvard.edu/manifests/view/drs:49186399$57i.

In her book...: Susan Wells, *Out of the Dead House*, 4-5.

Mary Ann had...: Mary Ann Evans to Elizabeth Blackwell, February 27, 1859, LOC.

That year, Elizabeth...: Blackwell, *Pioneer Work*, chap. 7.

My long-cherished...: Blackwell, *Pioneer Work*, chap. 7.

As she aged...: Boyd, *Excellent Doctor Blackwell*, 265.

Elizabeth's biggest goal...: Elizabeth Blackwell to Barbara Bodichon, June 16, 1869, CU.

Chapter 14: A Lady Doctor Gets Married

Back in 1862…: Blackwell, *Pioneer Work*, chap. 6.

I hope these…: Manton, *Elizabeth Garrett Anderson*, 187.

I am giving up…: Manton, *Elizabeth Garrett Anderson*, 184.

Her Royal Highness…: Manton, *Elizabeth Garrett Anderson*, 185.

Do you not…: Manton, *Elizabeth Garrett Anderson*, 190.

I had to find…: Manton, *Elizabeth Garrett Anderson*, 189.

I caught her…: Garrett Anderson, *Elizabeth Garrett Anderson*, 129.

While the impoverished…: Manton, *Elizabeth Garrett Anderson*, 195.

I cannot afford…: Manton, *Elizabeth Garrett Anderson*, 198.

Even the difficult-to-impress…: Garrett Anderson, *Elizabeth Garrett Anderson*, 143.

All the judges…: Manton, *Elizabeth Garrett Anderson*, 192.

Miss Garrett's abilities…: "Miss Garrett, M.D." *The Lancet*, October 29, 1870, p. 615, https://books.google.com/books?id=n3hMAQAAMAAJ.

Even The BMJ…: "Miss Garrett," *British Medical Journal*, June 18, 1870, p. 636, https://books.google.com/books?id=9DFHAAAAYAAJ.

One from Sophia…: Garrett Anderson, *Elizabeth Garrett Anderson*, 133.

Spite of all this…: Manton, *Elizabeth Garrett Anderson*, 193.

I have been…: Garrett Anderson, *Elizabeth Garrett Anderson*, 150.

Healthy women…: Elizabeth Garrett Anderson, "Sex in Mind and Education: A Reply," *Fortnightly Review*, May 1874, pp. 583-594, https://babel.hathitrust.org/cgi/pt?id=inu.30000070083922.

Seen at a…: Sally Mitchell, *Frances Power Cobbe: Victorian Feminist, Journalist, Reformer*, Charlottesville, VA: University of Virginia Press, 2004, p. 205.

In December…: Manton, *Elizabeth Garrett Anderson*, 210.

I love you more…: Manton, *Elizabeth Garrett Anderson*, 215.

My horizon was…: Elizabeth Garrett to Millicent Garrett Fawcett, December 25, 1870, LSE.

I do hope...: Elizabeth Garrett to Millicent Garrett Fawcett, December 25, 1870, LSE.

She was certain...: Manton, *Elizabeth Garrett Anderson*, 261.

The problem of...: *British Medical Journal*, January 7, 1871, p. 16.

The Lancet proposed...: "Minerva Medica Nupta," *The Lancet*, January 7, 1871, p. 22.

Next, she heard...: Garrett Anderson, *Elizabeth Garrett Anderson*, 170.

I have been...: Garrett Anderson, *Elizabeth Garrett Anderson*, 173.

Fancy my being...: Elizabeth Garrett to James Skelton Anderson, December 28, 1870, LSE.

They were to...: Garrett Anderson, *Elizabeth Garrett Anderson*, 173-174.

The Lancet declared...: "A New Hospital for Women," *The Lancet*, July 11, 1874, pp. 56-57.

An inpatient ward...: Manton, *Elizabeth Garrett Anderson*, 226-227.

People donated money...: New Hospital for Women Annual Reports, 1872-1877, LMA.

The Times reported...: Letter to the Editor from "M.D." "Medical Education for Women," *The Times*, March 4, 1875, *London School of Medicine for Women* press clippings, LMA.

Women came in...: New Hospital for Women Annual Reports, 1872-1877, LMA.

Four years prior...: Joseph Lister, *The Lancet*, www.thelancet.com/action/doSearch?searchType=authorLookUp&author=Lister,Joseph.

To be thoroughly...: Manton, *Elizabeth Garrett Anderson*, 229.

In the hospital's...: Elizabeth Garrett Anderson, "Clot in the Heart and Cerebral Embolism," *British Medical Journal*, December 14, 1872, p. 669, https://books.google.com/books?id=uHNMAQAAMAAJ.

Potassium bromide was...: JMS Pearce, "Bromide, the first effective antiepileptic agent," *Journal of Neurology, Neurosurgery & Psychiatry*, 2002, 72:412.

As the century...: A.N.M. Alamgir, *Therapeutic Use of Medicinal Plants and Their Extracts: Volume 1, Pharmacognosy*, Springer International Publishing AG, 2017, https://doi.org/10.1007/978-3-319-63862-1.

Laudanum was the…: Kang et al., *Quackery*, 65-68.

In one particularly…: Elizabeth Garrett Anderson, "Clot in the Heart and Cerebral Embolism," *British Medical Journal*, December 14, 1872, p. 669.

Lizzie published…: Elizabeth Garrett Anderson, *British Medical Journal*, www.bmj.com/search/advanced/author1%3Agarrett%252C%2Belizabeth.

When a journalist…: Manton, *Elizabeth Garrett Anderson*, 243-244.

Noise bothered her…: Garrett Anderson, *Elizabeth Garrett Anderson*, 192.

Now put on…: Louise Martindale, *The Woman Doctor and Her Future*, Plymouth, UK: The Mayflower Press, 1922, p. 61.

Chapter 15: The Campaign in Edinburgh Ends

Back when she…: Anna Blackwell, "Elizabeth Blackwell, M.D.," *The English Woman's Journal*.

Professors likewise…: Jex-Blake, *Medical Women*, Footnote 114.

A new obstacle…: Jex-Blake, *Medical Women*, Note A.

Part of my…: Jex-Blake, *Medical Women*, Note H.

She worked at…: Jex-Blake, *Medical Women*, Note H.

One male medical…: Todd, *The Life of Sophia Jex-Blake*, 294.

It is true…: Todd, *The Life of Sophia Jex-Blake*, 299.

Susan B. Anthony…: *The Revolution*, January 26, 1871.

Plainly dressed…: Todd, *The Life of Sophia Jex-Blake*, 311.

Sedate, quiet…: Todd, *The Life of Sophia Jex-Blake*, 311.

Those who wantonly…: Todd, *The Life of Sophia Jex-Blake*, 263.

The University must…: Roberts, *Sophia Jex-Blake*, 113-114.

The medical profession…: Jex-Blake, *Medical Women*, Note R.

If the students…: Jex-Blake, *Medical Women*, 107.

We availed ourselves…: Thorne, *London School of Medicine for Women*, 14.

Lucy, I do so...: Todd, *The Life of Sophia Jex-Blake*, 327.

I can count...: Jex-Blake, *Medical Women*, Note A.

In The Scotsman...: Jex-Blake, *Medical Women*, Note A.

I happened to...: Jex-Blake, *Medical Women*, Note A.

What began as...: Tuchman, *Science Has No Sex*, 209-210.

I have been...: Todd, *The Life of Sophia Jex-Blake*, 329.

Last night for...: Todd, *The Life of Sophia Jex-Blake*, 329.

It is a little...: Todd, *The Life of Sophia Jex-Blake*, 417.

Poets have always...: "The Cost of Notoriety," *The Lancet*, November 30, 1872, pp. 793-794.

We are on...: Todd, *The Life of Sophia Jex-Blake*, 364-365.

Even The Lancet...: Jex-Blake, *Medical Women*, Footnote 104.

Sophia claimed...: Todd, *The Life of Sophia Jex-Blake*, 337.

It had been...: Jex-Blake, *Medical Women*, Note T.

Sophia said the...: Jex-Blake, *Medical Women*, 124.

The Lord Ordinary...: Todd, *The Life of Sophia Jex-Blake*, 372.

Oh, sit down...: Todd, *The Life of Sophia Jex-Blake*, 340-341.

I do hope you...: Todd, *The Life of Sophia Jex-Blake*, 341.

If I felt I had...: Todd, *The Life of Sophia Jex-Blake*, 386.

Don't have any...: Todd, *The Life of Sophia Jex-Blake*, 362.

The whole opposition...: Jex-Blake, *Medical Women*, 85.

I have seen...: Todd, *The Life of Sophia Jex-Blake*, 379.

Oh Lucy, I'm...: Todd, *The Life of Sophia Jex-Blake*, 378.

There were no...: Thorne, *London School of Medicine for Women*, 14.

Most notably, Sir Littlejohn...: James O'Brien, *The Scientific Sherlock Holmes: Cracking the Case with Science and Forensics*, New York: Oxford University Press, 2013, pp. 14-15.

He spent 42 years…: "Sir Henry D. Littlejohn, M.D., Ll.D.Edin., F.R.C.S.E." *British Medical Journal*, Vol. 2, No. 2806, October 10, 1914, pp. 648–650, www.jstor.org/stable/25311426.

Never confide professional…: Student lecture notes, University of Edinburgh forensic medicine class taught by Henry Littlejohn, UE.

The Home Secretary…: Todd, *The Life of Sophia Jex-Blake*, 404.

It is not easy…: Robert Christison, *The Life of Sir Robert Christison, Bart.*, Edinburgh, 1876, p. 44.

Since I saw you…: Todd, *The Life of Sophia Jex-Blake*, 395.

The Prince of Wales's…: Todd, *The Life of Sophia Jex-Blake*, 395.

I was very…: Todd, *The Life of Sophia Jex-Blake*, Footnote 119.

At the end of…: Jex-Blake, *Medical Women*, 153.

We had therefore…: Thorne, *London School of Medicine for Women*, 16.

Chapter 16: Finding a Way Forward

Your want of…: Richard Symonds, *"Medicine," Inside the Citadel*, London: Palgrave Macmillan, 1999, pp. 100–123.

There was no 'failure'…: Jex-Blake, *Medical Women*, Preface to Second Edition.

The real solution…: Jex-Blake, *Medical Women*, Note EE.

I can imagine…: Todd, *The Life of Sophia Jex-Blake*, Appendix E.

One physician who…: Todd, *The Life of Sophia Jex-Blake*, 424.

Opponents, when the…: Todd, *The Life of Sophia Jex-Blake*, 450.

He explained…: Roberts, *Sophia Jex-Blake*, 161.

The BMJ raised…: "Minerva Medica," *British Medical Journal*, September 23, 1871, p. 356.

Before Edinburgh…: Jex-Blake, *Medical Women*, 62.

I had honestly…: Jex-Blake, *Medical Women*, 132.

I hope, even…: Jex-Blake, *Medical Women*, 133.

I think it very…: Todd, *The Life of Sophia Jex-Blake*, 419.

Chapter 17: Societies and Controversies

I do hope…: Garrett Anderson, *Elizabeth Garrett Anderson*, 255.

The conference president…: Manton, *Elizabeth Garrett Anderson*, 245.

Storms are brewing…: Elizabeth Garrett Anderson to James Skelton Anderson, August 4, 1875, LSE.

If you would…: Garrett Anderson, *Elizabeth Garrett Anderson*, 255–256.

We have had…: Garrett Anderson, *Elizabeth Garrett Anderson*, 255.

Pleased as we…: Obstetrical Society of London, Special Meeting March 4, 1874, p. 83, https://books.google.com/books?id=k3QFAAAAQAAJ.

The paper toasted…: Manton, *Elizabeth Garrett Anderson*, 236.

Smuggling implies…: Elizabeth Garrett Anderson, "The Proposed Admission of Women to the Obstetrical Society," *British Medical Journal*, March 14, 1874, p. 365.

To him, that…: Joseph Lister, Letter to the Editor, *British Medical Journal*, February 2, 1878.

Lizzie planned to…: Elizabeth Garrett Anderson, Inaugural Address, *London School of Medicine for Women*, October 1, 1877.

We have heard…: Tara Lamont, "The Amazons within: women in the BMA 100 years ago," *British Medical Journal*, Vol. 305, December 19, 1992, pp. 1529-1532, https://doi.org/10.1136/bmj.305.6868.1529.

I had a very big…: Elizabeth Garrett to Millicent Garrett Fawcett, October 22, 1890, LSE.

Consultant surgeon…: JF Geddes, "'Too high a percentage of failures'? Cover-up at the New Hospital for Women," *Journal of the Royal Society of Medicine*, Vol. 103, 9, 2010, pp. 348-351, https://doi.org/10.1258/jrsm.2010.100064.

I could not…: Brock, *British Women Surgeons and their Patients*, 38.

Six weeks later…: JF Geddes, "'Too high a percentage of failures'?" *Journal of the Royal Society of Medicine*.

Mrs Anderson reported…: JF Geddes, "'Too high a percentage of failures'?" *Journal of the Royal Society of Medicine*.

I consider the…: Boyd, *Excellent Doctor Blackwell*, 321.

When you shudder…: Morantz-Sanchez, *Sympathy and Science*, 195.

Shirking the responsibility…: JF Geddes, "'Too high a percentage of failures'?" *Journal of the Royal Society of Medicine*.

The temptations to…: Boyd, *Excellent Doctor Blackwell*, 321.

The uterus and…: Brock, *British Women Surgeons and their Patients*, 32.

Chapter 18: A Place All Their Own in London

After leaving her…: Hays, *Those Extraordinary Blackwells*, 192.

I feel much…: Boyd, *Excellent Doctor Blackwell*, 259.

Despite her major…: Hays, *Those Extraordinary Blackwells*, 193.

When Barbara once…: Elizabeth Blackwell to Barbara Bodichon, January 18, 1865, CU.

Sophia's future partner…: Todd, *The Life of Sophia Jex-Blake*, 447, 483.

She is in such…: Elizabeth Blackwell to Kitty Barry Blackwell, undated 1874, HU.

If I kept a record…: Todd, *The Life of Sophia Jex-Blake*, 424–425.

She claimed she…: Elizabeth Blackwell to Barbara Bodichon, August 28, 1874, CU.

The school's curriculum…: Garrett Anderson, Inaugural Address, *London School of Medicine for Women*, October 1, 1877.

Friendship was out…: Garrett Anderson, *Elizabeth Garrett Anderson*, 210.

I have just been…: Todd, *The Life of Sophia Jex-Blake*, 427.

You have fortunately…: Todd, *The Life of Sophia Jex-Blake*, 424.

The continually renewed…: Mary Putnam Jacobi, "Shall Women Practice Medicine?" *The North American Review*, 134, no. 302, 1882, pp. 52-75.

A few days…: Boyd, *Excellent Doctor Blackwell*, 259.

A few months…: Boyd, *Excellent Doctor Blackwell*, 261.

We had a grand…: Manton, *Elizabeth Garrett Anderson*, 243.

Because of all...: Thorne, *London School of Medicine for Women*, 19.

This curious old...: *Daily News*, March 13, 1877, *London School of Medicine for Women* press clippings, LMA.

Yet according to...: Thorne, *London School of Medicine for Women*, 19.

I have been...: Elizabeth Blackwell to Barbara Bodichon, October 12, 1874, CU.

Of all the...: Garrett Anderson, *Elizabeth Garrett Anderson*, 218.

An article in...: "London School of Medicine for Women," *The Lancet*, October 17, 1874, pp. 561–562.

I know of...: Elizabeth Garrett Anderson, "A special chapter for ladies who propose to study medicine," in Charles Bell Keetley, *The Student's Guide to the Medical Profession*, London, 1878, pp. 42–48.

Lizzie knew that...: New Hospital for Women Annual Report 1875, LMA.

With such friends...: Collection of press clippings on London School of Medicine for Women Annual Prizegiving Ceremony, June 2, 1875, LMA.

No amount of...: "General Council of Medical Education Session, 1875: Discussion on the Admission of Women to the Medical Profession," *British Medical Journal*, July 3, 1875.

One witty observer...: Roberts, *Sophia Jex-Blake*, 150.

When the warm-hearted...: "The Edinburgh Medical Students," *The Englishwoman's Review*, No. 6, April 1871.

Fancy a woman...: "General Council of Medical Education Session, 1875: Discussion on the Admission of Women to the Medical Profession," *British Medical Journal*, July 3, 1875.

The council's final...: "General Council of Medical Education Session, 1875: Discussion on the Admission of Women to the Medical Profession," *British Medical Journal*, July 3, 1875.

Feeling hopeful...: Todd, *The Life of Sophia Jex-Blake*, 432.

The council calls...: Letter from Robert Barnes, "The College of Surgeons and its Midwifery Board," *The Medical Times and Gazette*, March 25, 1876, p. 343.

She is now very...: Manton, *Elizabeth Garrett Anderson*, 247.

You were right...: Manton, *Elizabeth Garrett Anderson*, 248.

Help was needed...: Boyd, *Excellent Doctor Blackwell*, 257.

It was reported...: Discussion of the medical act amendment (foreign uni bill) in house of commons, LMA.

Miss Pechey has...: Todd, *The Life of Sophia Jex-Blake*, 435.

I met Mrs...: Roberts, *Sophia Jex-Blake*, 155.

Are they all...: Roberts, *Sophia Jex-Blake*, 155.

Now to see...: Todd, *The Life of Sophia Jex-Blake*, 438.

Lizzie was convalescing...: Manton, *Elizabeth Garrett Anderson*, 251.

As I was not...: Todd, *The Life of Sophia Jex-Blake*, 444.

The various tests...: Todd, *The Life of Sophia Jex-Blake*, 439.

As one of...: Letter to the Editor from Frances Elizabeth Hoggan, *The Standard*, March 6, 1877, LMA.

Stansfeld admired Sophia...: Roberts, *Sophia Jex-Blake*, 161.

The organizing secretary...: Roberts, *Sophia Jex-Blake*, 159.

About the best...: Todd, *The Life of Sophia Jex-Blake*, 448.

It is no exaggeration...: Garrett Anderson, Inaugural Address, *London School of Medicine for Women*, October 1, 1877.

I was then...: Elizabeth Garrett Anderson, notes for a speech, LMA.

Chapter 19: On to Separate Paths

What a comfort...: Todd, *The Life of Sophia Jex-Blake*, 458.

It was like...: Todd, *The Life of Sophia Jex-Blake*, 456.

I know you...: Todd, *The Life of Sophia Jex-Blake*, 460.

What pleases me...: Todd, *The Life of Sophia Jex-Blake*, 460.

My lecture went...: Todd, *The Life of Sophia Jex-Blake*, 495.

In the winter...: Todd, *The Life of Sophia Jex-Blake*, 497.

A woman must…: Elizabeth Smith, *Fragments, in Prose and Verse*, Boston, 1810, p. 131.

They might like…: Todd, *The Life of Sophia Jex-Blake*, 525-526.

My life is full…: Todd, *The Life of Sophia Jex-Blake*, 468.

Some twenty years…: Todd, *The Life of Sophia Jex-Blake*, 94.

By the time…: Emily Blackwell, Wikipedia, https://en.wikipedia.org/wiki/Emily_Blackwell.

When Elizabeth died…: Dean Smith, "A Persistent Rebel," *American History Illustrated*, January 1981, www.hws.edu/about/blackwell/articles/amhistory.aspx.

The work of…: Blackwell, *Pioneer Work*, chap. 7.

In 1881, there…: Laura Jefferson, et al., "Women in medicine: historical perspectives and recent trends," *British Medical Bulletin*, Vol. 114, Issue 1, June 2015, pp. 5–15, https://doi.org/10.1093/bmb/ldv007.

Epilogue: A Lasting Legacy

Janet Lane-Claypon…: *London School of Medicine for Women*, Notable Graduates, Wikipedia, https://en.wikipedia.org/wiki/London_School_of_Medicine_for_Women#Notable_graduates.

Lizzie's protégé…: "Eliza Walker Dunbar, M.D." *British Medical Journal*, vol. 2, 3376, September 12, 1925, pp. 496-497.

Matilda Chaplin…: "Matilda Chaplin," The University of Edinburgh, January 5, 2018, www.ed.ac.uk/equality-diversity/celebrating-diversity/inspiring-women/women-in-history/edinburgh-seven/matilda-chaplin.

Gertrude Herzfeld…: "'I wanted to do medicine when I was aged 5': Gertrude Herzfeld (1890-1981), Scotland's first practising female surgeon," The Royal College of Surgeons of Edinburgh Library and Archive, March 8, 2018, https://rcsedlibraryandarchive.wordpress.com/2018/03/08/i-wanted-to-do-medicine-when-i-was-aged-5-gertrude-herzfeld-1890-1981-scotlands-first-practising-femal-surgeon.

Mary Putnam Jacobi…: "Dr. Mary Corrina Putnam Jacobi," Changing the Face of Medicine, U.S. National Library of Medicine, National Institutes of Health, https://cfmedicine.nlm.nih.gov/physicians/biography_163.html.

After serving as…: "Dr. Rebecca J. Cole," Changing the Face of Medicine, U.S. National Library of Medicine, National Institutes of Health, https://cfmedicine.nlm.nih.gov/physicians/biography_66.html.

Mary Harris Thompson…: "Mary Harris Thompson," Wikipedia, https://en.wikipedia.org/wiki/Mary_Harris_Thompson.

Three years after…: "Dr. Anna Wessels Williams ," Changing the Face of Medicine, U.S. National Library of Medicine, National Institutes of Health, https://cfmedicine.nlm.nih.gov/physicians/biography_331.html.

Alum Sara Josephine Baker…: "Dr. S. Josephine Baker," Changing the Face of Medicine, U.S. National Library of Medicine, National Institutes of Health, https://cfmedicine.nlm.nih.gov/physicians/biography_19.html.

Recent research…: Tara Parker-Pope, "Should You Choose a Female Doctor?" *The New York Times*, August 14, 2018, www.nytimes.com/2018/08/14/well/doctors-male-female-women-men-heart.html.

In 2017…: Eve Glicksman, "A First: Women Outnumber Men in 2017 Entering Medical School Class," Association of American Medical Colleges News, December 18, 2017, www.aamc.org/news-insights/first-women-outnumber-men-2017-entering-medical-school-class.

In 1892…: "First Graduation of Female Students, 1893," The University of Edinburgh, Our History, http://ourhistory.is.ed.ac.uk/index.php/First_Graduation_of_Female_Students,_1893.

In 2019…: Brian Ferguson, "'Edinburgh Seven' to finally get degrees 150 years after campaign to allow women to study medicine," *The Scotsman*, April 4, 2019, www.scotsman.com/regions/edinburgh-seven-finally-get-degrees-150-years-after-campaign-allow-women-study-medicine-548642.

I do not consider…: Thorne, *London School of Medicine for Women*, 16-17.

INDEX